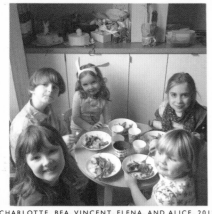

CHARLOTTE, BEA, VINCENT, ELENA, AND ALICE, 2012

ALLEGRA AND FLOSS WITH THE SCOTTS, 1977

SYBELLA, SALLY, AND GRAHAM, SARDINIA, 1987

LIZA AND HENRY, 1977

GEORGIA, JULIA, AND JONATHAN, 1972

JONNY, DUNCAN, AND PAULA, COLCHESTER, 1975

ANITA'S BIRTHDAY, 1975

JOHN AND NANA THORNTON, BROADSTAIRS, 1975

KAY WITH A FISH, PATTAYA, 1970

THE MANGANS & THE WOODS, MALLORCA, 1979

KAY WITH A SAUSAGE, BANGKOK, 1967

ALLEGRA AND FAMILY, DORSET, 1974

PHOTOGRAPHY BY GEORGIA GLYNN SMITH • DESIGN BY ANITA MANGAN

LEON
Family & Friends

BY KAY PLUNKETT-HOGGE
& JOHN VINCENT

Contents

LEON

We started Leon in order to make it easy for everybody to eat good food. And we decided that the best way to do that was to provide "good fast food." Food that tastes good and does you good. Food that's fun, fresh, fairly priced, and swiftly served by people who smile because they want to smile.

We opened our first Leon in Soho, London, at the end of Carnaby Street just across from Liberty, the famous department store. As the line formed outside on that very first day we had a great feeling of … you're ahead of me, aren't you … liberty.

People seemed as excited as we were about what we were doing. Of course, we made loads of mistakes, but we made plenty of great food, too. Enough for us to win "Best Newcomer" at the *Observer* Food Awards.

Word got around and we got busy. So busy, in fact, that we now have thirteen branches of Leon. Our secret plan, which we've actually told a lot of people, is to have Leons all over the world, making it easy for everyone everywhere to eat good food.

We have been supported by so many committed and wonderful people. Including those who come into our restaurants and eat with us. Thank you to all of you.

ABOUT KAY

Kay is a joy to work with, be with, and laugh with. Kay writes e-mails with "Yippee!" and "Yay!" Kay loves food. Not in an "I am a foodie, you know" kind of way, but in a really loving food kind of way. She finds it tasty. She finds the people who cook it interesting. She is positive about people. Positive about cooks and chefs she loves.

Kay is really sort of Thai. Her dad worked for Ford in England and then got a job selling tractors in Thailand, so they moved to Bangkok. Kay could speak Thai before she could speak English. Which today (literally today, because we have just come back from lunch in a Thai Café) makes trips to Thai restaurants more interesting, and which as a girl helped Kay learn all the culinary tricks of the family's cook.

Kay is married to Fred, who has been great at managing the administration of this book. They have traveled a lot, like inquisitive people do. Kay worked as a model agent for twenty years before realizing she wanted to make her hobby her work. Kay now works with me and Henry to develop recipes for Leon, and as luck would have it she is good. While we have both had a hand with the concept of this book, in writing the general sections, with the identity, and with pulling the team together, the bulk of the recipes are from Kay's brilliant mind and hands.

There are some people who marry loveliness and fortitude. Who live their life "on purpose." Kay is one.

JOHN

ABOUT JOHN

When I first met John my initial thought was … Blimey … he's loud. Big too. I still think the same thing (I'm only 5 feet 2 inches), but I've learned that the big and the loud applies to his heart, his mind, and his appetite, too. He's a man with big ideas. Like Leon.

John cofounded Leon with Henry and Allegra in 2004 with the simple but revolutionary idea of making fast food that's good for you. And written right through the middle of it is John's belief in better. Better meat, better veg, better nutrition.

The other big thing about John is his belief in family. Family's a big deal with Leon. That's why there are family photos all over the books, the web site, you name it. John understands inherently that family's not just about blood but about community. It's about the people you like and the people you work with, too. It's broad and inclusive.

John's family are from Wembley, Edmonton, and Tottenham, via Genoa, Sicily, and Livorno. His wife Katie's family come from Wilmslow, Yorkshire, Holland, and Brazil. Mine come from Lewisham, Ireland, Cookham, and Thailand, while my husband Fred's come from Suffolk, Jamaica, Canada, Devon, and Malaysia. So when we're all together, we're kind of a United Nations of Food. UNOF. Actually—that's a pretty good idea. John's the man to make it happen. He is unbelievably creative and supportive. He has a mind like a steel bear trap. And he likes my food.

Thanks, JV.

KAY

COOKING WITH KIDS

Learning to cook is an essential part of growing up, so these are our top tips for getting your youngsters interested in cooking.

1. **Role models:** As you know, kids like to copy adults and older kids. So the more they see you or their brothers and sisters or cousins cook when they are toddlers, the more they will want to get involved.

2. **Cooking judo:** As soon as they show the first signs of interest, go with it. Don't try to force them to cook what you want them to cook. Usually, it is a cake that first interests them. Make it "their thing." Natasha has made gluten-free pancakes her thing, and Eleanor bakes a cake that is basically a sponge cake … that is pink. And it is "her recipe." Last week she announced she was "presenting it" for this cookbook.

3. **Measuring with numbers:** In our experience kids like the process of measuring. Butter. Flour. Measuring cups and spoons are easy and fun for them to use. Start with a simple recipe that doesn't need to have exactly measurement ingredients.

4. **Break it down:** Teach them order from the beginning. It will help give them confidence and help them manage themselves as they get older. For example, lay out all the ingredients before you start cooking instead of rushing back and forth to the refrigerator.

5. **The whole routine:** Cooking, in the mind of a child, is the whole process from soup to nuts. It includes the talking about what food to make, shopping, peeling, licking the bowl, cleaning up, and sitting down to eat it. So let them enjoy each phase and celebrate with them as their dish is served out to everyone.

6. **Special occasions:** If you have a family gathering, let them make something that is their contribution for it. Maybe they can cook the little cookies at Christmas.

7. **Peeling can be fun:** You may be pleasantly surprised at how kids enjoy the things that you find dull. Eleanor, from the age of two, has really enjoyed peeling carrots and potatoes. It may take 20 minutes to do just a couple, but it is wonderful to watch.

8. **Find the magic:** The most fascinating dishes for kids are those that undergo the most magical transformations. Meringue. Or even popcorn.

9. **It's a gift:** Kids get most excited when what they are cooking becomes a present for a friend or member of the family.

10. **Food is relationships:** It's not really about the food is it? It is about the time you are spending with them. So make it fun. Be nice. And create some happy memories.

NUTRITION

It is easy to start an argument about nutrition. And there is a battle on in terms of who "owns" it. Doctors? Nutritionists? Biochemists? Us, the individuals listening to our own bodies?

Here are some points of view. Our points of view:

Eat like a scavenger with a spear. Our bodies are for the most part still made the way we lived for thousands of years. If you can't pick it or spear it, don't eat it. So, mostly eat vegetables (restrict potatoes and parsnips), berries, seeds, nuts, eggs, fresh herbs and spices, fish, chicken, and a little lamb and beef. Seeds, nuts and good olive oil (or avocado oil) will give you plenty of good fats, which is a GOOD THING.

Keeping your blood sugar low is critical. A little is a lot better than a lot. Foods that raise blood sugars include glucose, table sugar, white bread and pastries, white rice (apart from basmati), beer, and sugary cereals.

Keep it varied. Eat a variety of different vegetables and proteins. You'll get a good spread of goodness, and reduce the likelihood of building up an intolerance.

Keep your digestive system in tip-top form. By sometimes giving it a break, by chewing a lot, drinking water between meals, by doing plenty of relaxing exercise, by not stressing, and only eating when you are hungry.

Never ever drink "diet" carbonated drinks or eat "diet" anything else. It will screw with your head and body.

Eat sea salt instead of mass-produced sodium chloride. It is full of varied minerals, unlike factory-made salt, which as you know is just sodium chloride. Himalayan salt is particularly good for you.

Despite this, there is substance in the phrase "one man's meat is another man's poison." We are all different:

Many people would be better off without eating modern wheat and gluten. Try staying off it for a couple of weeks and see if you have more energy and more room inside your pants. In a good way.

Many people can't digest cows milk or cheeses made with cows milk. Two thousand years ago, before we worked out how to milk a cow and keep it inside the village fence, almost none of us had the enzymes to break down cows milk as adults. Many of us now do. Many of us still don't.

Your kidneys, liver, heart, intestines, and pancreas are not the same as everyone else's. Your genetics, the enzymes you produce and your blood type, make you special. It is worth working out whether you need less or more of certain foods. Should you keep potassium down?

Over time, your digestive tract may start to find it difficult to process certain foods, and you may build up an allergy. Saving up a little money to have a test to work out what makes your body respond badly may be a route to health and happiness.

Key to our recipe icons:

✓ LOW GLYCEMIC LOAD   ♥ LOW SATURATED FAT   WF WHEAT FREE
GF GLUTEN FREE   DF DAIRY FREE   V VEGETARIAN

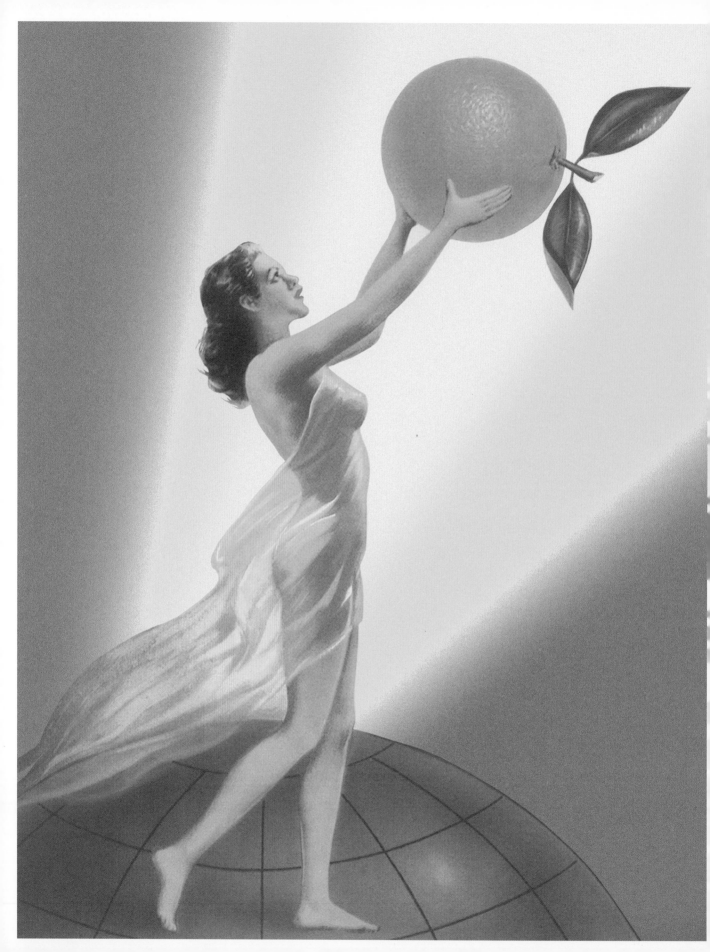

TODAY

Welcome to today. These are recipes with one thing in mind: making it easier for you to feed your family and friends good food. Today. Dishes that taste good, do them good, and are straightforward for you to shop for and make. In between performing your varied roles.

We also hope that there are recipes here that you can teach your children. Or that your best friend Sarah, who doesn't cook, can learn. If your best friend is not called Sarah, well, we can't help you.

BREAKFAST & BRUNCH

So we know it's called the most important meal of the day. Seems a little bit harsh on the others. But we get the gist. Nutritionally, if not emotionally. The trouble is, it has become owned by companies who want to fill rectangular boxes, and our bellies, with wheat, sugar, and corn.

Reclaim breakfast and make a better start to each day. And live your day as if you are the captain of your ship, just for today.

Energy Booster Smoothie

SERVES 4 • PREPARATION TIME: 5 MINUTES • COOKING TIME: NONE • ♥ WF GF DF V

The king of all smoothies. This bad boy (sorry, good boy—very good boy) is packed full of healthy omega-3 and is stuffed with all the vitamins in the alphabet. The secret weapon is avocado—one of nature's finest superfoods. As well as adding essential amino acids, it also brings a gorgeous creaminess to the smoothie.

1 **avocado**
2 handfuls EACH of any three of the following:
   hulled **strawberries, raspberries, blueberries,**
   blackberries, bilberries, loganberries
1 cup **orange juice**
1 tablespoon **flaxseed**, plain or toasted
2 ripe **bananas**

1. Put everything into the blender—it's not an exact science, just toss 'em all in—and blend until smooth.

TIPS

* When berries are in season, use them fresh— then freeze a load to use through the winter. Just put them straight into the blender, frozen, for a delicious chilled smoothie.

* Add soy milk instead of the orange juice, if you prefer. If you do, add a splash of honey or agave nectar to replace the sweetness the orange juice provides.

Ralph's Mango Lassi

SERVES 2 • PREPARATION TIME: 15–20 MINUTES • COOKING TIME: NONE • ♥ WF GF V

A wonderful, cooling drink, especially in hot weather, this is a great fruity way to start the day.

1¼ cups active **yogurt** (low-fat if preferred), chilled
4 ripe chilled **mangoes**, peeled, pitted,
   and chopped
2 tablespoons **honey**
1 tablespoon **lime juice**
2 cups of **ice cubes**
sprigs of **fresh mint**, to garnish

1. Combine the yogurt, mangoes, honey, and lime juice in a blender. Add ice and blend for 15 seconds, until smooth.

2. Serve garnished with sprigs of mint.

TIPS

* You can use buttermilk in place of the yogurt, if you prefer.

* If you can't find decent ripe mangoes, you can buy unsweetened mango pulp in cans at most large supermarkets.

* For a less sweet version, omit the honey and add a teaspoon of salt and a couple of pinches of ground cardamom.

Lovely Ralph Monthienvichienchai is literally MADD about mangoes, so much so that he opened a dessert bar of the same name in London. If you need to know *anything* about mangoes, he's your guy. Thanks to him for this delicious recipe.

RALPH, BANGKOK, 1988

Pick 'n' Mix

SERVES 8–10 • PREPARATION TIME: 5–10 MINUTES • COOKING TIME: 15–20 MINUTES • ✓ ♥ GF DF V

Most of us of a certain age have fond memories of going with a grown-up—in Kay's case, her Grandad Valler—to Woolworth's to buy a stash of assorted penny candies. Filling your own bag with whichever shapes and flavors you desired, sort of like a cut-price Willy Wonka ... No outing was complete without a trip to Horniman's Museum, fries and sausages, and a paper bag of Woolworth's penny candies (Kay particularly favored the milk bottles).

So, we thought: What a great idea for breakfast. Not the candies, obviously, but the concept. Build your own muesli or granola. With NO hidden salt, fats, or sugars.

The base:
4 cups gluten-free **oats**
½ cup **Omega seeds (pumpkin, sunflower, flaxseed, sesame)**—
    you can buy premixed at most health food stores, or create your
    own blend of your favorites

1. Heat the oven to 350°F.

2. Put the oats and the Omega seeds on a baking sheet and put into the oven for 15–20 minutes. Stir them from time to time or until the oats and seeds are toasted and golden brown—keep an eye on them, because they burn fast. Set aside to cool.

3. You now have your base. Time for the rest of it.

4. Just keep small jars of some or all of the following on hand:
   • dried goji berries • dried plums and apricots, chopped • dried blueberries and strawberries • dried strips of coconut • golden raisins • dried unsweetened banana chips, lightly crushed • dried unsweetened mango, chopped • dates, chopped • walnuts, chopped • almonds, chopped • dried figs, chopped • raisins • soft squishy banana coins • mixed dried berries

5. Then you and the kids can add what you like. Just take a ratio of 2 handfuls of base to one handful of pick 'n' mix. And *voilà*, different cereal experience every day.

6. Serve with milk, yogurt, fresh fruit, juice. We like a good squeeze of agave nectar or honey, too.

TIPS

* The base will keep in an airtight container, but we tend to just make up a batch every week or so.

* If you are not worried about gluten, use 4 cups of four-grain oatmeal mix instead, which you can find in most health food stores. We like one with a mixture of barley flakes, wheat flakes, oat flakes and rice flakes, but feel free to choose your own.

* Get creative—make your own custom-made pick 'n' mix combination and store it in your own labeled jar.

Happy Cakes

(BANANA, BUCKWHEAT & BLUEBERRY HOT CAKES)

MAKES 16–20 • PREPARATION TIME: 10 MINUTES • COOKING TIME: 2–3 MINUTES PER GRIDDLE CAKE • ✓ WF GF V

Yes, eating a griddle cake as good as this *is* enough to make you happy. This recipe has an added extra. And it's not illegal. Buckwheat. Somewhat like a sea lion is not a lion, buckwheat is not a wheat at all. In fact, it's more of a seed (and, strangely, it's part of the rhubarb family). There are those that say the rutin contained in buckwheat has antidepressant qualities. We're not experts, but we feel a darn sight happier after a plate of these.

These are smallish, thickish griddle cakes instead of the larger pancakes ...

1 cup **buttermilk**
2 **eggs**, lightly beaten
1 ripe **banana**, peeled and mashed
1½ cups **buckwheat flour**
1 teaspoon **gluten-free baking powder**
⅔ cup **blueberries**
1 tablespoon **vegetable oil**
a pat of **butter**
a good pinch of **salt**

1. Put the buttermilk and the beaten eggs into a large mixing bowl and mix until combined. Add the mashed banana and mix again.

2. Sift the buckwheat flour and baking powder into the wet mixture and beat in thoroughly. Stir in the salt and, very gently, the blueberries.

3. Let the batter sit for 5 minutes if you can to let it rest—it makes a fluffier cake.

4. Heat the vegetable oil and the butter in a skillet over medium heat until the butter starts to bubble slightly. Using a tablespoon, drop dollops of batter into the skillet (a 12 inch skillet can fit 4 in at once comfortably). Keep an eye on them. When you start to see them dimple on top, it's time to carefully flip them.

5. After another minute or so, flip them again and they should be ready to serve. You want them golden brown on each side, with some of the blueberries oozing purple juice. Remove from the skillet onto paper towels, then transfer them straight onto hot plates for serving.

6. Our favorite way to serve them? Good butter, plenty of maple syrup, and a side of crispy bacon.

TIPS

* If you can't find fresh blueberries, use about ½ cup dried blueberries.

* Try adding some ground cinnamon or grated nutmeg to the batter, or some grated orange zest.

Kow Mun Gai

(THAI CHICKEN & RICE)

SERVES 4 • PREPARATION TIME: 15 MINUTES • COOKING TIME: 1 HOUR 55 MINUTES • ✓ ♥ DF

This is a classic Thai breakfast dish, and you'll find food stalls dedicated just to this, serving from about 4 a.m. to noon, all over the country. You can spot them by the hanging chickens that adorn their stall. Kow Mun Gai tastes clean and delicious, and its zingy nam jim (dipping sauce) will wake up the most jaded palate. This is an easy version to make at home.

1 **chicken**, about 3¼ pounds (there will be leftovers)
1 small **onion**, peeled and chopped into chunks
4 **cilantro roots** (from the coriander plant, available in
   Asian grocery stores), crushed
1 clove of **garlic**, crushed
a ¾-inch piece of **cucumber**, chopped
1 tablespoon **fresh cilantro leaves**, plus extra to garnish
1½ cups **jasmine rice**, rinsed
peeled cucumber slices, to garnish
sea salt and **ground white pepper**

For the nam jim:
a 1½-inch piece of **fresh ginger**, peeled and finely sliced
2–3 **fresh Thai chiles**, sliced
a small handful of **fresh cilantro**, chopped
2 tablespoons **yellow bean sauce**
2 tablespoons **rice vinegar**
2 teaspoons **dark brown sugar** (palm sugar, if possible)
1 tablespoon **light soy sauce**

> Whenever I go back to Bangkok, this is the first breakfast I have, usually bought on the road to the hotel from the wonderful kow mun gai guy on Soi Saladaeng. It's especially restorative after a long flight.
>
> KAY

1. Put the chicken, onion, cilantro roots, and garlic into a heavy saucepan, cover with water, and season with the salt and white pepper. Bring to a boil, then reduce to a simmer and poach until the chicken is cooked, about 1 hour and 20 minutes or depending on the size of the chicken. (To test when it's done, jab a skewer or a fork into the thickest part of its thigh—if the juices run clear, not pinky red, it's done.)

2. Remove the bird from the pan and set aside. Strain and reserve all the poaching liquid and season to taste. It should be very mild and soothing.

3. To assemble the dish, cook your rice in the usual way using 1⅓ cups of the reserved chicken liquid instead of water. Let the rice rest for 5–10 minutes before serving. In a separate saucepan, boil the remaining chicken liquid.

4. Meanwhile, make the nam jim: Grind the ginger to a paste using a mortar and pestle. Add the chiles and cilantro. Mix together and combine well with the other nam jim ingredients, plus 2 tablespoons of the chicken liquid. Spoon out into a communal serving bowl.

5. Serve the chicken in slices beside the warm rice. Garnish with the cucumber and cilantro leaves, and accompany with a small bowl of liquid and the nam jim.

CLUCK-CLUCK!

Back in the 70s, the Americam Egg Board was established to promote eggs, so it's hardly surprising that, for many of us, breakfast's just not breakfast without an egg or two. We couldn't agree more.

 KEEPING CHICKENS

BY JOHN

Chickens provide both beautifully fresh eggs and wonderful metaphors. Cooped up, hen pecked, clipping my wings, pecking order, chicken feed, broody, ruffled feathers; they are a testament to man's close relationship with his birds.

Katie and I have been keeping chickens for three years. Here are our top tips:

The chicken or the egg?

While it is not clear which came first, I can highly recommend you buy chickens instead of eggs and hope they hatch. It's best to buy hens at 4–5 months; they will be on the cusp of laying and will be more straightforward to care for.

Some space

Your new friends will live outside in a coop, or any similar protected shack or shed. They will be happiest if you give them a perch, space to jog up and down, and a cozy area with sawdust to lay eggs. (Clear this every week.)

Food & water

Keep it simple: Buy chicken feed in a big sack, and some pellets. Chickens eat grit (as in very small stones) to help them digest and make good, hard eggs worthy of your breakfast table.

Outfoxing the fox. And Rambo.

I know two separate families who suddenly became fans of fox hunting after they saw what their local foxy predators had done to their chickens. So, keep your brood safe by protecting all the sides and top of your coop with chicken wire and make sure the fox can't dig underneath by burying the wire into the ground, or have a good heavy board at the bottom of the wire and keep your eyes open for the first sign of attempted tunneling. At night, your chickens will naturally go inside their coop to sleep—make sure they are locked in for double security. You also need to keep your eye on some breeds of dogs. Rambo, my brother-in-law's dog (yes, he was in the army), successfully scared most of our chickens away recently. On the flipside, the little springer was very useful in sniffing them out in the hedges, while on his leash.

What chickens?

We have two bantams (one hen, one cockerel) and five farmyard hybrids whose genealogy I am too inexperienced to judge. Hybrids tend to lay well, although our neighbors are fans of Brown Leghorn hens. From our six hens we get between five and eight eggs a day.

The great rooster question

A full-size rooster will keep you and your neighbors from waking too late. We have compromised and gone for a bantam rooster, who manages some mild cockadoodledooing and tries to lord it over his much bigger hens.

Clipping their wings

If your hens get too good at flying, it's a good idea to get a pair of strong scissors and shorten the long feathers at the tip of their wings. You'll find diagrams on how to do this on the Internet.

Loss of feathers

This winter and last winter two of our birds lost most of their feathers, to the point that they looked like they were only a few steps away from being in aisle four. They grew back, but I guess it is safest to seek expert advice if you start to see signs of disease.

Get the children involved

I am not going to get overly sentimental here, but chickens are a great way of getting the kids interacting with animals, and understanding that eggs don't come from the supermarket. Ours have been named by the girls after characters from *Glee* (Rachel is a great layer). They can hold them, feed them, clean them out, lock them away at night, count and collect the eggs in the morning, and, most lovely of all, walk straight back into the kitchen and crack the eggs into a skillet.

REGULARLY STORM YOUR CHICKEN COOP AS PART OF A 70S COP GAME

Perfect Scrambled Eggs

SERVES 2 • PREPARATION TIME: 5 MINUTES •
COOKING TIME: 5–10 MINUTES • ✓ WF GF V

In the short story *007 in New York*, Ian
Fleming gives one of the definitive recipes
for scrambled eggs with cream and finely
chopped *fines herbes*. But let's save the full
Bond for the weekend; for an everyday
breakfast, we won't be quite so indulgent.

> 5 medium **eggs**
> a dash of **milk**
> a good pinch of chopped **fresh
>   parsley**, or **basil**, or **cilantro**,
>   or **thyme** (optional)
> 1 tablespoon **butter**
> **salt** and **freshly ground
>   black pepper**

1. Crack the eggs into a bowl, add the
   milk, salt, and pepper (and the
   pinch of chopped herbs, if you're
   using them), and beat them all
   together with a fork.

2. In a heavy saucepan, melt the
   butter over medium heat until
   it starts to foam. Pour in the eggs,
   and start stirring at once with a
   fork or a wooden spoon. Keep
   stirring constantly as the eggs start
   to come together.

3. The question now is: How runny
   do you like them? As the eggs begin
   to come together, start turning
   down the heat—they'll keep cooking
   in the residual heat. Keep stirring
   until you've got them just how you
   like them, and serve out on to plates
   at once. Keep in mind, the eggs at
   the bottom of the pan will be firmer
   than the eggs you serve first—just in
   case some people prefer them one
   way or the other.

4. Garnish with an extra grind of black
   pepper and dig in.

Perfect Poached Eggs

SERVES 4 • PREPARATION TIME: 10 MINUTES •
COOKING TIME: 1.5 MINUTES • ✓ WF GF DF V

Kay never used to cook a lot of poached
eggs until chef Bryn Williams, of Odette's
in Primrose Hill, London, told her his
infallible method. As he says, if you have to
make fifty of the darned things a day, you
want something foolproof. This is it.

> 4 **eggs**
> 1 teaspoon **salt**
> 1 tablespoon **white wine vinegar**
> 1 bowl of **iced water**—if you're
>   not serving them immediately

1. Crack the eggs into 4 individual
   ramekins or small dishes.

2. Fill the deepest saucepan you can
   find with water, add the salt and
   vinegar, and bring to a rolling boil.
   One by one, add the eggs. They
   will sink to the bottom of the pan,
   and as they do, you will see the
   white coming up and around the
   yolk. After about a minute, the
   eggs will start to rise up through
   the water. At this point, if you're
   making them ahead of time, scoop
   the eggs out with a slotted spoon
   and plunge them immediately into
   the bowl of iced water to stop them
   from cooking. When they're cold,
   remove them from the water and set
   aside until you need them. If you're
   serving them now, cook them for
   another 30 seconds to 1 minute
   in a boiling water
   for a firm white and a
   good runny yolk.

3. To reheat, bring a
   saucepan of clean
   water to a boil, add
   the cooled eggs, and
   heat through for about
   30 seconds to 1 minute.

Perfect Soft-boiled Eggs

Ease an egg
into salted boiling
water and cook for

**3 MINUTES &
33 SECONDS**

Jonny Jeffery's Fluffy Eggs

SERVES 4 • PREPARATION TIME: 10 MINUTES • COOKING TIME: 8–10 MINUTES • ✓ V

This is a fantastic Sunday breakfast recipe from Kay's friend Jonny Jeffery. It's one of those classic family recipes—something his grandmother used to cook for the kids as a treat.

4 **eggs**
4 slices of **bread**
small handful of finely shredded **cheese—Cheddar**,
   Parmesan, **Swiss**, whichever you prefer
salt and **freshly ground black pepper**

1. Heat the oven to 375°F.

2. Separate the eggs, keeping the yolks whole, and whisk the egg whites into stiff peaks.

3. Lightly toast the bread, then put the slices on a baking sheet. Spread three-quarters of the egg white onto the semitoasted bread.

4. Make a small well in the egg white on each slice of bread, and stick in a yolk—one yolk per slice. Season each yolk with salt and pepper, then cover with the remaining egg white, making sure the yolk is sealed in.

5. Sprinkle a teaspoon of shredded cheese over each, then bake in the oven for 8–10 minutes, or until the top is nicely golden. This should give you a nice, runny yolk. If you prefer a firmer yolk, give it a little longer. Serve immediately.

TIPS

* When Jonny cooked this for us, he served it with some delicious pan-fried chorizo, but you could try it with bacon, smoked salmon, or even some sautéed mushrooms.

* Why not, as Jonny suggests, use duck eggs instead. Then you can call it Fluffy Ducks.

* The surface area of your slice of toast is important. The smaller the slice, the higher you must pile your egg whites, which slightly affects the cooking time. We recommend slices from a large white or whole wheat loaf.

JONNY, WITH DUNCAN AND
PAULA, ENGLAND, 1975

When we were kids, we used to call our grandma More Granny because we were always saying, "Please can we have some more, Granny". Her fluffy eggs were always one of my favorites.

JONNY

Deconstructed Huevos Rancheros

WITH A FRESH ROMANO PEPPER & CHILE SALSA

SERVES 4 • PREPARATION TIME: 15 MINUTES • COOKING TIME: 10 MINUTES • ✓ ♥ WF GF DF V

This Mexican breakfast dish is usually made with a fried egg, served on fried corn tortillas with refried beans and a cooked tomato and onion salsa on the side. All we've done here is pulled back on the oil by poaching the eggs, opted for a fresh salsa, and served some simple black beans and steamed corn tortillas on the side, making it brighter and lighter.

For the Romano pepper & chile salsa:
1 **Romano pepper**, seeded
1 **green Serrano chile**, seeded
2 **tomatoes**, seeded
1 **shallot**
2–3 cloves of **garlic**
a few leaves of **fresh basil**
a squeeze of **lime juice**
a dash of **olive oil**
salt and **freshly ground black pepper**

1 15-oz **can of black beans**
1 teaspoon **dried oregano**
4–8 **corn tortillas**
4 **eggs**
salt and **freshly ground black pepper**

1. First make the salsa: Finely chop the pepper, chile, tomatoes, shallot, and garlic, and mix them together in a bowl. Rip in the basil leaves, add the lime juice and olive oil, and season with salt and pepper. Stir together once again to make sure it's all evenly mixed. Taste for seasoning, then set aside.

2. Now empty the black beans into a saucepan—don't strain them, because you want their liquid. Gently heat them, adding the oregano and a pinch of salt and pepper. Set aside to keep warm.

3. Wrap the corn tortillas in a clean dish towel and steam over boiling water (preferably in a tiered steamer) until they are piping hot—for only a couple of minutes. Set aside to keep warm.

4. Finally, poach the eggs following our foolproof method on page 25. To serve, lay 1 or 2 warm corn tortillas on each plate, and top with the eggs, beans, and salsa.

TIPS

* Make sure to use pure corn tortillas. We've found that a lot of the commercial tortillas available have wheat in them.

* This is also delicious with some sliced avocado on the side, or with some of Kay's Guacamole on page 51.

Posh Poached Eggs in a Cup

WITH CHORIZO & TRUFFLED CHEESE

SERVES 4 • PREPARATION TIME: 5 MINUTES • COOKING TIME: 10–15 MINUTES

On our breakfast menu at Leon, we have what we call Egg Cups. We poach eggs in a small pot and add a few things—the don't-you-ever-take-it-off-the-menu combination is truffle, Gruyère, and sliced chorizo. No chorizo on hand? It also works well with shredded ham or bacon. And once you've tried it, it'll never come off your breakfast menu either.

4–8 **eggs**
4oz **chorizo**, thinly sliced
1 tablespoon **white vinegar**, for poaching
salt and **freshly ground black pepper**

For the cheese sauce:
2 tablespoons **unsalted butter**
¼ cup **chickpea flour**
1½ cups **milk**
1 cup shredded **Gruyère cheese**
½ teaspoon **truffle oil**

1. First make the sauce: Melt the butter in a saucepan over medium heat. Add the chickpea flour and whisk the two together until smooth and all the flour is incorporated in the butter and cooks out—about 2 minutes.

2. Add the milk a little at a time, whisking as you go, until you have a smooth lump-free sauce. Keep whisking until it thickens slightly, enough to coat the back of a spoon. Add the shredded cheese and the truffle oil and whisk well until everything is combined and glossy, then season with salt and pepper. Set aside and keep warm.

3. In a nonstick saucepan, heat the olive oil over medium heat and sauté the chorizo until the slices are cooked through and crisp. Remove the chorizo from the pan and drain on paper towels.

4. Poach the eggs (1 or 2 each, depending on how hungry everyone is) following the method on page 25.

5. Grind some pepper and a little sea salt on top of each egg, then put them into their cups (I use a small teacup or similar kind of thing). Sprinkle one-quarter of the chorizo on top of each egg, then pour one-quarter of the cheese sauce over it and grind a little more pepper on top.

6. Nummy nummy, as John's daughter Natasha used to say.

SPEEDY LUNCHES

So it turns out that I have a family motto, *festina lente*, which means "hasten slowly." For a long time, I thought this was sillily contradictory, but now I figure it means that, just because you're in a hurry, it doesn't mean you have to cut corners. In our lunch-on-the-run times, it turns out that this is good advice. In too much haste, we tend to grab something without any thought at all, forgetting that the wrong foods will make us dopey as our bodies work to digest them (it's called post-prandial torpor). But if, in the words of the wise Grail knight, we choose wisely, we can set ourselves up to face the afternoon with renewed vigor. On top of that, a good lunch helps us cut down on unnecessary snacking, which is a Good Thing.

We've worked hard to make sure that this chapter delivers on the Leon promise of fast food that's good for you. So packed herein you'll find soups, salads, wraps, dippers, and, if you need that massive jolt of pasta-driven energy, a bunch of sauces to liven up any plate of spaghetti.

KAY

Roasted Pumpkin Soup with a Zing

SERVES 4 • PREPARATION TIME: 15 MINUTES • COOKING TIME: 1 HOUR 15 MINUTES • ♥ WF GF V

Creamy and comforting, this colorful soup will cheer up even the darkest fall day. To jazz it up a little, we've added ground cumin and coriander for warmth.

4 lbs **pumpkin**, seeded, cut in wedges
3–4 sprigs of **fresh thyme**
2 tablespoons **olive oil**
3 cups good **vegetable** or **chicken stock**
1–2 teaspoons **ground cumin**

1–2 teaspoons **ground coriander**
2 **limes**, cut into wedges, to serve
2 teaspoons **dried red pepper flakes**, to garnish
salt and **freshly ground black pepper**

1. Heat the oven to 350°F.

2. Put the pumpkin wedges and the thyme onto a large roasting pan, coat with the olive oil, and season with salt and pepper. Place in the oven for 45 minutes to an hour, or until it's really soft and tender. Note, it could take even longer—every pumpkin is individual—just keep checking on it until it's done.

3. When the pumpkin is cooked, set it aside to cool, then scrape the flesh away from the skin. Cut larger chunks into ¾ inch chunks. Then put it into a saucepan with the stock and process with an immersion blender until you have a creamy consistency.

4. Add the spices and heat through for about 5 minutes. Then taste and add seasoning.

5. Serve in bowls, with the lime wedges and little piles of chiles on the side.

Leek & Potato Soup

SERVES 4 • PREPARATION TIME: 20 MINUTES • COOKING TIME: 45 MINUTES • WF GF V

This is the simplest and most soothing soup I know, and perfect for a stormy winter's day.

12oz **leeks**, cleaned and sliced
3–4 Yukon Gold **potatoes**, peeled and cut into chunks
2 teaspoons **sea salt**
4 cups **water**
½ cup **heavy cream**
1 tablespoon chopped **fresh flat-leaf parsley**
freshly **ground black pepper**

TIPS

* You can also serve this cold as a vichyssoise.
* Instead of the parsley, add a couple of bunches of fresh watercress for a delicious watercress and potato soup.

1. Put the leeks and potatoes into a heavy saucepan. Add the salt and the water and bring to a boil. Simmer until soft and cooked through, about 30–35 minutes. Then turn off the heat and, with an immersion blender, process until smooth.

2. Add the cream and stir it into the soup, then add the parsley and a few grinds of black pepper. Taste and adjust the seasoning, and serve with crusty bread.

Kay's Minestrone Maltese

SERVES 4 • PREPARATION TIME: 20 MINUTES • COOKING TIME: 30 MINUTES

When my parents first moved to Gozo in Malta, they quickly made friends with some of the local farmers who had fields on the slopes below the house, and my mom would often buy from them directly. One of those farmers, whose name I have long since forgotten, taught her the basis of this soup. It's not a thin soup; its hearty, filling, and packed with flavor.

1–2 tablespoons **olive oil**
1 **onion**, finely chopped
1 **carrot**, finely chopped
1 stick of **celery**, finely chopped
2 cloves of **garlic**, finely chopped
1 teaspoon **fresh rosemary**, chopped
5 cups **vegetable stock**
1 (14½-oz) **can of tomatoes**
1 **bay leaf**
1 piece of **Parmesan rind** (optional)
1 (15-oz) **can of cannellini beans**,
  drained and rinsed

3oz **little pasta shapes**
1 cup **peas**
1 **zucchini**, cut into chunks
a good grating of **nutmeg**
2½oz **bacon**, diced and cooked
  (optional)
a few **celery leaves**, chopped
freshly shredded **Parmesan cheese**,
  to garnish
salt and **freshly ground black pepper**

1. Heat the oil in a large, heavy saucepan over low to medium heat. Add the onion, carrot, celery, and garlic and soften gently for about 5 minutes. Then add the rosemary and cook for another 2 minutes or so to release its oils.

2. Now add the stock, tomatoes, bay leaf, and the Parmesan rind (if you're using it), and cook for about 5 minutes. Season with salt and pepper, add the beans, and simmer for another 15 minutes or so.

3. Add the pasta, and cook according to the package directions until done. About 5 minutes before the end, add the remaining vegetables.

4. Finally, add a couple of gratings of fresh nutmeg and stir it into the soup, and then season to taste. Add the bacon (if you are using it).

5. Serve garnished with chopped celery leaves and a good grating of Parmesan.

TIPS

* Minestrone simply means "a big soup," so you can pretty much put into it anything you like. Instead of the peas, why not add about 6 cups of trimmed and sliced kale or chard?

* If I want to add some bacon, I tend to cook them in a separate pan and add them as a garnish. This means I can serve this as a completely vegetarian soup. If you prefer, you can cook the bacon right at the beginning, before the onion, to add a deep porky note to the dish.

Marion's Lentil Soup

SERVES 6 • PREPARATION TIME: 10 MINUTES • COOKING TIME: 1 HOUR • ✓ WF GF

If chicken noodle soup is Jewish penicillin, this is North London Protestant penicillin.
Marion, John's mom, makes this for the family when it's cold, or when people have colds.
Make plenty in advance, and get it out of the freezer whenever the feeling or the need arises.

1 tablespoon **olive oil**
1 large **onion**, chopped
2 **leeks**, sliced
1 clove of **garlic**, crushed
4 slices of **smoked bacon**, chopped
2 **carrots**, sliced
3 sticks of **celery**, sliced
1 cup **red lentils**, washed and drained
½ teaspoon **grated nutmeg** or **turmeric**
5 cups **vegetable** or **chicken stock**
salt and **freshly ground black pepper**

JOHN'S MOM MARION, NICE, CA. 1957

1. Gently heat the oil in a large heavy saucepan. Add the onions and leeks and let them cook gently until they're transparent. Add the garlic and bacon and cook on medium heat for another 3–4 minutes.

2. Now stir in the carrots and celery, and cook for another 2–3 minutes. Finally, stir in the lentils and add the nutmeg or turmeric.

3. Pour in the stock and bring the soup to a boil. Simmer with the lid on for about 30–40 minutes, or until the lentils and vegetables are tender. Season the soup with salt and pepper, then blend until smooth.

TIPS

* Marion prefers to use an immersion blender for this recipe. If you're using a stand-alone blender, be very careful not to overfill it so you don't spatter the kitchen (and yourself) with boiling soup.

* For a thicker consistency, use more carrots and/or celery.

ABOVE: MARION'S LENTIL SOUP
BELOW: KATIE'S SPROUT & CARAMELIZED ONION SOUP

Katie's Sprout & Caramelized Onion Soup

SERVES 6 • PREPARATION TIME: 15 MINUTES • COOKING TIME: 1 HOUR 10 MINUTES • WF GF

Katie says: "I love making soups. They're generally easy, and yet everyone thinks you're terribly clever. This one was the result of overenthusiastic sprout-buying last Christmas; it was so popular it even made it onto the official Derham "Boxing Day" [Christmas holiday] menu this year—and believe me, that hasn't changed for about three generations."

4 **onions**, sliced
½ stick **butter**
1 tablespoon **sugar**
a handful of **fresh thyme**, leaves picked
1 lb **Brussels sprouts**, tidied up and halved
4 cups **chicken stock**
salt and **freshly ground black pepper**

1. Melt the onions in the butter. By this I mean don't brown them, just put them on the lowest possible heat in a heavy saucepan with the lid on and let them go transparent for about 40 minutes. (I found that heating them up, then putting them into the warming oven of the Aga was perfect; a low-temperature conventional oven would work, too.)

2. When they're really floppy, put them on the stove, turn the heat up a little, and add the sugar. Let them caramelize by cooking them for 5–10 minutes, stirring regularly, until they've started to color.

3. Stir in the thyme (strip the leaves off about 4 sprigs) and the sprouts, mix it all together, add a little salt and pepper, then add the chicken stock. (Bouillon cubes are naturally fine for this, although if you happen to have fresh stock already made or in the refrigerator, it will make the finished soup a notch superior.)

4. Simmer for about 10 minutes, or until the sprouts are tender. Process in a food processor or blender, being careful because the soup will be very hot. If you think it's looking a little thick, add a splash more stock to loosen the texture. Serve with a swirl of cream if you're feeling fancy.

KATIE, 1978

Katie is my wife and a very tremendous one. After we first met, I explained to her that she was going to marry me, and eventually the penny dropped and she did. OK, so there are some stories in between those two things, but I can tell you that in my view she would make a very good Queen of a small country. She is, in my view, pretty, interesting, interested, smart, great company, caring, a lovely Mom, good on the TV, sociable, a great team player, kind, has good posture, and I love her very much.

JOHN

The Wheel of Tomato-based Pasta Sauce

ALL DISHES SERVE 4-6 • PREPARATION TIME: 10 MINUTES • COOKING TIME: 30 MINUTES • ✓ ♥ WF GF V

The Hub of the Wheel

There's a lot you can do to change a simple tomato-base sauce into a variety of different dishes. Here's how. Two of the sauces opposite require a minor interruption to this simple process. In both cases, it comes at the onion and garlic stage.

1 tablespoon **olive oil**	1 tablespoon **tomato paste**
1 **onion**, chopped	2 teaspoons **dried basil**
2 cloves of **garlic**, chopped	1 teaspoon **dried oregano**
14½-oz can of **diced tomatoes**	**salt** and **freshly ground black pepper**

1. In a heavy saucepan, heat the olive oil over medium heat, then add the onion. Cook until it's soft and sweet smelling. Add the garlic and cook for another 2 minutes or so, or until it smells like good times. Add the tomatoes, then stir in the tomato paste and the dried herbs, and season with salt and pepper …

Pomodoro è Basilico

… add a pinch of sugar to cut the acidity, and simmer the sauce for 15–20 minutes. Then rip in the leaves from a small bunch of fresh basil, and serve over the pasta of your choice. We love this with linguine or spaghetti.

All'Arrabbiata

… depending on how you like it, seed and slice 1 or 2 red chiles and add them alongside the garlic (the second interruption). Then add the tomatoes, tomato paste, dried herbs, and salt and pepper, as before.

All'Amatriciana

… the first interruption: At the very beginning, cook 2½oz cubed pancetta in a dry saucepan until it's not quite golden. Then add the onions, followed by the garlic, along with a pinch of dried red pepper flakes. Then add the tomatoes, tomato paste, dried herbs, and salt and pepper, as before. This is terrific with penne or rigatoni.

Papalina

… this is exactly the same as the pomodoro è basilico, except that you add ¼–½ cup heavy cream before the basil leaves and stir it in well.

Con Tonno è Piselli

… once you've made the tomato sauce, add a drained 5-oz can of tuna, ½ teaspoon dried thyme, and 1⅓ cups frozen peas. Reduce the sauce for about 20 minutes, and serve with conchiglie.

Zucchini

… add a pinch of sugar to cut the acidity. Then trim the ends of 2 zucchini and, depending on your preference, cut them into sticks or circles. After the tomatoes have simmered for about 10 minutes, chuck them in. This sauce is great with penne or fusilli.

* In all these sauces, we like to add ½ cup white wine, just for that extra depth and dimension. You don't have to if you don't want to.

Wrap 'n' Roll

When we started Leon, even before we opened Carnaby Street, we made a list of all the foods that are held by hand. Burgers, sandwiches, satay sticks … you get the idea. We launched our menu with both hot wraps and cold wraps. We temporarily took cold wraps off the menu for what was meant to be a few weeks and haven't yet, seven years later, put them back on.

We have plans to fix that, because wraps and rolls make wonderful lunches.

Whether you make them in advance or let your family have the fun of preparing them real-time, they have to be one of the easiest ways of getting through a lunchtime or afternoon snack time unscathed.

As a variation on a theme, John's sister-in-law Qing (married to Richard in Toronto) has taught the kids to make sushi rolls. They love it, the activity, the sense of achievement, and the taste. Her simple recipe is included here.

Let's wrap 'n' roll …

Fish Stick Wrap

SERVES 2 • PREPARATION TIME: 10 MINUTES • COOKING TIME: 20 MINUTES • ✓ ♥

Every kid's favorite … in a wrap.

4 **fish sticks**
2 good-quality **flatbreads**
2 tablespoons good **tartar sauce**
4–6 **pickles**, sliced

Romaine lettuce leaves, shredded
a pinch of chopped **fresh dill**
a squeeze of **lemon juice**
salt and **freshly ground black pepper**

1. Cook the fish sticks according to the package directions. If you cook them in the oven (our preferred method), you can always add the flatbreads at the bottom of the oven, or just heat them up as per package directions.

2. Spread some tartar sauce onto the warmed flatbreads, and top with a few slices of pickle. Add some lettuce, then the crisply cooked fish sticks. Add a little sprinkling of freshly chopped dill, season with salt and pepper, and get fancy with a squeeze of fresh lemon juice to finish. Wrap and eat.

Leon's Muenster Wrap

SERVES 2 • PREPARATION TIME: 10 MINUTES • COOKING TIME: 6 MINUTES • ✓ V

This is based on the popular wrap we had on the menu for a while. Time to bring it back?

2 tablespoons good **mango chutney**
2 **gluten-free flatbreads**, or the **flatbread**
  of your choice
7oz **Muenster or mozzarella cheese**,
  sliced and marinated in **olive oil**, **garlic**,
  and **thyme**
2 **carrots**, peeled and shredded
2 tablespoons **fresh flat-leaf parsley**, chopped
salt and **freshly ground black pepper**

1. Spread the mango chutney thinly on the flatbread of your choice.

2. Drain the cheese and broil it for 3 minutes or so on each side, until golden brown.

3. Pop half the cheese into each flatbread (heat them up, if you like) and add the carrot, parsley, and freshly ground pepper. And some salt if you really want it. Wrap and eat.

TIPS

* Marinate the cheese in olive oil with a crushed clove of garlic and some fresh or dried oregano.

Natasha's Chicken Fajitas

MAKES 4 • PREPARATION TIME: 10 MINUTES • MARINATING TIME: 15 MINUTES, LONGER IF POSSIBLE
COOKING TIME: 5 MINUTES • ✓ DF

John's daughter Natasha's favorite dinner is fajitas. Saturday night, Sunday night, any night. In front of *Glee*: eleven-year-old girl heaven.

> 3 small **chicken breasts**, cut into strips
> 2 teaspoons **dried oregano**
> a good pinch of **chili powder**, or to taste
> 1 teaspoon **ground cumin**
> 1 **onion**, sliced thinly
> 2 **red bell peppers**, sliced thinly
> 3 tablespoons **olive oil**
> 4 **flatbreads** of your choice, or some **soft tortilla**
> **salt** and **freshly ground black pepper**

1. Put the chicken, oregano, chili, cumin, onion, and bell peppers into a bowl with 2 tablespoons of the olive oil and mix well. Season with salt and pepper and set aside to marinate for as long as you can.

2. Heat the remaining tablespoon of olive oil in a sauté pan over medium heat and add the chicken, onion, and bell peppers. Cook until the onions have caught some color, the peppers are soft, and the chicken is cooked through—about 7–10 minutes. You may need to do this in 2 batches to make sure the chicken browns nicely.

3. Serve in a flatbread or tortilla, with a bowl of the Romano pepper and chile salsa on the side (see page 29), or with Kay's Guacamole (see page 51).

Kay's California Rock 'n' Roll Wrap

SERVES 4 • PREPARATION TIME: 10 MINUTES • COOKING TIME: 12–15 MINUTES • ✓ ♥

This is loosely based on the idea of the California roll you get in Japanese restaurants.

12oz **salmon fillet**
2 tablespoons **light soy sauce** or **tamari**
¼ cup **good mayonnaise**
½ teaspoon **wasabi powder** (more if you like it hot)
4 **wraps** of your choice, warmed
3 **scallions**, shredded lengthwise
1 **avocado**, sliced
1–2 tablespoons **toasted sesame seeds**
1 **lime**, quartered (optional)

1. Heat the oven to 400°F or preheat the broiler.

2. Marinate the salmon in the soy sauce for a few minutes. Then either broil or bake it in the oven for about 12–15 minutes, depending on its thickness, or until it's cooked (you can follow the recipe for Sweet Soy Salmon on page 116, if you like).

3. Mix the mayonnaise with the wasabi powder.

4. Put the salmon into the wrap with some shredded scallion, sliced avocado, wasabi mayonnaise, and a sprinkling of toasted sesame seeds. Serve with a wedge of lime, if you desire.

Shrimp Satay Wrap

SERVES 4 • PREPARATION TIME: 10 MINUTES PLUS MARINATING • COOKING TIME: 10–15 MINUTES • ✓ ♥

This one should please the whole family. It's sweet, nutty, salty, and a little spicy.

10½oz **raw peeled shrimps**
2 teaspoons **Madras curry powder**
½ teaspoon **turmeric**
¼ cup **coconut milk**
a dash of **Thai fish sauce**
4 good-quality **wraps**, warmed
Romaine lettuce leaves, shredded
a good handful of **fresh cilantro**, coarsely chopped
½ **lime**, to serve

For the sauce:
¼ cup **sugar-free chunky peanut butter**
1 tablespoon **soy sauce** or **tamari**
1 teaspoon **Madras curry powder**
a pinch of **dried chile**
2 teaspoons **palm sugar** or **dark brown sugar**
a dash of **white vinegar**
1 tablespoon **coconut milk**
3–4 tablespoons **water**, to loosen

1. Put the shrimp, curry powder, turmeric, coconut milk, and fish sauce into a bowl and mix together. Set aside to marinate for about 30 minutes (or as long as you can).

2. To make the sauce, put all the ingredients into a bowl and stir them until combined, adding the water a little at a time until the consistency is to your liking. If it seems a little thick, just add a little more water. Taste and adjust the seasoning.

3. Heat a grill pan and cook the drained shrimp until cooked—about 8–10 minutes. Put them straight into the warmed wraps, add a dollop or two of the sauce, and top with some shredded lettuce, chopped cilantro, and a squeeze of lime.

Aunt Qing's Sushi Roll

MAKES 3 ROLLS, ENOUGH FOR 2 • PREPARATION TIME: 30 MINUTES PLUS COOLING
COOKING TIME: 15 MINUTES • WF GF DF

John's brother-in-law is called Richard. He's Katie's brother. He looks enough like the British Prime Minister David Cameron that we think we should start a lookey-likey agency. Richard is married to Qing. She is Chinese. With us so far? When they come over for Christmas, Qing makes sushi with the kids. It is involved enough to give them real satisfaction at having made it, it's fun to make and eat, and it's not as tricky as you might think. And at Christmas, it is an oasis of fresh exotica in amid the meaty, potato-y Yuletide carnage.

2 cups **glutinous** or **risotto rice**, rinsed thoroughly
2 tablespoons **rice vinegar**
1 tablespoon **sugar**
1 teaspoon **salt**
3 **nori (seaweed) wrappers**
2 tablespoons **mayonnaise**
½ an **avocado**, thinly sliced
½ a **cucumber**, thinly sliced
soy sauce and **wasabi**, to serve

* You will also need a bamboo mat, which you can find in most good Asian supermarkets

TIPS

* Add some cooked crabmeat to make it a California roll.
* If you want to add raw fish, make sure it's "sushi grade."
* You can cool the rice with a fan to speed up the process.
* To avoid sticky fingers, keep on hand a bowl of water with a couple of drops of vinegar in it so you can rinse them when you need to.

1. Put the rice into a saucepan with 2 cups of water and place on the heat to cook.

2. Meanwhile, mix together the rice vinegar, sugar, and salt to make a rice seasoning.

3. When the rice is cooked, spread it out in a wide wooden salad bowl to cool. While it's still warm (about 104°F), sprinkle it with the rice seasoning and stir it in, spreading it through the rice, making sure it doesn't become too clumpy.

4. Lay out a sheet of nori on your bamboo mat, with its rough side facing upward. Press a small handful of rice onto the nori and spread it evenly over the whole sheet, leaving a ¾ inch strip at the bottom so you can seal the wrap closed. Spread the rice with one-third of the mayonnaise.

5. Mix together the avocado and cucumber, then take one-third of this mixture and lay it on the mayonnaise. Try to make sure the sliced vegetables lie as closely together as possible.

6. Use the bamboo mat to roll up the sushi tightly. Keep it tight as you roll, putting pressure on all the way, otherwise it will fall apart. Chop the roll into slices—cut it in the middle first, then work out to the ends to ensure neat, elegant pieces. The rice often sticks to the knife, so rinse the blade whenever you feel it's too sticky. Serve the sushi rolls with a small bowl of soy sauce and with wasabi on the side, for dipping.

① ④

SNACK PLATES

If snacks are going to be the order of the day, you really can't beat a crudité and a dip to dunk it in. Be it carrots, bell peppers, celery, cucumber, tomatoes, or toast, homemade dips hold the key to healthy snacking. Totally transparent. What you see is what you get. And they make for a superspeedy lighter lunch, too.

① Hummus

SERVES 4–6 • PREPARATION TIME: 10 MINUTES •
COOKING TIME: NONE • ✓ ♥ WF GF V

Everybody loves hummus. Our supermarkets sell it by the ton—literally. But have you seen what's written on the label? Try this homemade version, and cut out the additives.

> 1 (15-oz) can of **chickpeas**,
> drained
> 1–2 cloves of **garlic**, peeled
> 2 tablespoons **tahini**
> 2 tablespoons **olive oil**
> ⅓ cup **water**
> the juice of ½ a **lemon**
> a large pinch of **salt**
> a drizzle of **extra virgin olive oil**
> a sprinkle of **ground sumac** and/
> or **ground cumin** (optional)

1. Just place everything except the extra virgin olive oil and the sumac/cumin in a food processor and process until smooth. Taste and adjust the seasoning.

2. Serve in a bowl, drizzled with a little extra virgin olive oil. Sprinkle with the sumac and/or cumin, if you desire.

② Lentil Masala Dip

SERVES 4–6 • PREPARATION TIME: 5 MINUTES PLUS COOLING
COOKING TIME: 10-20 MINUTES • ✓ ♥ WF GF V

Fragrant with curry and very delicious.

> ¾ cup **red lentils**
> 1 teaspoon **Madras curry powder**
> a pinch of **ground ginger**
> a small handful of **fresh**
> **cilantro**, chopped
> **salt** and **freshly ground black pepper**

1. Rinse the lentils well under running water—you want to get rid of any grit or sand. Put them into a saucepan and cover them with fresh cold water.

2. Bring to a boil and simmer for about 15 minutes, or according to the package directions. Drain and set aside to cool.

3. Once the lentils have cooled, process them in a food processor with the curry powder, ground ginger, salt, and pepper. Taste and adjust the seasoning.

4. Stir in the chopped cilantro and serve.

③ Tangy Cheese Dip (Cheez Whiz)

SERVES 4 • PREPARATION TIME: 10 MINUTES • COOKING TIME: NONE • ✓ ♥ WF GF V

Cottage cheese isn't just for diet fruit plates.

> 1¾ cups **cottage cheese**
> 1 clove of **garlic**, peeled and chopped
> 1 tablespoon **Worcestershire sauce**
> 1 teaspoon **ketchup**
> ½ teaspoon **Tabasco sauce**
> a good squeeze of **lime** or **lemon juice**

> 1 tablespoon chopped **fresh chives**
> 4 **cherry tomatoes**, seeded and chopped
> a small handful of **fresh cilantro**, chopped
> 1 large **red chile**, seeded and slivered
> (optional)
> **salt** and **freshly ground black pepper**

1. Process everything except the chives, tomatoes, cilantro, and chile in a food processor. Taste and adjust the seasoning. You want a little spice, some sharpness, and some sweetness.

2. Pour into a serving bowl and gently stir in the chives and tomatoes. Sprinkle some chopped cilantro and the slivered chiles on top.

④ Kay's Guacamole

SERVES 4 • PREPARATION TIME: 10 MINUTES •
COOKING TIME: NONE • ✓ ♥ WF GF DF V

Rich, green, and good for you.

> 1 clove of **garlic**, peeled
> 2 ripe **avocados**, peeled and
>   flesh scooped out
> the juice of ½ a **lime**
> 2 **scallions**, trimmed and
>   finely chopped
> a small handful of **fresh cilantro**,
>   finely chopped
> ½–1 **green serrano** or **jalapeño**
>   **chile**, seeded and finely
>   chopped (optional)
> 4 **cherry tomatoes**, sliced (optional)
> **sea salt**, to taste

1. Using a big mortar and pestle or a molcajete, grind the garlic to a paste. Add the avocado and pound until mashed. Add the lime juice.

2. Stir in the chopped scallions and the chopped cilantro. If using, stir in the chiles and tomatoes. Season to taste with salt.

FOOD FACT

OH-OH-AVOCADO
Avocados are the James Bond of superfoods. They're one of Nature's true wonders. Underneath that alligator-y skin lies a creamy green powerhouse of amino acids, vitamins (B, E, and Kay's favorite … K) and healthy fats. They have 35 percent more potassium than bananas. We've even heard you can use them to wean a baby—but we're not recommending it.

FOOD FACT

SUMAC
Sumac is the fruit of a shrub that grows in the Middle East and the Mediterranean. In its dried, ground form, it's a beautiful brick red and has a tart, citrusy tang.

⑤ Roasted Carrot & Cumin Dip

SERVES 4–6 • PREPARATION TIME: 10 MINUTES
COOKING TIME: 50 MINUTES • ♥ WF GF DF V

Healthy and simple. And bright orange.

> 10–12 **carrots** (about 1½ lbs),
>   coarsely chopped
> 3 tablespoons **olive oil**
> a pinch of **sugar** (optional)
> 1 teaspoon **ground cumin**
> 1 clove of **garlic**, peeled
>   and coarsely crushed
> 2 tablespoons **water**
> **salt** and **freshly ground**
>   **black pepper**

1. Heat the oven to 400°F.

2. Tumble the carrots in a roasting pan with 1 tablespoon of the olive oil, a pinch of sugar (if you feel like it), and a good sprinkle of salt and pepper.

3. Cover with aluminum foil and roast for 45–50 minutes, or until a knife goes through the carrots easily.

4. Remove from the oven and cool slightly.

5. Once the carrots have cooled, put them into the food processor or blender and process, adding the cumin, garlic, and the remaining 2 tablespoons of olive oil and the water, until you have a nice creamy consistency. Serve at room temperature.

JAZZING IT UP

Every so often, I'll rummage through a kitchen cabinet for an ingredient and find cans and boxes that have been there for years. I know I'm not alone in this. So I resolved to cook more with the contents of my cabinets. The thing is, we've all been encouraged (a) to cook from fresh, and (b) to cook seasonally—both of which are Very Good Things. But we've forgotten the importance of making use of all those foods we store so we can enjoy them unseasonally. So dust off that can of sardines or beans, and let's make them new again.   KAY

Anchovies

Drain a 2-oz can of anchovies. Blend with some fresh rosemary, olive oil, lemon juice, a couple of cloves of garlic, and a glug of Cognac. Serve spread on toast or use it to melt into a gravy or sauce for beef dishes.

Drain a can of anchovies and chop them finely. Melt some unsalted butter—about ½ stick— in a saucepan. Add the anchovies and stir over gentle heat until melted together and smooth. Add some freshly ground black pepper and a good squeeze of lemon juice. Add a handful of halved cherry tomatoes and heat through. Toss with some cooked pasta, preferably capellini.

Tuna

Well, of course, there's the pasta sauce on page 40. But there's more we can do with the humble can of tuna.

Boil 2 or 3 large, peeled potatoes. Drain and mash them well with a little butter and milk, salt, and pepper. Drain a can of tuna and mash it into the potato. Add a pinch of ground cumin and/or some finely grated lemon zest and chopped fresh parsley and/or some chopped pickles and/or some capers and chopped scallions—whatever you want. Form the mixture into patties and lightly coat them with a little rice flour (optional). Cook gently in a little olive oil until they're golden brown on both sides.

Toss a salad of lettuce, endive, scallions, and cucumber. Mix together a dressing of lime juice, Thai fish sauce, a pinch of sugar, 1 chopped Thai chile, and a handful of chopped fresh cilantro. Drain a can of tuna and sprinkle it the salad. Pour over the dressing over the top. A tasty Thai Yum Tuna.

Sardines in oil

Make a deconstructed *Sardines en Saor*—thinly slice an onion and cook it in a little olive oil until it's softened. Add a tablespoon of red wine vinegar to the saucepan, bubble it for a minute or two, and season with salt and black pepper. Pour this over the drained sardines and garnish with raisins, toasted pine nuts, and chopped parsley.

Heat some olive oil in a saucepan. Sauté a chopped clove or two of garlic. Add a can of drained sardines. Break them up a little. Add a can of tomatoes. Mix well, stirring it all together. Add a few pitted black olives, some capers, and some dried red pepper flakes or lemon zest, if you desire. Pour it all over pasta and top with some chopped fresh parsley.

Beans

Beans are a treasure trove.

Bean purée—roast 2 whole bulbs of garlic by wrapping them in some aluminum foil with a dash of olive oil and a sprig or two of fresh thyme, salt, and pepper. Put into the oven at 350°F for about 45 minutes, or until soft and cooked through. Let cool a little, just so you can handle them. Squeeze out the garlic into a blender or food processor. Add the drained, rinsed cannellini beans. Add 2 tablespoons good olive oil and some salt and pepper. Add some water to thin if the consistency is a little thick. Serve on toast, with a squeeze of lemon and some chopped fresh parsley, or as a side to any broiled meat—it's particularly good with the Midweek Lamb on page 130.

Kidney beans—how about a Quick 'n' Easy Jamaican Red Pea Soup? Sauté some diced bacon in a little olive oil with a few chopped scallions and the leaves from a sprig of fresh thyme. Add a can of drained, rinsed kidney beans. Add enough water to cover well. Add a small piece of Scotch bonnet chile, with the seeds and membrane removed. Bring to a boil. When the beans are cooked, use an immersion blender or put into a food processor to blend the soup (be careful: it will be HOT). Taste and add salt and pepper, if desired. Serve with some hot sauce on the side and few chopped scallions on top. This was Grandma Southby's (Fred's grandma's) favorite!

SALADS & BRAIN FOOD

We are what we eat, or so the saying goes. But it's only recently that scientists have begun to understand the biochemical relationships between our diet and our bodies.

Salads deliver the fibers and the raw vibrancy that cooked foods sometimes don't. That straight-from-the-earth quality that I love for both the taste, and the sheer immediacy. Pull up a beet. Wash it. Grate it. Squeeze over some orange juice. Sprinkle on some raisins. Eat it. Job done.

As for brain food, here we've focused on ingredients that deliver omega-3s. We're still learning how much they do for us, but all the evidence seems to point to their being key not just to the development of the growing brain, but to supporting its everyday function in adults as well. So here's to the good stuff.

KAY

Mackerel Skies Salad

SERVES: 4 AS A MAIN DISH, OR 6 AS AN APPETIZER • PREPARATION TIME: 15 MINUTES • COOKING TIME: NONE ✓ ♥ WF GF DF

This is FULL of omega-3 fatty acids and vitamin C, and packed with wonderful agrodolce flavor. It's quick to make, and it's colorful, too—just like a sunrise on a plate.

We've included it here as a lunch, but Kay often serves it as an appetizer, especially before a rich roast dinner.

1 large **carrot**, grated into long strips
1 small **red bell pepper**, seeded and sliced into strips
¼ of a small **green cabbage**, shredded
1 small **raw beet**, peeled and grated
½ a large **cucumber**, peeled and sliced into small cubes
7oz **hot-smoked mackerel**, peeled and flaked
1 tablespoon toasted **flaxseed**

For the dressing:
3 tablespoons **olive oil**
the juice of ½ a large **orange**
3 teaspoons **red wine vinegar**
a good pinch of **sea salt**
freshly ground black pepper

1. Mix all the vegetables together in a large bowl. Mix the ingredients for the dressing together in clean screw-top jar, shake, and stir thoroughly into the vegetables.

2. Stir in the flaked, smoked mackerel, or sprinkle it on the top. Up to you. Finish with the toasted flaxseed.

TIPS

* Instead of mackerel, you could use hot-smoked trout or salmon. Smoked chicken works, too.

* Sometimes Kay omits the fish and uses the salad as a base for leftover duck or turkey.

* Mix up the seeds—we love the crunch and flavor of toasted flax seeds, but pumpkin or sunflower seeds would be great, too, as would walnut pieces.

A few words about mackerel

Iridescent, shiny, and as fast a bullet; as fish go, it's just about as healthy as it's possible to be. It's full of omega-3 fatty acids, vitamin B_{12} and selenium. At the time of writing, it's one of the most sustainable fish in the sea. (Let's hope it stays that way.) And it's delicious. Smoked, broiled, steamed, or roasted—and even raw—it's packed with flavor. Here are a couple of easy suggestions for mackerel-base lunchtime salads.

Justin Ovenden's Mackerel Ceviche

SERVES: 4 • PREPARATION TIME: 15 MINUTES • COOKING TIME: NONE • ✓ ♥ WF GF DF

First things first: Ceviche is not raw fish (that's sushi). You're cooking it chemically in the acid from the lime juice. Even so, you want *really* fresh mackerel for this, the fresher the better.

Justin says: "This is very much a 'what's in the garden, how's it looking' dish, so don't worry if you go a little over or under on the measurements".

> 4 large **mackerel fillets**, skinned and boned
> the juice of 1 (or 2) **limes**
> 1 tablespoon **olive oil** or **canola oil**
> 1–3 **small red chiles**, finely chopped,
>   depending on heat tolerance
> a small handful of **fresh chives**, finely chopped
> a handful of **arugula leaves**
> a small handful of **fresh cilantro** and/or **hyssop**
> a small bunch of **baby asparagus**, lightly steamed
> **kosher salt** and **coarse ground black pepper**

1. Cut the mackerel into roughly ½ inch squares or strips. Mix it with the lime juice, oil, chiles, and chives, and season with salt and pepper.

2. Let stand for 5–10 minutes, giving it an occasional stir. Then mix it with the leaves, herbs, and asparagus and serve.

FOOD FACT

HYSSOP

Hyssop is an ancient herb with a slightly bitter, minty flavor. It's great to plant in your garden or in your windowbox because the bees absolutely love it. However, be careful when you're cooking with it. Like sage, it has a tendency to dominate.

Mackerel is in my top three fish to eat raw. I have a wonderful memory of fishing for mackerel off the Dorset coast in England in mid-summer with friends, when I first ventured into trying sashimi (of sorts). Since then, I've gone fishing a hundred times, where, upon catching the first mackerel, I whip out some mustard and start sharing with whoever doesn't look at me like I'm crazy.

The love of my life, Niamh, has always expressed a distaste for this ritual, due to the fact that "It's a bit too Boy!" Max, our beautiful son, is a little too young for punchy mustard, so we came up with our ceviche. It's simple, which makes it perfect to have as a quick snack, or to prepare in large quantities for visiting friends and family.

JUSTIN

JUSTIN, 1975, NIAMH, 1978, AND MAXI, 2011

CONDIMENTS

Gomasio

MAKES ABOUT ⅓ CUP • PREPARATION TIME: NONE • COOKING TIME: 15–20 MINUTES • ✓ ♥ WF GF V

Gomasio is used a lot as a condiment in macrobiotic diets, although it originates from Japan. We use it to cut down on added salt and to add a delicious nutty flavor to soups, salads, cereals, and vegetables. Sesame seeds are little treasure stores, too—full of protein, iron, zinc, and amino acids. You can buy gomasio in health food stores, but it's just as easy to make at home.

> ½ cup **sesame seeds**
> 1 tablespoon **sea salt**

1. Heat a wide, dry skillet over low heat and toast the sesame seeds until they are golden and fragrant—be careful with this; you don't want them to burn. It should take about 10–15 minutes. Keep an eye on them and stir them occasionally.

2. Remove from the heat and let them cool.

3. Put them into a mini-blender or coffee grinder with the salt and process until you have a coarse sprinkle—you want some texture, so don't let it get too powdery. Keep in an airtight jar and use as needed. It should keep for about 4–6 weeks.

4. Some health food stores sell toasted sesame seeds, so you could just skip the toasting part. And feel free to play with the proportions.

Kay's Cajun Magic

MAKES ABOUT ⅓ CUP • PREPARATION TIME: 2 MINUTES • COOKING TIME: NONE • ✓ ♥ WF GF V

I used to buy Cajun spice by the case for my Dad when he lived in Gozo, Malta. He used to put it on everything, and I think we must have tried just about every brand on the market at one point or another. In the end, I realized it was much more economical (and a lot less salty) to make my own. Here it is.

> 2 tablespoons **ground paprika**
> 1–2 tablespoons good **sea salt**
> ½ tablespoon **ground black pepper**
> 2 tablespoons **cayenne pepper**
>
> 2 tablespoons **dried oregano**
> 2 tablespoons **dried thyme**
> 1 tablespoon **garlic powder**
> 1 teaspoon **dried roasted red pepper flakes**

1. Spoon all the ingredients into a clean, screw-top jar. Put the lid on and shake well to combine everything thoroughly. Process into a powder in a mini-chopper.

2. Store with your other spices until you need it.

3 Sisters Superfood Salad.

SERVES 4 • PREPARATION TIME: 15–20 MINUTES • COOKING TIME: 35 MINUTES • ✓ ♥ DF V

These 3 sisters—corn, beans, and squash—and their friends really pack a punch: a vibrant, delicious, colorful salad that showcases big, bold flavors influenced by the fusion of the new and old worlds.

12oz **pumpkin**, peeled, seeded, and cut into 1–1½ inch cubes (about 3 cups)
4–6 small **purple potatoes**
a little **olive oil**
2 cobs of **corn**
4 large handfuls of **mixed salad greens**
2 cups **bean** and **seed sprouts**
4 **scallions**, trimmed and sliced on the diagonal
1 **avocado**, cut into ¾–1 inch pieces

½ cup **pomegranate seeds**
a handful of **pumpkin seeds**
a good sprinkling of **gomasio** (see page 57)

For the dressing:
2 tablespoons **lemon juice**
½ tablespoon **tamari**
1 tablespoon **rice vinegar**
3 tablespoons **mild olive oil**

1. Bring 2 large saucepans of lightly salted water to a boil. Put the pumpkin pieces into one and simmer until they are just tender—about 8–10 minutes. Stick a knife in to test for doneness—we want them tender but not collapsing. Drain, run under some cold water to stop them from cooking, then set aside to cool.

2. In the other saucepan, add the whole purple potatoes and cook until just done, about 15–20 minutes, depending on your potato size. Drain and set aside to cool.

3. Meanwhile, heat a grill pan. Lightly oil the corn cobs and place them on the heated pan. Keep turning them until they are cooked through and have some nice charmarks on the sides—about 10 minutes. Remove and set aside to cool.

4. To make the dressing, mix all the ingredients together well. Taste and adjust the seasoning if you like. We want a salty/sour/umami flavor.

5. Now take a sharp knife and, holding the corn vertically, gently slice off the kernels.

6. Divide the greens evenly among 4 bowls and sprinkle the bean and seed sprouts on top.

7. Slice the potatoes into disks and add them, together with the pumpkin, scallions, avocado, and corn kernels, to the bowls. Sprinkle the pomegranate seeds over each portion.

8. Pour the dressing over the top, and sprinkle with the pumpkin seeds and gomasio to serve.

TIPS

* This salad stands up well on its own, but you can also add broiled chicken or fish. If that's how you'd prefer to serve it, these proportions will serve 6.

THE 3 SISTERS

The 3 Sisters—corn, beans, and squash—are central to Native American cooking and agriculture. Planting them together, in a process called companion planting, aids the growth of all three. The beans climb the corn stalks, the pumpkins' leaves shade all their roots, and the beans trap nitrogen in the soil to fertilize the corn naturally. Better yet, they're all superfoods in their own way.

P-P-PICK UP A POMEGRANATE

Ruby red and glistening, these seeds are high in anti-oxidants and full of vitamins C, E, and A—more than just a pretty sprinkle …

PERK UP YOUR PUMPKIN

We often feel for the pumpkin, dragged out just once a year to be carved into scary faces. But there is so much more to our orange friend. It's flesh is full of beta-carotene, helping to protect us from heart troubles and respiratory problems, and its seeds are bursting with zinc, iron, calcium, and the B–complex vitamins. So perk up that pumpkin in as many ways as you can.

Gill's Spinach, Chorizo & Halloumi Salad

SERVES 4 • PREPARATION TIME: 15 MINUTES • COOKING TIME: 20 MINUTES • ✓

Actually, this was created by Gill's friend Jane, but it comes to us via Gill, so we're putting her name on it. It's a salad that uses up the things you find in the refrigerator during the summer.

> 4 large handfuls of **baby spinach leaves**, washed
> 8oz **Halloumi cheese**, cut into 4 pieces
> 2 fat cloves of **garlic**, crushed
> ¼ cup **extra virgin olive oil**, plus extra for tossing and drizzling
> 24 spears of **fresh asparagus**, trimmed
> 5oz **chorizo**, thinly sliced
> ¼ cup **balsamic syrup** (see tip below)
> **salt** and **freshly ground pepper**

1. Divide the spinach among 4 large plates.

2. Lay the cheese flat in a bowl. Mix the crushed garlic and olive oil together and pour it over the pieces of cheese, letting them sit for a few minutes to marinate.

3. Put a grill pan over medium to high heat until it's very hot. Put the asparagus into a bowl and toss it in a little olive oil until it's well coated. Season with a pinch of salt, then chargrill the asparagus spears until they are nice and lined or charred. You may want to cut a few in half lengthwise before putting them in the pan if they are really fat. Divide the asparagus among the bowls.

4. Now cook the slices of cheese, pouring the marinade into the pan with them. Cook the cheese until it starts to turn golden on the outside. Divide the cheese evenly among the salad bowls, laying it on top of the asparagus.

5. Finally, pan-fry the chorizo in a clean skillet. As it cooks, it will release plenty of its spicy oils. This is a good thing! When the sausage starts to get a little crispy on the outside, divide it up, along with the juices, on top of the salad bowls.

6. Drizzle over more olive oil that you might think is needed, and finish off with a little salt, plenty of pepper, and a tablespoon of balsamic syrup per serving.

TIPS

* You can buy balsamic syrup in the stores, but it's very easy to make your own. Pour 1 cup of balsamic vinegar into a small saucepan, bring to a boil over medium heat, and reduce it by at least half. Set aside to cool. Then behold your syrup.

A WALK IN THE PARK

Growing up in North London suburbia, I came to value the pockets of green one could escape to on a Sunday. If Saturdays were about sport and parties, Sundays were about homework. Around the time I couldn't take any more math or my head was too full of French, my mom would suggest an outing to Grovelands, or if we were feeling adventurous, to Forty Hall or Whitewebs or Trent Park. All of them were pockets of preserved greenery that had escaped urbanization. We would come back to the house with color in our cheeks, clear heads, and with clarity about how to tackle that equation.

Then when I was older, Katie and I would escape to Hyde Park on a Sunday afternoon. And later we'd do the same with the girls.

These recipes are, by their description, meant to be easy ways of putting things in the oven so they'll be ready to greet you with an aromatic hello when you get back.

JOHN

Chicken & Tarragon Casserole

SERVES 4–6 • PREPARATION TIME: 20 MINUTES • COOKING TIME: 1 HOUR 20 MINUTES • ✓

Tarragon is a perfect foil for chicken, adding sweetness and bags of flavor. No wonder it's become such a classic combination. Here, we've used it to add a big herby accent to a one-dish meal. Bundle everything in, go out for a coffee or to the gym for an hour (or have that walk in the park), then come home to dinner.

6–8 **chicken thighs**, depending on their size
1 tablespoon **olive oil**
1 **onion**, chopped
1 stick of **celery**, chopped
1 **carrot**, chopped
1 clove of **garlic**, crushed
3 cups **chicken stock**
1 **bay leaf**
1 small bunch of **fresh tarragon** or 1 teaspoon **dried tarragon**
1 **red bell pepper**, seeded and cut into squares
1 small **cabbage**, trimmed and cut into quarters through the root
1 tablespoon **crème fraîche** or **sour cream**
1 tablespoon **Dijon mustard**
salt and **freshly ground black pepper**

1. Heat the oven to 350°F.

2. Trim any excess fat off the chicken thighs. In a heavy casserole dish or dutch oven, heat the olive oil over medium heat. Brown the chicken thighs in batches on both sides, then remove and set aside.

3. Now turn down the heat and cook the onion, celery, and carrot until soft. Add the garlic and cook for another 2 minutes before adding a dash of the stock. As it bubbles up, scrape up any sticky cooking residues off the bottom of the dish.

4. Return the chicken to the dish, along with the herbs, red bell pepper, and cabbage. Pour in enough stock to cover the chicken, season with salt and pepper, then put the lid on the dish and bake in the oven for about an hour.

5. Take the casserole dish out of the oven and place it on the stove. Transfer the chicken, cabbage, and red peppers to a plate and reduce the cooking liquid by half, boiling hard for about 3–4 minutes. Then turn down the heat and stir in the crème fraîche and the mustard.

6. Finally, blend the sauce with an immersion blender for an extra silky finish. Taste and add more salt and pepper, if necessary. Return the chicken, cabbage, and peppers to the dish to coat them with the sauce and serve immediately.

TIPS

* You could serve this with new potatoes or some wide flat noodles.

Chili Game Stew

SERVES 4–6 • PREPARATION TIME: 15 MINUTES • COOKING TIME: 1 HOUR 15 MINUTES • ✓

This was the product of indecision: chili or lamb stew? Our solution—why not combine them?

12oz **venison**
12oz boned **pheasant breasts**
4oz **pigeon breasts**
2 tablespoons **olive oil**
4 cloves of **garlic**, chopped
1 large **jalapeño chile**, chopped
½ cup **red wine**
1 (14½-oz) can of **diced tomatoes**
4 teaspoons **ground cumin**
1 teaspoon **chili powder** (or to taste)
1 teaspoon **ground cinnamon**
2 teaspoons **dried oregano**
¾oz **semisweet chocolate**
2–4 **potatoes**, depending on size, peeled and thinly sliced
½ cup shredded **cheddar cheese**
a little **melted butter**, to glaze
salt and **freshly ground black pepper**

1. Heat the oven to 350°F.

2. Chop the venison, pheasant breast, and pigeon breast into small pieces or pulse in the blender. Be careful: We don't want a mush. Set aside.

3. Heat the oil in a heavy casserole dish or dutch oven and gently cook the garlic and chile until softened. Add the game and cook until it's browned. Add the red wine and let it all bubble, then add the canned tomatoes, cumin, chili powder, cinnamon, oregano, chocolate, and salt and pepper. Stir and bring to a simmer. Let it simmer for about 20 minutes, then taste and more salt and pepper, if necessary. Set aside to cool slightly.

4. Layer the potatoes on top of the game chili in overlapping circles. Brush with a little melted butter and sprinkle half the shredded cheese over the top. Put into the oven for about 40 minutes, then add the rest of the cheese and cook for another 5–10 minutes, or until bubbly and golden brown.

5. Serve with some simply cooked or sautéed green vegetables.

TIPS

* Feel free to make your own combination of game, or do without the game altogether and make this with lamb or chiuck beef.

Joyce-Ann's Jamaican Curried Lamb Shanks

SERVES 6 • PREPARATION TIME: 15 MINUTES • COOKING TIME: 3 HOURS 30 MINUTES • ✓

When we first started talking about this book, we initially thought of writing recipes to mark events across the year. Well, the inspiration for this dish comes from a Jamaican party that Fred's mom, who moved to London in the early 60s to become a stewardess for BOAC, cooked with her apartment mate Maureen to celebrate the leap year in 1964.

Back then, they were trying to make curried goat, but had to make do with mutton from the North End Road market, just around the corner from their apartment on Talgarth Road. We're using lamb shanks here, simply because you'll find them easier to source than goat, kid, or mutton. But if you can track some down, goat will make this dish more authentic.

¼ cup **vegetable oil**
6 **lamb shanks**
2–3 cloves of **garlic**, peeled but left whole
2 **onions**, chopped
¼ cup **Jamaican curry powder** (see opposite)
2 **scallions**, trimmed and cut into chunks
2 **carrots**, sliced
2 large **potatoes**, peeled and cubed
1 **bay leaf**
2 sprigs of **fresh thyme**
1 **Scotch Bonnet chile**, seeded and finely chopped
2 cups **stock**, any flavor (or 1¾ cups if using coconut milk)
⅔ cup **coconut milk** (optional)
the juice of ½ a **lime**
salt and **freshly ground black pepper**

JOYCE, HEATHROW AIRPORT, 1962

1. Heat the oven to 325°F.

2. In a heavy skillet, heat 2 tablespoons of the vegetable oil and brown the lamb shanks thoroughly over medium heat. When they're done, put them into a large casserole dish or dutch oven with a well-fitting lid.

3. Add the garlic cloves to the skillet and cook until they're nutty brown, then add them to the lamb. Now add the remaining vegetable oil to the skillet and, when it's hot, add the onions. Stir them through the oil, then add the curry powder. Cook, stirring, for about 5–7 minutes.

4. While the onions are cooking, add the carrot, potatoes, scallions, herbs, and the Scotch bonnet to the dish.

5. When the onions are soft and deliciously fragrant, add a ladleful of the stock to the skillet, stirring everything together into a sauce, and scraping up any cooking residues from the bottom of the skillet. Pour it over the lamb and vegetables.

6. Add the rest of the stock and the coconut milk, if using, and season with salt and pepper. If the vegetables are not covered with the liquid, top up with water. Bring to a boil on the stove, cover, then transfer the dish to the oven and cook until the lamb shanks are tender – about 3 hours. Remove from the oven, skim off the excess fat, then stir in the lime juice.

7. Serve piping hot, with rice (or rice and peas). Joyce-Ann recommends serving with some good mango chutney, too.

JOYCE-ANN & MAUREEN'S MENU
FEBRUARY 29, 1964

Curried goat, made with mutton

Rice & peas

Boiled green banana

Steamed cho-cho

Pineapple with rum & nutmeg

Drizzle of Red Stripe & Appletons

TIPS

* Scotch bonnets are superiery, so to tone down the heat, just use half the chile or put it in whole. (However, it does carry the inherent risk of the chile exploding in the sauce, defeating the purpose.) If you want it hotter, leave the seeds in. And if you want it hotter still, add a generous slug of Grace's Hot Pepper Sauce.

* Some people wash the lamb shanks in the lime juice before they brown them. This changes the flavor of the curry, giving it a caramelized limey base note instead.

Jamaican Curry Powder

MAKES ABOUT 1½ CUPS • PREPARATION TIME: 5 MINUTES • COOKING TIME: 10 MINUTES • ✓ ♥ WF GF DF V

As a general rule, you don't find any chile in a Jamaican curry powder—they use fresh Scotch bonnets to add the heat.

2 tablespoons whole **coriander seed**
2 tablespoons whole **cumin seed**
2 tablespoons whole **fennel seed**
1 tablespoon **black mustard seed**
1 tablespoon whole **fenugreek**
1–2 tablespoons **allspice berries**
1 teaspoon **ground cinnamon**

1 teaspoon **freshly grated nutmeg**
1 teaspoon **ground ginger**
1 teaspoon **garlic powder**
½ teaspoon **mustard powder**
3 tablespoons **turmeric**
1 tablespoon **dried thyme**

1. In a dry skillet, toast the whole seeds, fenugreek, and allspice over low heat, stirring all the time to prevent them from burning, until they're really fragrant. Then grind them in a pestle and mortar or with an immersion blender and pour them into a clean, dry, screw-top jar.

2. Add the remaining ingredients, screw the lid on, and shake well to combine everything together. This will keep for 4–6 weeks in a sealed container.

Storecupboard Daube

SERVES 4 • PREPARATION TIME: 30 MINUTES • COOKING TIME: 2 HOURS 30 MINUTES • ✓ DF

Our version of the Provençal classic. As the title suggests, this was born from Kay's pantry, the refrigerator, and the little patch of herbs on the roof.

1 lb **chuck steak,** cubed
1 tablespoon **flour seasoned
 with salt and pepper**
1 tablespoon **olive oil**
2½oz **bacon,** diced
1 large **carrot,** coarsely chopped
1 large **onion,** coarsely chopped
4 cloves of **garlic,** coarsely chopped
1 (2-oz) can of **anchovies in olive oil,**
 drained and chopped
¼ cup **brandy**

1 bottle of **red wine**
2 big sprigs of **fresh rosemary**
 or 1 teaspoon **dried rosemary**
a few sprigs of **fresh thyme**
 or 2 teaspoons **dried thyme**
2 strips of **fresh or dried orange peel**
1 (14½-oz) can of **diced tomatoes**
½ cup pitted **black olives**
small handful of **chopped
 flat-leaf parsley,** to garnish
salt and **freshly ground black pepper**

1. Toss the steak in the seasoned flour and shake off the excess (see tip, below).

2. Heat the olive oil in a casseroledish or dutch oven over medium heat and brown the meat on all sides. Remove and set aside. (You may have to do this in batches—don't overcrowd the dish, or the meat will turn a nasty gray and you won't get the flavor.)

3. Add the bacon, carrot, and onion to the oil and cook to soften slightly. After a couple of minutes add the garlic and continue to cook for another 2–3 minutes. Then scoop everything out and set it all aside with the beef.

4. Add a splash more oil, if needed, then add the anchovies, stirring and crushing them into the oil until you get a kind of emulsion. Add the brandy and let it bubble furiously for a couple of minutes, scraping up any cooking residues on the bottom of the dish with a wooden spoon.

5. Now return the meat, bacon, and vegetables to the dish and add the red wine, rosemary, thyme, orange peel, and diced tomatoes. Season with salt and pepper, and bring the whole lot to a boil. Then put the lid on the casserole dish and put it into the oven for about 2 hours.

6. About half an hour before it's due to be ready, open it up and throw in the olives.

7. When it's ready, taste the sauce and adjust the seasoning, if necessary. Serve sprinkled with chopped flat-leaf parsley, and accompanied by a bitter leaf salad and some crusty bread or boiled new potatoes.

TIPS

* Kay tosses the beef in the seasoned flour to thicken the finished sauce. If you want to use a gluten-free alternative, you can replace the flour with buckwheat.

AFTERNOON SNACKS

Each meal we eat together has a meaning and a particular role. The afternoon is an especially interesting time to me.

At Leon, we often hear snippets of conversation from people who leave their offices or escape from shopping at around 4 p.m. The occasions are ritualistic, the conversations often a little conspiratorial. This is the time of day, it seems, to talk about people you fancy, bosses who are frustrating you, and jobs you would prefer.

At home, Katie and I have recently encouraged anyone in our house at 4 p.m. (even if we're not there) to sit down and spend time together, with a cup of tea and a small treat in nice cups and on nice plates. This has been partly inspired by our finding the records of a lady who lived in our house before us; back around 1910, Mary insisted on doing the same thing.

But that is not what after-school time with kids is mostly like. It's about kicked-off shoes, mud on the carpet, bags slung across the couch, and children who are hyper one day and tired the next.

Whether your afternoon treats are old-fashioned or modern, we hope you find some rituals here.

JOHN

Things on Potatoes

Sometimes there's nothing better than a hot baked potato, crusty on the outside and steaming and soft within, just begging to be buttered. But what else can we do with them? Here are some suggestions from family and friends to making the best baked potatoes ever…

1. Pick your potato—this is very important. Buy a variety that bakes well—high-starch types are best. We recommend russets.

2. Heat the oven to 425°F.

3. Wash the potatoes under cold, running water. Shake them a little to remove the excess water, but don't dry them completely.

4. Roll them in some sea salt.

5. Put them straight into the oven, directly onto the shelf. Bake them for about an hour—it depends on the size of your potato. Just poke them with the tines of a fork to test for "give" and doneness.

6. Take them out and let everyone admire their crispy exterior and wow at their fluffy insides.

Some ideas for toppings, from left to right:

Georgia's Eggy Potato

This comes from our photographer Georgia. Scoop out the insides of the cooked potato. Mash it in a bowl with a lightly beaten egg, then season with salt and black pepper. Add some crisply fried bacon bits (or leftover ham or bacon), and some cheese if you desire … or any pieces of cooked veggies you have on hand. Scoop it all back into the potato skin, top with a little pat of butter, and put back in the oven for 15 minutes, or until it's puffy and crispy on top.

Cheesy Spinach & Mushrooms

This is for Abi and Issy, the vegetarian element of our team. Sauté some sliced mushrooms in a little olive oil and butter with a sprinkle of garlic and parsley, and set aside. Then wilt down a handful or two of spinach in the same saucepan. Season with salt and black pepper. Pile it onto the potato with the mushrooms and top with some cubes of Gruyère or Swiss cheese.

GEORGIA'S EGGY POTATO

CHEESY SPINACH & MUSHROOMS

ELEANOR'S MAKE THE GRADE POTATOES

Eleanor's Make the Grade Potatoes

Eleanor is John's younger daughter. One day at school in first grade she was allowed to sit with Mr. and Mrs. Heinrich, and to have baked potatoes with her favorite topping: plenty of butter and EXTRA shredded cheddar cheese, salt, and black pepper. Now that's what we call making the grade.

Beet, Crème Fraîche & Chives

Simply chop some cooked (not pickled) beet into cubes. Spoon some crème fraîche onto the buttered potato. Sprinkle with the beet and finish with chopped fresh chives, salt, and black pepper.

Herb Butter

Very retro, but very good. Make the herb butter of your choice—we use finely chopped fresh parsley, garlic, fresh thyme, and salt and black pepper mashed into some softened, unsalted butter. If you have time, using some plastic wrap or aluminum foil, roll the soft butter into a log shape, and refrigerate it. Then just slice off a few disks and place them artfully in a steaming, split potato.

The Leftovers Potato

Baked potatoes take to leftovers like ducks to water (actually, leftover duck would be fantastic). There are plenty of recipes in this book that will provide suitable pals for your potato: the Romano Pepper & Chile Salsa on page 29, Natasha's Chicken Fajitas on page 44, Hummus and the Lentil Masala Dip on page 50, the Ragù alla Toscana on page 134, Salsa Verde on page 170, Diamond Jubilee Chicken on page 186, not to mention the Quick Convenience Store Curry on page 267, and many, many more. So use 'em up.

BEET, CRÈME FRAÎCHE & CHIVES

HERB BUTTER

LEFTOVERS POTATO

THE LEFTOVERS POTATO

Things on Toast

Toast, glorious toast. Sometimes we just need to jazz it up a little. Here are some suggestions from the Leon team:

Brown Crab, Lemon & Dill

Spread some thick brown crabmeat on your toast. Squeeze over some lemon juice. Finish with freshly ground black pepper and a sprinkling of chopped fresh dill.

Marmite, Avocado, Tomato, Basil & Gomasio

Kay's favorite: Spread a smear of good, unsalted butter on the toast. Then a smear of Marmite. Follow this with sliced avocados and halved cherry tomatoes. Sprinkle a few fresh basil leaves on top and finish with a good grinding of black pepper and a sprinkle of our Gomasio (see page 57).

Graig Farm's All Meat Sausage on Fig Preserves

Broil or oven-roast some sausages until cooked. Spread the toast with a thick layer of fig preserves. Slice the sausages in half lengthwise and lay them on the toast.

Poached Egg & Sautéed Mushrooms

Slice some mushrooms and sauté them with some garlic in a little olive oil. Sprinkle in a few leaves of fresh thyme or some chopped fresh parsley. Set aside to keep warm. Meanwhile, poach an egg (see page 25), then pile the mushrooms on the toast with the poached egg on top.

Goat Cheese, Honey, Thyme & Walnuts

Cut a goat cheese log (the type with rind) into slices. Place 2 or 3 slices overlapping on each slice of toast. Place under a hot broiler for 1 minute or so, just to get the cheese slightly melt-y. Drizzle with honey and sprinkle with chopped walnuts and fresh thyme.

Cinnamon Butter with Sliced Apples

Mix some softened butter with a good pinch of ground cinnamon and a squeeze of agave nectar. Spread on the toast. Place slices of raw apple on top. Sprinkle with a final dusting of cinnamon.

Miss Morton's Lemon Cake

SERVES 10 • PREPARATION TIME: 15 MINUTES PLUS COOLING • COOKING TIME: 50 MINUTES • V

This is a Hogge family institution. We've calculated the ingredients for measuring cups and spoons, although Kay uses imperial measures. For some reason, it never works when she tries to make it metric. We think that's because the ghost of Miss Morton disapproves …

1 stick **butter**, softened
¾ cup **superfine** or **granulated sugar**
1⅓ cups **all-purpose flour**
2 **eggs**
1 tablespoon **gluten-free baking powder**
¼ cup **milk**
grated zest of 1 **lemon**

For the icing:
juice of 1 **lemon**
¾ cup **confectioners' sugar**, sifted

1. Heat the oven to 350°F. Grease and line an 8 x 4-inch loaf pan with parchment paper.

2. Put the cake ingredients into a food processor and whoosh it together until you have a smooth batter.

3. Pour into the loaf pan and bake in the oven for about 50 minutes. To test if it's cooked, stab the cake with the tines of a fork. If it comes out clean, it's done.

4. Remove from the oven and let cool in the pan for 10 minutes. Then turn out of the pan and prick the cake all over with a fork.

5. To make the icing: Mix the lemon juice and confectioners' sugar together to make a thick white paste. Spoon and pour it over the top of the cake, smoothing it on with a rubber spatula knife. Let set, then devour.

OK—this one's a little convoluted. Miss Morton was a village schoolteacher and leader of the local Brownies in Ferndown, Dorset. She was a good friend of Fred's great-great-aunt Mary Walker, known as Little Old Auntie. When Fred's granny brought his dad, Phil, to England for the first time in May, 1945 (they'd been evacuated to Australia from Singapore in 1942), they went to stay with Little Old Auntie until Fred's grandfather came home from the war. Phil says: "We used to go to tea with Miss Morton. It was always a treat. I think I can remember scones and hot buttered toast, but I can definitely remember her lemon cake. My mother kept the recipe and handed it on to your mother, too."

FRED'S GRANDFATHER, ARTHUR, HOLDING PHILIP, PENANG, 1941

Flatplanet Brownies

MAKES: 12–16 SLICES • PREPARATION TIME: 10 MINUTES PLUS COOLING
• COOKING TIME: 1 HOUR 25 MINUTES • WF GF V

Although Leon is his first love, John has also spent some time on a little concept called Flatplanet. It's his attempt at creating a little café that re-creates what was best about the original coffee shops, where people experience positivity, energy, good food, and good ideas.

He's not the biggest fan of modern wheat. So at Flatplanet, they cook spelt flatbreads and wheat-free and gluten-free cakes. The most popular of which is this brownie.

Originally developed by Sarah Jenkins, these brownies are now made for Flatplanet by Sarah Hale and served with amazing energy instore by Ot.

4 sticks **butter**, chopped
1 lb **chocolate** (minimum 50 percent cocoa solids), chopped
2 cups **superfine** or **granulated sugar**
6 **eggs**
3 cups **ground almonds** (almond meal)

1. Heat the oven to 250°F.

2. Over very low heat, melt the butter in a large saucepan. When almost melted, add the chocolate and stir until smooth. Remove the pan from the heat and stir in the sugar.

3. In a separate bowl, beat the eggs lightly together with a balloon whisk. Then use the balloon whisk to beat them into the pan of chocolate mixture. Add the ground almonds, again mixing them in with the balloon whisk until there are no large pockets of almonds remaining.

4. Grease and line a 10 x 14-inch baking pan. Pour the batter into the pan and bake in the oven for 1 hour 10 minutes, or until starting to crack on the surface.

5. Let the brownies cool in the pan for about an hour, because they will still be very soft.

6. When cool, slice, then remove from the pan and enjoy.

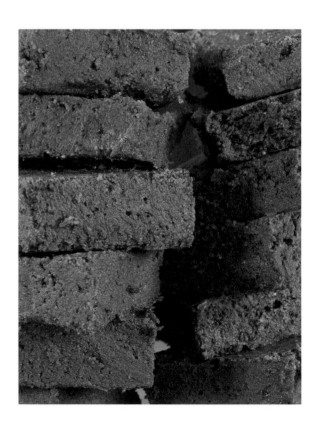

Zucchini Cupcakes

MAKES: 12 • PREPARATION TIME: 20 MINUTES PLUS COOLING • COOKING TIME: 30 MINUTES • ✓ GF V

There is a small deli in John's nearest town and the thing John likes most about it is the gluten-free zucchini cupcakes. This is our version of the little beauties.

1 stick **butter**, softened
½ cup **firmly packed light brown sugar**
2 **eggs**
1⅓ cups Bob's Red Mill or similar **gluten-free all-purpose flour**
2 teaspoons **baking powder**
1 teaspoon **ground cinnamon**
½ teaspoon **ground allspice**
juice and zest of 1 **orange** or 1 **lemon**
1½ cups shredded **zucchini**
¼ cup coarsely chopped **walnuts** (optional)

For the lemon or orange cream cheese frosting:
2 tablespoons **unsalted butter**, softened
¼ cup **cream cheese**
1¼ cups **confectioners' sugar**
the juice and zest of ¼ of a **lemon** or **orange**

1. Heat the oven to 350°F. Line a 12-cup muffin pan with cupcake liners.

2. Beat the butter and sugar together in a mixing bowl so it goes all creamy. Add an egg and stir it in. Do the same with the second egg.

3. Sift the flour, baking powder, cinnamon, and allspice into a bowl. Fold the flour mixture into the butter, sugar, and eggs, stopping halfway through to add the orange or lemon juice and zest. Then stir in the zucchini, and walnuts (if using).

4. Scoop a large tablespoonful of the batter into each cake liner and stand the pan on a baking sheet. Put it all into the oven for 30 minutes.

5. Listen to the radio while you're waiting.

6. Then take the cakes out of the oven and cool them on a rack if you have one, or anywhere clean if you don't.

7. To make the frosting, beat the butter and cream cheese together, and gradually add the confectioners' sugar and the lemon or orange juice and zest. Spread over the cakes once they have cooled down.

TIPS

* Why not make these with less sugar and have them for breakfast?

Susanna Mattana's Amaretti Macaroons

MAKES: 24 • PREPARATION TIME: 20 MINUTES PLUS COOLING • COOKING TIME: ABOUT 40 MINUTES • WF GF V

Our friend Susanna can *really* cook. This macaroon recipe has been handed down to her from her grandma via her mother. No saint's day, wedding, or feast in her native Sardinia would be complete without these glorious almond clouds …

> 5 cups **ground almonds** (almond meal)
> 1½ cups **superfine** or **granulated sugar**
> the zest of 1 **lemon**
> 6 **egg whites**
> 24 **whole blanched almonds**

1. Heat the oven to 325°F. Line a large baking sheet with parchment paper.

2. In a large bowl, thoroughly mix the ground almonds, sugar, and lemon zest using your hands.

3. In a separate bowl, beat the egg whites into stiff peaks—really give them a good seeing to! Then gently fold them into the almond mixture, a spoonful at a time, mixing carefully but thoroughly.

4. Now form them into 24 "meatballs" (as Susanna says). Place them on the baking sheet, push a blanched almond gently into the top of each one, and put them into the oven for about 40 minutes. They should be golden brown and smell gorgeous. Cool before serving.

SUSANNA, COSTA SMERELDA,
SARDINIA, 1982

Susanna Mattana and Massimo Usai run a wonderful, warm Sardinian restaurant in Putney, southwest London, called Isola del Sole. Their handmade pastas are to die for. Susanna's pumpkin or artichoke raviolis are sigh inducing, like angels' pillows. Massimo supports the soccer team Arsenal.

CRUNCH!

SQUISH!

SLURP!

Food's not just about the look and the taste of it. Eating employs every one of our five senses. Sight, taste, and smell are a big part of the process, but let's not forget hearing and touch. Mouthfeel matters. And so does sound. Half the joy of eating crackling is that glorious sound it makes as you bite into it. And think of how the perfect sauce can feel silky on your tongue.

So the following recipes are here to explore a little more of the tactility of food.

KAY

Ot's Chicken Ton-katsu

Traditionally, ton-katsu is a breaded, deep-fried piece of pork cutlet or tenderloin, served sliced, with shredded cabbage and rice. But, as Ot says: "It doesn't have to be pork. And it doesn't need to be covered in bread crumbs or deep fried." Here are her secrets.

4 **boneless chicken breasts**, about 1 lb in total
1 good handful of **rice flour**
2 **eggs**, beaten
1 good handful and a little bit extra of **rolled oats**
   (if the oats are too big they fall off easily, so you may
   want to whoosh them quickly in a blender)
3 tablespoons **olive oil**
salt

OT & HER DAD (TAKEN BY HER MOM),
HOKKAIDO, JAPAN, 1983

1. Cut the chicken fillets into strips no more than ½ inch thick and season with salt.

2. Prepare 3 shallow plates. Put the rice flour in one, the beaten eggs in the next, and the oats in the third.

3. One by one, dust the chicken pieces in the rice flour, making sure they're thoroughly covered, but shaking off any excess. Then, again one by one, dip them into the egg. Then, finally, dredge them through the oats. When all the pieces are well coated, shake off the excess oats. (This is a good opportunity to put the kids to work; you want a little factory assembly line, with one person in charge of dunking the chicken into each plate!)

4. Heat the olive oil in a skillet over medium heat and fry the chicken in batches until each piece is cooked through and golden brown. Try not to move them around the skillet too much so that the crumbs stay intact.

5. Serve with lettuce and "bulldog" sauce (see tip below).

TIPS

* Bulldog sauce can be very expensive outside Japan. So here's Ot's legendary, patented quick version: mix equal parts of ketchup and Worcestershire sauce. Job done.

* Why not add some dried basil or parsley to the oats? You can also flavor the cooking oil by sautéing a little garlic, then removing it when it's golden brown, before cooking the chicken. Serve with a little salad of baby tomatoes and basil.

* YOU MUST MAKE EXTRA PIECES AND PUT THEM IN THE REFRIGERATOR FOR TOMORROW. Ot has a point. The katsu sandwich is something else. In fact, they sell more katsu sandwiches in Japan than actual ton-katsu.

Ot is a ball of fire—she's our go-to fix-it girl, and she's John's right-hand woman. Frankly, without Ot, the wheels would've come off the bicycle long ago. She's from Hokkaido, an island in the north of Japan. And she has such a great palate, I think she's a supertaster. But she won't say if this is true. Or not.

OPPOSITE: PAPER CHICKEN BY ABI

Chef Ann's Malaysian Shrimp

SERVES: 4 • PREPARATION TIME: 10 MINUTES • COOKING TIME: 20 MINUTES

Spicy, creamy shrimp with a crunch.

1¼ lbs big **peeled shrimp**
2 **eggs**
cornstarch, for coating (or all-purpose flour is fine)
2 cups **sunflower oil** or **vegetable oil**, plus extra to cook the egg
10 **curry leaves**
1 whole **Thai chile**
1¼ cups **whipping cream** or **heavy cream**
chicken bouillon cube, to taste
a handful of **gluten-free oats** (optional)
salt and **freshly ground black pepper**

1. Season the shrimp with salt and black pepper. Beat one of the eggs in a bowl and coat the shrimp, then roll in the cornstarch (or all-purpose flour—I've used both).

2. Heat the oil in a wok or deep skillet—when a dribble of egg dropped in sizzles, then it's hot enough. Deep-fry the shrimp until golden brown. (This part of the recipe can be done well in advance.) Drain the shrimp on paper towels.

3. Heat up a skillet with a small drizzle of oil and sauté the curry leaves and chile for a minute. Add the cream, a sprinkle of crumbled chicken bouillon cube (or bouillon powder) and a pinch of salt.

4. When the cream has thickened, add the shrimp and toss everything together so that they are all covered in cream and are utterly self-indulgent.

5. This dish can easily be eaten now (and believe me, it will be scoffed very quickly), but a little crunch is an excellent addition, so here comes the really clever part. Separate the second egg and beat the yolk (you can freeze the white for meringues). Clean your wok, then heat 1 inch of oil until very hot. Deep-fry the yolk by dribbling it very slowly into the very hot oil. Swirl it around until it looks like a kind of crispy egg bird's nest. Golden, crispy egg is what you're after. If you can get it in a single strand, you win a prize. If not, it'll taste good anyway—serve it with the shrimp. If that seems complicated, try quickly frying some oats (this only takes a minute at most—you want them golden, not dark!).

6. You can serve this as an appetizer or as part of a real feast, with maybe a meat dish and a noodle dish as well as a big bowl of rice.

We spent last New Year in Malaysia at the ritzy and incredibly friendly resort of Tanjong Jara. The monsoon was late—either that or we'd misread the weather section of our travel guide—and it rained. A lot. To keep the whole family entertained, we learned to cook some local dishes. The resort's head chef, Chef Ann, taught us how to make this simple but incredibly delicious dish.

KATIE

Bo-That's Bananas

SERVES: 4–6 • PREPARATION TIME: 10 MINUTES • COOKING TIME: 8–10 MINUTES • V

This is a simple version of a Thai dish called *gluay buat chee*, which means "bananas that have been ordained as nuns." We guess it's because they are clothed in white milk, the same color as the robes of Thai Buddhist nuns. It's really delicious, and very simple to make. This version is named after Kay's elephant Bo-That, because he *loves* bananas.

> 4–6 **bananas**
> 1 cup **coconut milk**
> a 2-inch piece of **pandan (screwpine) leaf**
>   or a drop of **pandan essence**
> 2 tablespoons **palm sugar (jaggery)** or **brown sugar**
> a large pinch of **salt**
> ⅔ cup **coconut cream**

1. Peel the bananas and slice them in half lengthwise, then chop them into 3 so that each banana gives you 6 pieces.

2. Heat the coconut milk with the pandan leaf and, when it comes to a boil, add the banana pieces, sugar, and salt. Bring back to a boil and add the coconut cream.

3. Gently bring back to a simmer and let the bananas cook for 3–4 minutes. Remove the pandan leaf and serve warm or at room temperature.

TIPS

* Kay eats this dish for breakfast, hot on a cold morning or chilled on a hot morning.

* You can find pandan leaves or pandan essence in most Asian stores. If you can't find them, don't worry. It's just as good without.

* Look for coconut cream in Asian stores (don't use the sweet stuff for making cocktails). If you can't find it, use an extra ⅔ cup of coconut milk.

OPERATION DUMBO DROP, MAE HONG SON, 1993

I was in Thailand working on a Disney movie in the early 90s when I met Bo-That. We'd flown in a movie star elephant from Hollywood (yes, really), but we used Thai elephants as extras. At the end the shoot, we found an orphaned elephant. The company bought him and put him into the safe hands of the Thai Elephant Conservation Center in Lampang. He was just 5 at the time. He's now a strapping although stroppy bull elephant of 22. If I can say this about someone who's 10 feet tall, he's still my baby boy.
KAY

Jenny's Sago Gula Melaka

SERVES: 4–6 • PREPARATION TIME: 10 MINUTES PLUS RESTING / CHILLING
COOKING TIME: 30 MINUTES • WF GF DF V

This cool, soothing Far Eastern classic comes to us from Kay's friend, the food writer Jenny Linford. It's their childhoods in a nutshell. Don't be put off by the fact that it resembles frog spawn—just focus on the fact that it tastes like nectar.

> 1⅓ cups fine **sago starch** or **tapioca pearls**
> 1⅓ cups **palm sugar (jaggery)** or **brown sugar**
> 1 cup **water**
> 2 **pandan leaves** (see tip on page 89)
> 1¾ cups **coconut milk**
> a pinch of **salt**

1. Bring a large saucepan of water to a boil. Add the sago starch and return the water to a boil, stirring. Cook for 10 minutes, stirring. Then remove from the heat, cover, and set aside for 10 minutes.

2. After 10 minutes the sago should be translucent. Uncover the pan and drain it in a strainer. Rinse the sago under cold running water, then let it stand the strainer to drain thoroughly.

3. Transfer the sago to 4 or 6 individual small bowls rinsed with cold water, let cool, then chill until ready to serve.

4. Place the palm sugar in a heavy saucepan with the 1 cup of water. Tie a pandan leaf in a knot and add to the pan. Bring to a boil and simmer until the palm sugar has melted into a syrup. Strain into a small bowl and set aside to cool.

5. Pour the coconut milk into a saucepan. Tie the other pandan leaf in a knot and add to the coconut milk with the salt. Bring to a boil, then simmer, stirring, until slightly reduced. Strain into a small bowl, cool, and chill.

6. To serve, slide a knife around each portion of sago and transfer onto serving dishes. Pour over some coconut milk and a little of the palm sugar syrup and enjoy!

Although Jenny was born in London, she spent much of her childhood living in the tropics, especially in Singapore. She says: "My memories of it are very vivid—particularly of the food. I remember going with my cousins down to the harbor, which in those days was filled with boats, on velvety warm tropical nights. In the humid tropical heat, a serving of sago gula melaka was a treat to be savored—the cool gelatinlike sago combined with rich creamy coconut milk and dark, bitter, caramel-flavored palm sugar syrup. Comfort food for the tropics.'

JENNY & HER MOM LYDIA, SINGAPORE, 1970

Watermelon Slurpie

SLURP!

SERVES 2–4 • PREPARATION TIME: 10 MINUTES • COOKING TIME: NONE • ♥ WF GF V

All over Thailand, you see carts advertising *ponlamai puun*, or "spun fruit." These icy cool fruit drinks come in myriad flavors—perfect for the tropical heat. Our favorite is the watermelon—pink, refreshing, and sweet.

> 1 smallish ripe **watermelon** (4½–6½ lbs), peeled, seeded, and diced, preferably chilled
> ½ teaspoon **salt**
> a few **ice cubes**
> 2 tablespoons **simple syrup** (see page 229)

1. Blend the watermelon in a blender with the salt and ice cubes. Only add the simple syrup if the watermelon is not sweet enough.

TIPS

* To be Very Thai, you could finish the slurpie off with a spoonful or two of sweetened condensed milk or some coconut milk.
* Add a few fresh mint leaves and a squeeze of lime.

Date Shake

SERVES 2–4 • PREPARATION TIME: 5 MINUTES • COOKING TIME: NONE • WF GF V

> 15 whole **dates**, pitted and coarsely chopped
> 1 cup unsweetened **soy milk**
> 1 ripe **banana**, peeled and chopped
> 2–4 **ice cubes**
> a pinch of **ground cinnamon** or **ground cardamom**

1. Put everything into a blender and process on high power until it's really well blended, thick, and creamy. Pour and serve immediately.

TIPS

* You could use whole milk or skim milk or rice milk—it's up to you.
* Try replacing the banana with a scoop of good vanilla ice cream or another handful of pitted dates.

Toph's Strawberryade

SERVES 2 • PREPARATION TIME: 5 MINUTES • COOKING TIME: NONE • WF GF V

> ¾ cup **water** or **sparkling water**
> 1–2 tablespoons **agave nectar** (depending how sweet you like it—I like it tart, so I just use 1 tablespoon)
> ¼ cup **lemon juice** (about 2 lemons)
> 5–6 fresh **strawberries**, hulled and chopped

1. Blend all of the above together (add a little ice if you desire, but if you do, then drop the water).

LEFT TO RIGHT: DATE SHAKE; WATERMELON SLURPIE; TOPH'S STRAWBERRYADE

THE BENEFITS OF HONEY BY JOHN

OK, so I like it when Katie dresses up. What can I tell you. But that is not why I bought Katie a beehive for her birthday last year. Apart from doing what we can to protect the bee population, and apart from the joy of being so connected with one's surroundings, honey is rich in vital life-giving nutrients.

There's a lot of research going on, and views will continue to develop. Here's what I know so far:

Honeys are not created equal
The honeys at the top of their game are the raw, unheated, unprocessed ones. They are darker in color and, unless you have your own hive, more expensive. Unfortunately, when mass-produced honey is made, it's heated and processed, and this means that the vitamins and enzymes and other good things are pretty much destroyed.

The best of the best
Apart from locally made honey, the honey with the best reputation today is Manuka honey, a natural honey from New Zealand that scores highly for its antibacterial and antiseptic properties. Vying for the top spot is eucalyptus honey, aka stringy bark honey, which is made by adding eucalyptus oil to natural honey, and this has become popular as an antibacterial and anti-inflammatory and even as an antidepressant.

Honey & blood sugar
Let's start with the bad news. Mass-produced honey is no better for you than sugar or syrup. Honey comprises 40 percent fructose (low GI), 30 percent glucose (very high GI), and 1 percent sucrose and 9 percent other sugars. Which means it has a similar makeup to inverted sugar syrup, and around a net GI of 60, which is the same as sucrose (table sugar). The good news: Some natural honeys have low GIs because of the balance of sugars. Look for locust honey (not made from locusts) with a GI of 32, yellow box honey with a GI of 35, and stringy bark honey with a GI of 44. These are the best honeys to cook with or use as a sweetener.

The treasure chest
Beyond the sugars, however, honey provides a small but rich treasure chest. It's not so much about depth as breadth. Whereas table sugar has no nutritional benefit, a good honey has more than 600 natural ingredients—principally vitamins, minerals, enzymes, and antioxidants. Vitamins include vitamins B1, B2, B3, B5, B6 and B9 (I have matured enough to resist any bee jokes) and vitamin C. Minerals include iron, zinc, manganese, copper, calcium, potassium, sodium, magnesium and phosphorus. Honey also contains 18, of the 22 amino acids humans need—but admittedly only in small quantities. Manuka honey, almost uniquely, has wound-healing powers inside the body. Take a look at the work of Professor Peter Molan at the University of Waikato in New Zealand.

Local honey & prevention of allergies
When Katie came back from her first bee-keeping lesson (she got stung only once), one of the things that struck me were the claims about the antiallergenic effects of eating natural honey that has been produced locally. The theory is that the bees have used pollen from all the local flowers and provide you with a small, almost vaccinelike, amount of local pollen that protects you from developing allergic reactions. There is some research to support this and anecdotal evidence, but more would be welcome.

Topical antiseptic
There are now many people (scientists with white coats and normal people with jeans and sneakers) who use the raw Manuka and eucalyptus honeys for cleaning wounds and cuts and sores. There is now consensus that it has good, practical antiseptic, antifungal, anti-inflammatory, and antimicrobial properties. In Australia and other countries, it is used to heal burns. But I suggest you do your own research.

Tiger's Milk

SERVES: 1 • PREPARATION TIME: 3 MINUTES • COOKING TIME: 2–3 MINUTES • WF GF V

Tiger, Tiger, burning bright … No, no—not THAT kind of tiger! You think we're mad enough to try to milk one? No, this was the only way anyone could get the small Kay to drink milk. The tale went that it was "tiger's milk" because it was stripy … Kay can't for the life of her believe that she fell for that one! The honey "stripes" disappear after about three seconds, so she must have been an extraordinarily gullible child!

She says: "It wasn't until I was re-creating this that I discovered that the mixture of cinnamon, honey, and warm milk has a mildly soporific effect, perfect for prebedtime imbibing. It has been firmly reinstated here, stripes or no stripes …"

Adults could add a tot of something fortifying …

1 mug of **milk**
1 small **stick of cinnamon**
1 tablespoon **honey**
an extra pinch of **ground cinnamon** (optional)

1. Heat the milk in a saucepan until it's just warm—you don't want it too hot. Then use an immersion blender to froth the milk. This guarantees you will get stripes.

2. Put the cinnamon stick into the mug and pour the warmed milk over it. Now—watch for it—drizzle the spoonful of honey into the milk, from a height, in concentric circles. See those stripes? Stir it in with the cinnamon stick and add an extra pinch of cinnamon, if you desire.

3. Sweet dreams.

LUNE & KAY, 1965

Lune was a huge part of our family and was my nanny when I was growing up. She was also the manufacturer of this particular tall tale. We adored each other. Except for when she tried to comb the tangles out of my perpetually wayward hair. Then I wasn't so fond.

KAY

OOH HONEY HONEY!

Spiced Honey & Orange Cake

Kay's husband Fred is obsessed with those gooey, sticky but oh-so-good honey cakes sold in Middle Eastern bakeries. He often reminisces, misty eyed, about the ones he had when traveling through Lebanon and Syria … This one has the taste he remembers, but without the flour. It's a moist, dense cake, drenched in honey and orange flower syrup. Best served in small squares with mint tea or strong coffee. Or eaten straight out of the pan, as seems to be the habit with our friends …

1 large **orange**
3 **eggs**
1 cup **superfine** or **granulated sugar**
1 tablespoon **orange blossom honey**
1½ cups **ground almonds (almond meal)**
½ cup **walnuts**, ground
2 tablespoons **buckwheat flour**
1 teaspoon **gluten-free baking powder**
¼ teaspoon **ground cinnamon**
¼ teaspoon **ground ginger**
the seeds from 8–10 **cardamom pods**, lightly crushed
a pinch of **salt**

For the syrup:
¼ cup **orange blossom honey**
2 tablespoons **orange flower water**

1. Put the orange into a large saucepan of boiling water. Bring back to a boil and simmer for 50 minutes to 1 hour, until tender. Drain and set aside to cool slightly. Cut the orange into quarters, remove any seeds, and place in a food processor. Blend until smooth.

2. Heat the oven to 350°F. Grease a 9 x 9-inch cake pan and line with wax paper.

3. Put the eggs and sugar into a bowl and beat together. Add the tablespoon of honey and beat again. Add the ground almonds and walnuts, the buckwheat flour, and the spices. Add the pureed orange and stir well to combine.

4. Scrape the batter into the prepared pan, then put it into the oven for 50–60 minutes, or until a little springy and deep golden brown. Cool completely in its pan.

5. To make the syrup, heat the honey and orange flower water in a saucepan over a gentle heat until combined.

6. When the cake has cooled, lift it out of the pan, keeping it on its wax paper, then drizzle the syrup over it with a spoon (if you try to pour it directly from the pan, it tends to gloumph—technical term—out in a big splotch.) Let soak in, then cut into squares and serve.

John's Ultimate Cold-Buster

SERVES 1 • PREPARATION TIME: 5 MINUTES • COOKING TIME: NONE • WF GF V

There aren't many upsides to being ill, but this is one of them. In fact, I often have one of these just in case I might be going to get ill. The more expensive the glass, the better it tastes. Try it in one of those bulbous-y, tallish brandy type glasses. For kids, leave out the brandy.

> 1 teaspoon **Manuka honey**
> a mug of **hot water** (i.e. boiled water that has cooled a little)
> ½ a slice of **orange** with 8–12 **cloves** spiked into it
>   (where the segments meet the rind)
> 1 stick of **cinnamon**
> a slug of **brandy** or **your favorite sticky alcohol**
>   (Cointreau or Glayva perhaps)

1. Stir the honey into the hot water. Then put in the slice of orange with its cloves on.

2. Add the cinnamon stick and then the brandy to taste. Not hard. Very good.

Kay's Hard Core Cold-Buster

SERVES 1 • PREPARATION TIME: 5 MINUTES • COOKING TIME: 10 MINUTES • ♥ WF GF V

This sounds so horrible, but truly, it's not. I got it from a naturopath when I was in college, and it's never failed me. Just take it before bed when you have a horrible cold. Yes, you may sweat garlic through the night, but you'll wake up feeling tons better.

> 2 mugs of **water**
> 20 cloves of **garlic**, peeled
> 2 teaspoons **dried sage**
> 1 tablespoon **raw honey**

1. Bring the water to a boil in a saucepan. Add the garlic and simmer for about 8 minutes, or until the water has reduced to about a mugful. Remove from the heat and stir in the sage and honey.

2. Strain through a strainer into a mug and drink immediately. Sleep.

TIPS

* You can use any honey, but raw untreated honey seems to work better, and Manuka honey seem to work best.

Honey & Rose Baklava

MAKES: 18–24 PIECES • PREPARATION TIME: 35 MINUTES PLUS COOLING • COOKING TIME: 1 HOUR • V

These are just one of the most beautiful things going—thin, crispy sheets of filigree-like pastry, delicate rose water, and fragrant honey.

12 sheets of **phyllo pastry** (have a few more on standby if you're clumsy)
1¾ sticks **unsalted butter**, melted
an extra tablespoon of **orange blossom honey**, to finish (optional)

For the syrup:
⅓ cup **orange blossom honey**
¼ cup **water**
¼ cup **superfine** or **granulated sugar**
2 tablespoons **rose water**
a pinch of **ground cinnamon**
2 **star anise**

For the filling:
1 cup **firmly packed soft brown sugar**
1 cup shelled **pistachios**
1 cup **walnut pieces**
1 cup **ground almonds (almond meal)**
¼ cup **flaxseed**, toasted
1 teaspoon **ground cinnamon**
the seeds from 10 **cardamom pods**
1 tablespoon **dried rose petals** (optional)

1. Heat the oven to 350°F. Grease a 12 x 8½-inch baking pan.

2. Put all the filling ingredients into a food processor and process until broken down. You want some texture so don't grind it to a paste. Tip into a bowl and set aside.

3. Unroll the phyllo pastry and cut the sheets in half—they should be about 12 x 8 inches when cut. (Cover the sheets with a damp dish towel, because they dry out.)

4. Layer the pastry sheets in the pan, one at a time, brushing each sheet with melted butter until you have stacked 10 sheets. On top of the tenth sheet, spoon over a nice layer of filling. Then place another sheet on top and butter again. Add another layer of filling and repeat the layers until the filling is used up—it will probably take 2 more layers. Finish with 10 sheets of phyllo layered on top, remembering to butter every sheet as you work and give the top sheet a final buttering.

5. Cut the baklava diagonally into diamond shapes.

6. Place in the oven for 45 minutes to 1 hour. (Check them after 45 minutes: you want a golden brown, crisp exterior.)

7. Meanwhile, make the syrup. Gently heat the syrup ingredients in a saucepan over medium heat and simmer for 5–10 minutes, or until thick and fragrant. Remove from the heat and let cool.

8. As soon as the baklava comes out of the oven, pour the cool syrup evenly over the surface. Finish by drizzling the extra tablespoon of honey over the top, if you want to, and sprinkle with any leftover filling. Let the baklava cool in the pan before gently removing and putting on a serving plate. If you're feeling fancy, decorate the cooled baklava with some dried rose petals.

M   T   W   T   F

SUPER WEEKDAY DINNERS

I never saw the point of a frozen dinner. Takeouts, yes (you can't always be bothered to cook and, besides, with Bangkok's food stalls, I grew up in a takeout culture), and restaurants, of course. But frozen meals? They're neither one thing nor the other, neither freshly made nor especially good for you. So ever since I left home, I've cooked. It's more about habit than anything else. But is it really any harder to put some chicken thighs in a pan than to prick holes in the top of some foil? They both take forty minutes in the oven.

Most of these recipes are quick and convenient. A couple take a little effort, but that's a good thing. And I've always found, after a not-so-great day at the office, that there's something very soothing and karmically restorative about taking your wrath out on the onion you're chopping.

KAY

FOUR
RISOTTOS

Sometimes, there's nothing more comforting than a bowl of piping hot risotto. It's healthy, soothing, and much easier to make than some people think. So if you haven't made one before, give it a try.

Here, we give you one basic method with four variations. And we are departing a little from tradition. Risotto is usually made with butter. But to be that little bit healthier, we're using olive oil with just a dash of butter so you should get that creamy flavor with less risk of a coronary.

Basic Risotto Bianco

SERVES 4 • PREPARATION TIME: 5–10 MINUTES • COOKING TIME: 25–30 MINUTES • WF GF

4 cups **chicken** or **vegetable stock**
2 tablespoons **olive oil**
1 teaspoon **butter**
1 **onion**, finely chopped
2 cups **risotto rice**

½ cup **white wine**
2 tablespoons freshly grated **Parmesan cheese**
salt and **freshly ground black pepper**

1. Pour the stock into a large saucepan and bring it to a gentle simmer. Keep it there, quivering away.

2. In a separate saucepan, heat the oil and then the butter over medium heat. When the butter begins to foam, add the onion and cook gently for about 5 minutes, until it's soft and translucent. Now add the rice and stir for about 2 minutes, until all the rice is evenly coated with butter and oil.

3. Now add the wine, stir it into the rice, and, when it's almost completely absorbed, add the first ladle of hot stock—just enough to cover the rice. Turn down the heat to low-to-medium, and keep stirring so that the rice doesn't stick. (When you've done this a few times, you don't have to stir it religiously, but you have to pay it appropriate attention.)

4. As the rice absorbs the liquid, keep adding stock in smaller and smaller quantities, even if you have to do so quite frequently, until the rice is cooked; you don't want a soupy, runny risotto, the rice should be al dente. It should be creamy, and not-exactly-dry. This can take up to 20 minutes and sometimes longer.

5. Season with salt, pepper, and Parmesan and there you have a simple *risotto bianco*.

TIPS

* Rice likes to rest. So when cooked, cover with a lid and let it stand for 5 minutes to let it relax.

* With risotto, the cooking temperature is crucial. If it's too high, the rice won't cook evenly and the grains will be chalky inside. Too low, and the rice will be claggy. You'll get the hang of it.

OPPOSITE ABOVE: TRAFFIC LIGHT RISOTTO
BELOW: PEA & HAM RISOTTO

Pea & Ham Risotto

WF GF

Peas and ham—just made to go together.

  1 quantity **basic risotto bianco** (see page 103)
  4oz shredded **ham**
  1⅓ cups **peas** (we often use thawed frozen peas for this)
  1 teaspoon **fresh thyme leaves**

1. Make the basic risotto bianco as per the method on page 103. When the rice is cooked, stir in the ham, peas, and thyme before you season with salt, black pepper, and Parmesan, then serve.

2. You could use a ham stock when making the risotto. Just make sure it's not too salty.

Grilled Asparagus & Lemon Risotto

WF GF

These are fresh and sunny flavors. Grilling the asparagus adds an extra smokey dimension.

Variations to the basic risotto bianco:
change the wine for ⅓ cup **white vermouth**
add 1 clove of **garlic**, finely chopped, when you sauté the onion

Then add:
1 pound **asparagus**, trimmed
1 tablespoon **olive oil**
2 sprigs of **fresh thyme**, leaves picked
the juice of ½ a **lemon**
the zest of 1 **lemon**
1 tablespoon finely chopped **fresh parsley**, plus extra to garnish
salt and **freshly ground black pepper**

1. Heat a ridged grill pan until you can *really* feel the heat rising off it when you hold your hand about 2½ inches above it.

2. Dry the asparagus thoroughly, then toss it in the olive oil. Season it with salt and balck pepper, and sprinkle it with the thyme leaves.

3. Grill the asparagus, turning occasionally, for about 5 minutes, or until it's nicely soft, with elegant black char lines on it. Remove from the heat and set aside. When it's cooled a little, cut it into bite-size pieces.

4. Now for the risotto: Make the risotto as per the method above, substituting the vermouth for the wine and adding the garlic when the onion is halfway there.

5. When the rice is cooked, add the grilled asparagus, lemon juice, lemon zest, and parsley. Stir everything together, and finish with salt, black pepper, and Parmesan as usual. Serve garnished with a little extra parsley.

Traffic Light Risotto

♥ WF GF

Peppery and sweet—this is a colorful favorite.

1 quantity **basic risotto bianco** (see page 103)

2 tablespoons **olive oil**

3 cloves of **garlic**, peeled and thinly sliced

1 mild **red chile**, sliced (seeds are optional, depending on how spicy you like it)

1 **red bell pepper**, cut into ½–¾-inch chunks

1 **yellow bell pepper**, cut into ½–¾-inch chunks

1 **green pepper**, cut into ½–¾-inch chunks

2 tablespoons **fresh flat-leaf parsley**, finely chopped

1. Make the basic risotto bianco as per the method on page 103.

2. While you're cooking the rice, heat the olive oil in a skillet over medium heat. Add the garlic and sauté until it begins to color. Then add the chile and the bell peppers and stir. Season with a pinch of salt and cook, stirring occasionally, until the bell peppers are soft and hot. Set them aside until the risotto's ready.

3. When the rice is cooked, remove it from the heat and stir in the bell peppers, then taste, adjust the seasoning as required, and serve.

Summer Squash & Nasturtium Risotto

WF GF

By squash, we mean summer squash: pattypans, yellow crooknecks, and so on. If you can't find them in the supermarket, you can substitute zucchini. The nasturtium flowers add a shock of color, as well as a sweet-peppery bite.

1 quantity **basic risotto bianco** (see page 103)

2 tablespoons **olive oil**

2 cloves of **garlic**, finely chopped

2 tablespoons chopped **fresh thyme**

2 cups **coarsely chopped summer squash cubes**

a few **fresh basil leaves**, torn

8 **nasturtium flowers**

1. Make the basic risotto bianco as per the method on page 103.

2. While the rice is cooking, heat the olive oil in a separate skillet over medium heat. When it's hot, add the garlic and sauté until it just begins to color. Add the thyme, stir for another minute, then add the squash. Let it color and the garlic turn a nutty brown. Then remove the skillet from the heat and set aside.

3. When the risotto is cooked, add the squash and the basil leaves, then stir everything together. Serve, garnishing each bowl with a pair of nasturtium flowers.

Tasty Herby Chicken Thighs & Salad

CHICKEN

SERVES 4 • PREPARATION TIME: 10 MINUTES • COOKING TIME: 50 MINUTES • ✓ WF GF

An old standby in the Plunkett-Hogge household.

> 8 **chicken thighs**
> 3–4 cloves of **garlic**
> 1–2 tablespoons **olive oil**
> a small bunch of **fresh lemon thyme**
> 4 **Boston lettuces**
>   or 4 large handfuls of **baby leaves**
> 2 bunches of **watercress**
> 1 cup **white wine**
> 2 tablespoons **butter**
> **salt** and **freshly ground black pepper**

1. Heat the oven to 400°F.

2. Trim the excess fat off the chicken thighs and place them, skin side up, in a roasting pan. Throw in the garlic cloves, then drizzle everything with the olive oil—try to make sure everything's well covered.

3. Now strip the leaves off the lemon thyme stems, and sprinkle them into the pan. Season the chicken thighs with salt and black pepper and put them into the oven for 45 minutes, or until they're cooked through.

4. While the chicken's in the oven, trim the lettuce and slice them into ¾-inch strips. Put them into a bowl and toss them with the watercress, then divide the salad equally among your plates.

5. When the chicken's ready, remove it from the oven and place on top of the salad. Deglaze the roasting pan with the wine, scraping up all the cooking sediment from the bottom of the pan and squashing the roasted garlic into the sauce.

6. Finally, whisk in the butter for a nice glossy finish. Pour the sauce over the chicken and salad, and serve.

TIPS

* If you prefer a change from chicken thighs, this will work perfectly well with drumsticks or with entire thigh/leg sections. We don't make it with chicken breast because it tends to dry out.

* Try using different herbs—you can make this with pretty much any herb you like, but go easy on the sage.

* For a sweeter, less peppery salad, why not substitute pea shoots for the watercress?

* If you don't want to use wine, just use a good chicken stock to deglaze the roasting pan.

Grilled Chicken Angelus

SERVES 4 • PREPARATION TIME: 30 MINUTES PLUS MARINATING • COOKING TIME: 40 MINUTES • ✓ ♥ WF GF DF

Herby and spicy, this features a dry-rub that's halfway to Cajun. Try it on the barbecue.

1 heaping tablespoon **allspice berries**
1 teaspoon **cayenne pepper**
1 teaspoon **ground paprika**
a good pinch of **ground cumin**
1 teaspoon **dried oregano**
1 teaspoon **dried thyme**
a good pinch of **salt**
2 cloves of **garlic**, chopped
2 **scallions**, trimmed and chopped
a couple of grinds of **black pepper**
1 tablespoon **olive oil**
1 **chicken**, butterflied
the juice of ½ a **lemon**

1. Grind the allspice berries with a mortar and pestle. Add the other ground spices and the dried herbs and grind together a little more. Now add the salt, garlic, and the scallions and grind to a paste. Add the black pepper and olive oil and mix together. You should have a loose, fragrant putty to smear over the bird.

2. Slash the back and thighs of the chicken with a sharp knife. Rub the putty well into the bird, especially into the slashes, then let marinate in the refrigerator for up to 4 hours. (But, of course, if you only have 20 minutes, that'll do.)

3. Grill (or broil) the chicken over medium heat for about 30–40 minutes, until it's completely cooked through.

4. When it's done, squeeze over the lemon juice. Serve with a salad and some extra lemon wedges on the side.

This is named for the street where we often stay in Los Angeles, at my great friend Sue McNamara's house. Sue has a wonderful indoor/outdoor kitchen which inspires me to grill whenever we're there.

KAY

Pesto Chicken

SERVES 4 • PREPARATION TIME: 20 MINUTES • COOKING TIME: 25 MINUTES • ✓ WF GF

We also like to make this with fresh pesto when we have a little extra time (see tip below).

1½ pound boneless, skinless **chicken breasts**,
  sliced ½ inch thick
2 tablespoons **olive oil**
2 tablespoons **butter**
2 cloves of **garlic**, peeled and finely chopped
1 cup **white wine or chicken stock**
2 tablespoons **pesto sauce**
a squeeze of **lemon juice**
sea salt and **freshly ground black pepper**

1. Season the chicken breast slices with a little salt and black pepper.

2. In a heavy skillet, melt the oil and butter over medium heat and, in batches, sauté the chicken until it's cooked through. Each batch should take about 5–7 minutes to cook and the chicken will be golden in color. Set aside.

3. Reduce the heat and add the garlic to the residual oil in the skillet. Cook, stirring gently from time to time, until it begins to color for about another 2 minutes. Now increase the heat and add the wine or stock. Bubble until reduced by about half its volume, scraping up any cooking sediment from the skillet.

4. Stir in the pesto and the lemon juice, and season with salt and black pepper to taste. Return the chicken to the skillet, toss it through the sauce, and serve.

TIPS

* If you have time, this homemade pesto will make it taste all the fresher:

1 tablespoon **pine nuts**, toasted
1 clove of **garlic**
a pinch of **sea salt**
a large handful of picked **fresh basil leaves**
¼ cup **freshly grated Parmesan cheese**
⅔ cup **olive oil**

1. Using a small immersion blender, process the pine nuts and garlic together with a pinch of salt. Add the basil, the cheese, and ½ cup of the oil and process again until you have a rough paste.

2. If you don't want to use it immediately, spoon it into a jar, top with the remaining oil, and store in the refrigerator. It should keep for a couple of days.

Back in the 80s, a jar of pesto was the height of sophistication, so this quick, simple staples dinner was something of a weekly favorite when I was growing up. Pesto is still something I keep in the refrigerator—you never know when it will come in handy.
FRED

Deb Henley's Chicken Enchiladas Verdes

SERVES 4–6 • PREPARATION TIME: 20 MINUTES • COOKING TIME: 50 MINUTES • WF GF

Our friend Deb always roasts a chicken especially for her enchiladas. She devised this particular recipe when she moved back to London from Mexico City in the summer of 2000, after all her Mexican friends kept asking her: "Please cook us something from home."

1 x 28-ounce **can of tomatillos**
2 **serrano** or other **medium-hot green chiles**,
   or 1 **jalapeño chile**
1 clove of **garlic**
1 small **onion**, chopped
1 tablespoon of **fat** from roasting your
   chicken (optional)
a bunch of **fresh cilantro**, finely chopped
½ cup **chicken stock**
8–12 **soft, pure corn tortillas** (see tips opposite)
2½ cups **shredded, cooked chicken**
⅔ cup **heavy cream**
½ cup **shredded young Manchego cheese**
sea salt

1. Heat the oven to 350°F.

2. Drain the tomatillos and set them aside in a bowl.

3. Put the chiles into a small saucepan and add ½ cup of water. Bring to a boil, simmer for 5 minutes, then remove from the heat. Put the chiles and their cooking water, the tomatillos, garlic, and onion into a blender or food processor, and process until smooth.

4. If you're using the chicken fat, put it into a deep saucepan and heat gently. Add the blended salsa verde (the tomatillo mixture) and 2 tablespoons of the chopped cilantro and cook for about 5 minutes over medium heat. Add the chicken stock, season with salt, and cook until it thickens up a little—about 4 more minutes. Keep the salsa warm while you prepare the enchiladas.

5. Wrap the tortillas in a clean dish towel and steam them, preferably in a tiered steamer, over boiling water for 1–2 minutes. You may want to do this in batches of 4–6 to prevent them from sticking together.

6. Put a good portion of the shredded chicken onto each tortilla, roll them up like fat cigars, and lay them side by side in a 2½ inch deep baking dish about 12½ x 9 inches. . Pour the green salsa over the tortilla, then the cream, and finally sprinkle with the shredded cheese. Bake in the oven for about 30 minutes.

7. Serve sprinkled with the rest of the chopped cilantro.

* You can buy cans of tomatillos online.

* Traditional corn tortillas are 100 percent corn, making them gluten free, and about 6 inches in diameter. However, in supermarkets, I've found many that are a mix of wheat and corn that are larger, so just keep that in mind.

* Deb roasts a small chicken and uses its meat for this but, if you prefer, you could just poach what you need. You can also use roasted chicken leftovers.

* If you have fresh tomatillos, you'll need 1¾ pounds. Just simmer them in enough boiling water to cover them for 5–10 minutes, or until their color changes from a bright to a drab green. Drain the tomatillos and the chile, reserving ½ cup of the water. Continue with the recipe as normal, being careful when you process the sauce, so that you don't burn yourself.

DEB, SYDNEY, 1970

Deb Henley is from Sydney, Australia. She is Kay's Pilates teacher and a great friend. She first moved to Mexico City in the mid-1990s to work as a ballet dancer and soon fell in love with the culture. Luckily for us, she then moved to London.

Kim's Spanish-style Chicken

SERVES 4–6 • PREPARATION TIME: 10 MINUTES • COOKING TIME: 1 HOUR 35 MINUTES • ✓ DF

Kay's sister Kim has two strapping teenage sons who can look at a refrigerator the way that locusts look at a farm. So she specializes in big, chunky recipes that go the distance. This one does just that.

8 **chicken thighs**
1 tablespoon **olive oil**
4oz **chorizo**, sliced ½-1cm thick
1 **onion**, finely chopped
1 x 15-oz **tin of cannellini beans** or **lima beans**,
   drained and rinsed
a couple of sprigs of **fresh oregano**
a couple of sprigs of **fresh tarragon**
a pinch of **cayenne pepper**
1 bulb of **garlic**, halved horizontally
   through the middle
a strip of **orange zest**
a glass of **white wine** or **dry sherry**
1 teaspoon ground **paprika**
12 **cherry tomatoes**
1¾ cups **chicken stock**
1 tablespoon chopped **fresh parsley**, to garnish
salt and **freshly ground black pepper**

My big sister Kim (who's actually really rather small) is everything I'm not: organized, efficient, green-fingered … and a parent. When we were little, she used to order me to fetch her lemonades and snacks, since she was so exhausted from school back in England. Once again, I fell for it. I have forgiven her. She's a bundle of energy, and a real inspiration.

KAY

KIM, JOMTIEN, 1963

1. Heat the oven to 350°F.

2. Clean and dry the chicken thighs, cutting away any excess fat. Put a heavy, nonstick skillet over medium heat, then add the olive oil. Thoroughly brown the chicken thighs all over, then set them aside in a large casserole.

3. When you've browned all the chicken, cook the chorizo slices for about 3 minutes each side, until they release their oil into the skillet and are cooked through. Add them to the casserole.

4. Reduce the heat under the skillet, add the onion, and sauté until soft. While it's cooking, add the beans, herbs, cayenne, garlic, and orange zest to the casserole.

5. When the onions are cooked, pour the wine or sherry into the skillet and bring to a rapid simmer, scraping all the cooking sediment off the bottom of the skillet with a wooden spoon. Add the paprika and stir it in. Pour everything into the casserole, add the cherry tomatoes, then top it up with enough chicken stock to cover the thighs.

6. Season with salt and black pepper, put on the lid, and put the casserole into the oven for about 1 hour and 10 minutes. Serve in big bowls with plenty of bread for dunking, with sautéd greens or a simple green salad.

Sweet Soy Salmon with Mushrooms & Pea Shoots

SERVES 4 • PREPARATION TIME: 15 MINUTES • COOKING TIME: 8–10 MINUTES • ♥ DF

A Japanese-inflected salmon. The wasabi provides a punch that salmon takes really well. For an extra kick, try adding a pinch of dried red pepper flakes.

4 **salmon steaks**, about 4–5oz each
¼ cup **tamari**
1–2 teaspoons **wasabi paste**, or to taste
2 teaspoons **sugar**
4 teaspoons **rice vinegar**
1 tablespoon **olive oil**, plus 1 teaspoon
a ¾-inch piece of **fresh ginger**, peeled and finely slivered
4 **scallions**, trimmed and sliced on the diagonal
3 cloves of **garlic**, chopped
4oz **fresh shiitake** and/or **chanterelle mushrooms**, trimmed and sliced
a pinch of **dried chile** (optional)
a squeeze of **lemon juice**
¾ cup **pea shoots**
salt and **freshly ground black pepper**

TIPS

* When pea shoots are out of season, use watercress or arugula leaves.
* You could also mix in ⅔ cup of frozen peas or some edamame (fresh soybeans) beans when cooking the mushrooms.
* Experiment with different mushrooms—cremini mushrooms work just as well, as do enoki.

1. Heat the oven to 400°F.

2. Put the salmon into a small roasting pan. Mix together the tamari, wasabi, sugar, vinegar, and the teaspoon of oil in a bowl, and pour it over the fish, coating it well.

3. Divide up the slivers of ginger and half the sliced scallions into 4 little piles, and sprinkle one evenly over each piece of salmon. Season with a pinch of black pepper, and roast for about 8 minutes, or until the salmon is just cooked through.

4. While the salmon is in the oven, heat the tablespoon of olive oil in a skillet over medium heat. When it's hot, add the garlic and cook until soft but not browned. Now add the mushrooms and cook for a few minutes, making sure that all the water evaporates out of them, otherwise they'll be soggy (mushrooms are 90 percent water). Add the pinch of chile (if you desire), a squeeze of lemon, and the rest of the scallions and continue cooking for a few minutes. Remove from the heat, and season with a little salt and pepper.

5. Remove the salmon from the oven and put it onto 4 plates. Top with the mushroom mixture and finish with an even sprinkling of the pea shoots.

Salmon in a Bag Three Ways

SERVES 4 • PREPARATION TIME: 10–15 MINUTES • COOKING TIME: 15–20 MINUTES

Even people who say they don't really like fish seem to like salmon. Pink and juicy, it's packed with all kinds of good-for-you goodies. It's high in protein, in vitamins D and B12, and don't forget those omega-3 fatty acids—good for the heart, limbs, and the old brain. Top food.

This method of cooking salmon (*en papillote*) is super quick and easy. Essentially, you're steaming the fish in a "bag" so you lose none of its goodness. Here are three of our favorites.

Provençal Salmon	St. Clement's Salmon	Thai Salmon
✓ ♥ WF GF DF	✓ ♥ WF GF DF	✓ ♥ WF GF DF
These flavors always remind us of summers in France.	Oranges and lemons, say the bells of St. Clement's …	Exotic and warming, with some fiery red chile …
4 **salmon fillets,** about 5oz each	4 **salmon fillets,** about 5oz each	4 **salmon fillets,** about 5oz each
8 **cherry tomatoes,** or 4 **larger tomatoes,** halved	4 thin slices of **lemon**	1 **red Thai chile,** seeded and finely chopped
16 **black olives**	4 thin slices of **orange**	2 **cilantro roots,** chopped
2 cloves of **garlic,** peeled and chopped	2–3 sprigs of **fresh dill,** finely chopped	2 cloves of **garlic,** chopped
a handful of **fresh basil leaves,** plus a little extra to garnish	2 cloves of **garlic,** peeled and chopped	1 tablespoon **Thai fish sauce**
a drizzle of **olive oil**	the juice of ½ a **lemon**	2 **scallions,** trimmed and chopped
a splash of **dry white vermouth**	the juice of ½ an **orange** (you should have about ¼ cup of liquid from the two halved fruits)	2 tablespoons **lime juice**
salt and **freshly ground black pepper**	a drizzle of **olive oil**	a good grinding of **white pepper**
	a few sprigs of **fresh dill,** to garnish	a bunch of **fresh cilantro,** to garnish
	salt and **freshly ground black pepper**	

1. Heat the oven to 350°F.

2. Put each salmon fillet onto a square piece of either parchment paper or aluminum foil measuring about 14 x 14 inches. Then add the flavorings and the liquids, depending on which version you're making. Seal the "bag" with tight folds, making sure there's room inside for the salmon to steam. If you're using parchment paper, don't scrunch instead of folding because this may unravel, spilling all the juices.

3. Place the packages in a baking pan and cook them in the oven for 15 minutes, or until the salmon is just cooked through.

4. Remove from the oven and place carefully onto plates. Then rush them to the table so that everyone can open their own bag and add their own garnish.

Easy Pad Thai

SERVES 2 • PREPARATION TIME: 10 MINUTES PLUS SOAKING • COOKING TIME: 5–10 MINUTES • WF GF DF

This has nothing on the Pad Thai at Pratu Pee (the Ghost's Gate) in Bangkok, but it's pretty darn good, and streamlined for speed.

It's better to make this in small batches, so the recipe here feeds two.

5oz **rice noodles**
1 tablespoon **vegetable oil**
3 cloves of **garlic**, chopped
5–8oz **fresh peeled shrimp**
2 **eggs**, lightly beaten
2 handfuls of **bean sprouts**
2 **scallions**, trimmed and chopped
2 tablespoons **dried shrimp**
2 tablespoons **unsalted, roasted peanuts**,
   coarsely chopped
3 tablespoons **Thai fish sauce**
2 tablespoons **lime juice**
2 tablespoons **sugar**
½ teaspoon **tamarind paste**
¼ teaspoon **chile powder**

For the garnish:
2 **scallions**, trimmed and chopped
1 tablespoon **fresh cilantro**, leaves picked
a few slices of **cucumber** (optional)
½ tablespoon **unsalted, roasted peanuts**,
   coarsely chopped
2 **lime wedges**

1. Soak the rice noodles in warm water for 5–10 minutes, or until they're just malleable. (The instructions on the package will probably say to soak them for 15–20 minutes, but this will make them too soggy for the finished dish.) Drain, rinse, and set aside.

2. Heat the oil in a wok over high heat. Add the garlic and stir-fry quickly until just turning golden. Add the fresh shrimp and stir-fry for a minute or two. Then add the noodles and stir through before adding the eggs, bean sprouts, scallions, dried shrimp and peanuts, stirring after each addition.

3. When everything is well combined, add the fish sauce, lime juice, sugar, chile powder and tamarind paste. Stir thoroughly, then serve immediately, garnished with scallion, cilantro, cucumber, and peanuts, with lime wedges on the side.

TIPS | * If you prefer, you can change the shrimp for the same amount of chicken or pork.

West Indian Seafood Curry

SERVES 2 • PREPARATION TIME: 15 MINUTES • COOKING TIME: 15 MINUTES • ✓ ♥ WF GF

This is based on a dish Kay had when she went to visit Fred's extended family in Montego Bay, Jamaica. It kind of sums up all the ethnic influences on the island. It's a melting pot of a dish.

1 teaspoon **coriander seeds**
1 teaspoon **black mustard seeds**
1 teaspoon **cumin seeds**
2 **allspice berries**
¼ teaspoon **dried red pepper flakes**
1 tablespoon **vegetable oil**
1 **shallot**, peeled and chopped
1 clove of **garlic**, peeled and chopped
1 x 14½-oz can of **chopped tomatoes**
½ teaspoon **tamarind paste**
the juice of ½ a **lime**
2 **fresh kaffir lime leaves**
1–2 teaspoons **superfine sugar**
a couple of drops of **hot pepper sauce** (optional)
½ teaspoon **sea salt**
12oz **white fish fillets**—anything firm and
    sustainable: haddock, pollock, farmed cod—
    cut into chunks
2 tablespoons **Greek** or **plain yogurt** (optional)
¼ **red bell pepper**, thinly sliced, to garnish
freshly ground black pepper

1. Heat a dry skillet and toast the spices over low heat for 3–4 minutes, or until fragrant. Grind them in a mortar and pestle or a coffee grinder and set aside.

2. Heat the vegetable oil in a wide, heavy saucepan, and soften the shallot and garlic. Add the spices and stir for 30 seconds more. Add the canned tomatoes, tamarind paste, lime juice, one of the kaffir lime leaves, sugar, hot pepper sauce (if using), the sea salt, and a grinding of black pepper. Simmer for 1 minute.

3. Add the fish and simmer for another 3–5 minutes, or until the fish looks white and is falling apart.

4. Taste for seasoning. If you want, swirl through some yogurt. Serve with rice and garnish with the other lime leaf, slivered into ribbons, and strips of red bell pepper.

TIPS

* If your sauce seems a little thick, add a splash of water to loosen it up.

Linguine with Crab & Tomato

SERVES 4 • PREPARATION TIME: 10 MINUTES • COOKING TIME: 10–12 MINUTES • DF

This is Kay's absolute favorite pasta sauce.

1 lb **linguine**
3 tablespoons **olive oil**
2 cloves of **garlic**, finely chopped
1 **red serrano** or other **medium-hot chile**,
   seeded and sliced into small pieces
8–12 **cherry tomatoes**
8oz **white crabmeat** or 2 x 6-oz **cans of crab**
2 tablespoons **dry white vermouth** or **white wine**
2 tablespoons **dark crabmeat**
1 tablespoon **fresh flat-leaf parsley**, chopped
salt and **freshly ground black pepper**

1. Bring a large saucepan of salted water up to a rolling boil. Check the cooking time on your pasta package—we find, normally, for al dente pasta, that it takes a little less time than advertised—and add the linguine to the pan.

2. Meanwhile, heat 2 tablespoons of olive oil in a large sauté pan over medium heat. Add the garlic and stir until you can just smell it. Now add the chile and tomatoes. Stir until the garlic just begins to brown, then add the white crabmeat or canned crab. Stir for a moment or two, then add the vermouth or wine, the dark crabmeat, and a good pinch of the parsley. Season with salt and pepper and stir together well. In total, this should take no more than 5 minutes.

3. If the pasta isn't quite cooked, set the sauce aside to keep warm. When the linguine's done, drain it and toss in the remaining tablespoon of olive oil. Stir the crabmeat sauce through the pasta and serve with a sprinkling of parsley and a good grind of black pepper. Oh, and with a good glass of crisp Italian white.

TIPS

* We often make this with canned crab and without the dark crabmeat—it's a quick and easy pantry staple. But if you really want to go for it, buy prepared crab meat—we like to mix the white and dark crabmeat.

* The wine or vermouth adds an important dimension to this dish, but you can substitute water if you'd prefer.

* To make the sauce a little spicier, why not use a pinch of dried peperoncino or some rinsed green peppercorns instead of the chile.

* Sometimes, for an extra seaside flavor, Kay replaces the tomatoes with 5oz of sea asparagus.

Henry's Meatballs with Herb Salad

MAKES 12 • PREPARATION TIME: 20 MINUTES • COOKING TIME: 20 MINUTES • ✓ WF GF

These lightly spiced meatballs contain a surprise within. Make sure there are no holes or the cheese will ooze out.

For the meatballs:
8 **cardamom pods**
2 teaspoons **coriander seeds**
4 **cloves**
4 large cloves of **garlic**
a large pinch of **salt**
12oz **ground sirloin beef**
6oz **ground pork**
½ teaspoon **turmeric**
chile powder, to taste
1 **egg**, beaten
1–2 tablespoons **peanut oil**
½ cup **cream cheese**

1½ cups **halved baby plum tomatoes**
1 tablespoon **plain yogurt**

To serve:
2–3 tablespoons chopped **fresh cilantro leaves**
2 tablespoons **slivered almonds**, toasted
4 **shallots**, finely sliced and deep-fried

For the salad:
5 cups mixed **salad greens**
2 tablespoons finely chopped **fresh mint leaves**
2 tablespoons finely chopped **fresh chives**
2 tablespoons finely chopped **fresh flat-leaf parsley**
2 tablespoons finely chopped **fresh oregano**
1 teaspoon **white wine vinegar**
1 teaspoon **English mustard**
3 tablespoons **olive oil**

1. Take the seeds out of the cardamom pods, place them in a coffee grinder or mortar and pestle with the coriander seeds and cloves, then grind to a fine powder. Chop the garlic with the salt until it forms a paste, or add it to the mortar and pestle.

2. Put the beef and pork into a large bowl and mix together vigorously to soften the texture—this will help stop the cheese from escaping.

3. Add the ground spices, turmeric, chile powder, and garlic to the meat and mix really well with your hands, then add the beaten egg and combine well.

4. Wet your hands, then take pieces of the mixture and roll into balls the size of ping-pong balls. You should have about 12 meatballs.

5. Lightly oil a clean work surface with a little of the peanut oil and gently press the meatballs into flattened circles.

6. Put a teaspoon of cream cheese in the center of each meat circle and carefully bring the meat up around it to enclose the cheese completely, making larger meatballs. Roll gently and make sure there are no holes.

7. Heat a large skillet until hot, then add the remaining oil and cook the meatballs over medium-high heat for 10 minutes, turning regularly, until browned and cooked through. Put the meatballs into a serving dish and keep warm.

8. Increase the heat under the skillet, then add the tomatoes and cook them quickly. Remove the skillet from the heat and stir in the yogurt.

9. For the salad, toss together the greens and herbs in a large bowl. Whisk the vinegar, mustard, and olive oil together and season with salt and black pepper. Toss together with the salad greens.

10. To serve, arrange the salad around the edge of a serving platter and place the meatballs in the center. Pour the tomato mixture over the meatballs and garnish with the chopped cilantro, almonds, and fried shallots.

THE DIMBLEBY FAMILY IN THE DORDOGNE, 1976

"My mom used to love making us dishes with surprises in them: ice cream bombes which spilled grated chocolate, puddings with hidden custards, and stuffed meatballs. This recipe is my take on a dish that appeared in her alliteratively named *Marvellous Meals with Mince* in the 80s—a book of its time."

HENRY

Quick Guay Tiew Nam Moo

(PORK MEATBALL NOODLE SOUP)

SERVES 4 OR 2 GREEDY PEOPLE • PREPARATION TIME: 15 MINUTES • COOKING TIME: 15 MINUTES • DF

A superquick shortcut to a tasty Thai pork noodle soup. You can find variations on this theme on practically every street corner in Thailand. To be honest, it's perfect at any time of day. And it's great for the morning after the night before …

For the meatballs:
1 teaspoon **white peppercorns**
2 fresh **cilantro roots** (from the coriander plant)
2 cloves of **garlic**
a pinch of **salt**
8oz **ground pork**
a dash of **Thai fish sauce**

For the soup:
4oz medium-width **rice noodles**
1 tablespoon **vegetable oil**
1 clove of **garlic**, smashed
5 cups **stock**, any flavor
2 tablespoons **light soy sauce**
2 tablespoons **Thai fish sauce**
100g **bean sprouts**
1 head of **bok choy**, coarsely chopped
3 **scallions**, trimmed and finely chopped
a handful of **fresh cilantro leaves**, chopped

TIPS

* In Thailand, you get this served with a selection of condiments called *kruang prung*. These could be some ground, roasted dried chiles, rice vinegar with mild chiles sliced into it, Thai fish sauce with finely sliced Thai chiles; lime juice; sugar; plain Thai fish sauce and crushed peanuts.

1. Fill a large bowl with water and put in your rice noodles; this just softens them and gets rid of a lot of the starch, which would otherwise make your soup "gummy."

2. In a mortar and pestle, pound the peppercorns, coriander roots, garlic, and the salt to a paste. Then, in a clean bowl, mix the paste with the ground pork and fish sauce, mushing it thoroughly with your hands. Form the mixture into 16 meatballs and set them aside.

3. Now for the soup. Heat the oil in a large saucepan and, once it's hot, add the smashed clove of garlic. Cook for a minute or so until it's really fragrant—but don't let it brown. Pour in the stock and bring to a boil. Add the soy sauce and the nam pla, bring it back to a boil, then add the meatballs. When they're cooked through—in about a minute or two—add your drained noodles.

4. Bring it all back to a boil and add your bean sprouts and bok choy. Bring back to a boil again and cook for 3 minutes. Check that the noodles are cooked—by this time your vegetables will be ready. You want them with a little bite.

5. Divide among bowls and top each bowl with a few pieces of scallion and some chopped cilantro.

Midweek Lamb

SERVES 4 • PREPARATION TIME: 15 MINUTES • COOKING TIME: 40 MINUTES • ✓ WF GF DF

This is an incredibly easy dish that tastes as though you've spent loads of time on it.

a small bunch of **fresh rosemary**
1 boned **leg of lamb**, about 2¾ lb in weight
6 **anchovies**—about half a 2-oz can
2 large cloves of **garlic**, peeled
the zest of ½ a **lemon**
2 **dried chiles**
1 tablespoon **olive oil**
salt and **freshly ground black pepper**

1. Heat the oven to 425°F.

2. Strip the leaves off the rosemary and set aside. Sprinkle the twigs in a roasting pan. Open out the lamb, pat it dry and lay it on top of the rosemary twigs.

3. Now put all the remaining ingredients into a food processor with the rosemary leaves and process to a paste. Spread the paste over the lamb.

4. Roast in the oven for 40 minutes, or until the lamb is still nicely pink inside. Set it aside to rest for at least 15 minutes before serving.

TIPS

*   Deglaze the roasting pan with 1 cup of wine, stock, or water to make a luscious yet simple gravy.

*   Feel free to substitute black olives for the anchovies—say about 18 large ones.

*   If you want more of a one-dish meal, chop up some red bell peppers and a bulb or two of fennel and sprinkle them in the bottom of the roasting pan. Drizzle with a little olive oil and moisten with a splash of stock, wine, or water, then lay the lamb on top and roast as above.

John's Big Bowl of Sunday Night Lamb

SERVES AS MANY AS YOU LIKE • PREPARATION TIME: 20 MINUTES PLUS MARINATING
COOKING TIME: 20–25 MINUTES • WF GF DF

This is a simple dish I used to cook, normally on a Sunday night, when we lived off the Edgware Road in Kilburn come Maida Vale in London.

These are all ingredients that I bought from the Middle Eastern store behind the bus stop opposite the Islamic Center. In a nutshell, it ends up as a big bowl of basmati rice with dried fried onion, plenty of broiled marinated lamb chops and a little chopped cilantro. I used to serve it with fava beans.

Kids will eat two chops each, and you will eat as many as you want, don't let me decide.

1. Marinate the **lamb chops** in whatever you prefer: **olive oil**, **lemon juice**, **salt and black pepper**, **garlic**. Try **rosemary**. Try anything once. Let marinate for 15 minutes at least, longer if possible.

2. Cook ½ a cup of **white basmati** or **long grain rice** per person with double the amount of **water**. Add a little **salt** and **olive oil** because that seems to be the done thing.

3. Broil the lamb chops under medium heat. To keep them a little pink, turn them after a couple of minutes. Longer if you want them to, but they won't taste as good. Cook on the other side for the same time.

4. Fill a high-sided serving bowl with the drained, cooked rice, and open a package of **fried onions**. Sprinkle them over the rice, maybe folding some in, but leaving a lot on top as if they are savoury candy sprinkles.

5. Place the lamb chops on top, then sprinkle with some coarsely chopped **fresh cilantro** or **flat-leaf parsley**.

6. Serve with some **green beans** or **fava beans** to make you feel good and look good.

7. Ta daaaa. You can now put it on the table and feast, either elegantly or carnivorously—you choose.

JOHN AT BROADSTAIRS, AGE 3

TIPS

* I buy my onions already prepared for this. You can find them in most Asian supermarkets in plastic jars or packages. Alternatively, you can heat a couple of tablespoons of vegetable oil in a wok until it's very hot, then throw in a couple of finely sliced shallots or one finely sliced onion, stir-frying for a couple of minutes until they're golden brown. Remove immediately with a slotted spoon and drain on paper towels. When they're cool, store them in a plastic container or a food bag.

Fred's Ragù alla Toscana

MAKES ENOUGH SAUCE TO SERVE 8 EASILY
PREPARATION TIME: 30 MINUTES • COOKING TIME: I HOUR 30 MINUTES • ✓ DF

This is rich, meaty, and well worth the effort. Fred was taught it in Florence from his landlady, Signora Capelli. Apparently, she used to say that some things can cook fast, and some things can't. And to deny time to the things that can't is to cook without love.

So why is this in a Weekday Dinners chapter? Because it makes twice as much as you need, and tastes just as good when reheated.

3 tablespoons **olive oil**
1 **onion**, finely diced
1 stick of **celery**, finely diced
1 **carrot**, finely diced
1 clove of **garlic**, sliced as thinly as you can
12oz good-quality **ground sirloin beef**
4oz **chicken livers**, cleaned and chopped
⅔ cup **red wine**
1 28-oz can **tomato puree** or **tomato sauce**
a 4-inch sprig of **fresh rosemary**
salt and **freshly ground black pepper**

FRED, FAWLEY, 1975

I met Fred over a sponsorship deal. It involved many martinis. A proposal of marriage wasn't meant to be one of his deliverables, but somehow it turned out like that after a flirtation involving the copious swapping of … recipes. He's an amazing cook, a great barman, and, with a crazy Jamaican background and a love of travel, has broadened my food horizons more than I can say. (He's also *really* annoying!)

KAY

1. Heat 2 tablespoons of the oil in a large saucepan. Add the onion, celery, and carrot and cook over low heat for 10 minutes, stirring occasionally—you don't want the vegetables to catch or burn.

2. Add the garlic and cook for another 5 minutes or so, then remove from the pan and set aside. They should be warm and golden and sweet smelling.

3. Add another tablespoon of oil to the pan and brown the ground beef and liver in batches. Remove the meat from the pan and set aside. We want sticky, rich, meaty bits left on the bottom of the pan.

4. Deglaze the pan with the wine, scraping up all the yumminess on the bottom with a wooden spoon. Return the vegetables and meat to the pan. Add the tomato puree, rosemary, and season with salt and black pepper.

5. Bring to a boil, then simmer over the lowest heat possible for at least an hour, stirring occasionally. The sauce is done when it's thick and rich.

6. Serve with the pasta of your choice—we prefer fettucini or tagliatelle for this, but hey, sometimes you want shells, sometimes spaghetti …

TIPS

* For an extra special kick, substitute rabbit livers for the chicken livers. It gives the sauce a game-y flavor that is irresistible.

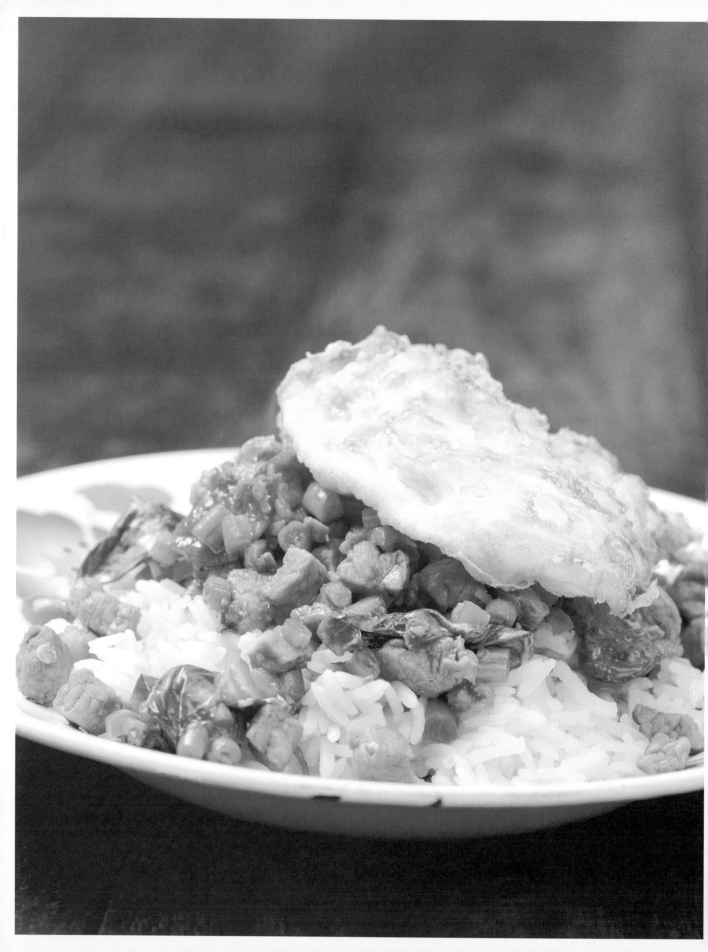

Kay's Pad Krapow Neua

(STIR-FRIED BEEF WITH HOLY BASIL)

SERVES 2 AS A MAIN DISH OR 4 AS PART OF A LARGER THAI MEAL
PREPARATION TIME: 10 MINUTES • COOKING TIME: 5 MINUTES • ✓ DF

This is one of my favorites, a real Bangkok staple, and my ultimate comfort food whenever I find I'm missing Thailand. I like to serve it as a single meal over a plate of plain rice, with a Thai-style fried egg on top, just waiting to ooze out its yellowy goodness. It provides a creamy counterbalance to the salty-spiciness of the dish.

4–6 **Thai chiles**

1 medium–large red **chile**, cut into chunks

6 cloves of **garlic**, peeled

a pinch of **salt**

2 tablespoons **dark soy sauce**

1 tablespoon **light soy sauce**

1 tablespoon **Thai fish sauce**

2 tablespoons **water**

a pinch of **sugar**

1–2 tablespoons **vegetable oil**

8–12oz **top sirloin steak**, finely chopped

a large handful of picked **bai krapow,**
   or **Thai holy basil leaves**—the more the
   merrier—plus a few to sprinkle at the end

1 cup **green beans**, topped, tailed and
   cut into ½-inch pieces

TIPS

* You can really use anything you like in this: shrimp, duck, tofu, chicken, finely sliced beef, and so on.

* If you can't find Thai holy basil, you can substitute it with *bai horapha* (sweet basil) or regular basil.

* Traditionally, this is served with some *nam pla prik* on the side. To make this, chop up a few Thai chiles and cover with 2–3 tablespoons of Thai fish sauce.

1. In a mortar and pestle, pound the chiles, garlic, and salt together into a coarse paste, then set aside.

2. Now mix the soy sauces, fish sauce and water together in a small bowl, and stir in the sugar. (This is a shortcut to speed things up at the wok. Properly, you should add them individually.)

3. Heat the oil in a wok until it's really hot. Throw in the chile-garlic paste and stir-fry for a few seconds—until you can really smell everything in the pan, but not long enough to brown the garlic. Add the beef and stir-fry until it's almost cooked through. Then add the green beans and keep stir-frying until the beef is done.

4. Finally, add the soy sauce mixture and stir, keeping it moving in the wok and letting it bubble up before adding the basil and wilting it into the dish.

5. Serve over steamed jasmine rice, and finish with a sprinkling of a few extra basil leaves.

6. For a very Thai touch, heat about a 1–1½-inch depth of vegetable oil in another wok and, when it's superhot, crack in an egg. Fry until the white is crispy on the outside, and the yolk runny within—it should take about a minute. Drain, and serve on top of your *pad krapow* and rice. Everyone should have their own egg, or there'll be fighting.

Cabbage, Peas & Pancetta

SERVES 4 • PREPARATION TIME: 10 MINUTES • COOKING TIME: 15 MINUTES • ✓ WF GF

This is a great combo, and the pancetta brings out everything that's glorious about cabbage.

3oz **pancetta**, cubed
½ head of a **savoy cabbage**, sliced
a couple of sprigs of **fresh flat-leaf parsley**
2 tablespoons **butter**
1⅓ cups **frozen peas**, thawed
salt and **freshly ground black pepper**

1. In a small, nonstick skillet, cook the pancetta until golden. Set aside.

2. Put the cabbage into a large saucepan with a good-fitting lid. Add a splash of water, no more than ½ inch deep. Add the parsley, butter and some salt and black pepper, put the lid on, and place the whole thing over medium heat.

3. When you see steam starting to escape, throw in the peas, give the pan a good shake, and cook for 3–5 minutes, or until the cabbage is soft but still retains some bite.

4. Strain off the buttery water, leaving a little to coat the leaves. Then toss the pancetta through the cabbage and serve immediately.

Fragrant Cardamom Basmati Rice

SERVES 4 • PREPARATION TIME: 5–10 MINUTES • COOKING TIME: 15–20 MINUTES • WF GF V

The smell of this turns our kitchen into an exotic, faraway land … at least, with our eyes closed.

1 tablespoon **vegetable oil** or **butter**
1 tablespoon finely chopped **onion**
1 cup **basmati** or **long grain rice**, rinsed and drained
5–6 **cardamom pods**, lightly crushed
a pinch of **saffron**
1¼ cups **water**
a pinch of **salt**

1. Heat the oil in a saucepan with a tight-fitting lid. Add the onions and sauté gently for a few minutes, or until they're just softening.

2. Stir in the rice. Add the crushed cardamom pods and the saffron and stir again. Add the water and a pinch of salt, then bring to a boil. As soon as it comes to a boil, reduce the heat to low, cover and cook for 10–12 minutes.

3. Check to see that the rice is cooked and all the water has been absorbed, then turn off the heat and let the rice sit with a lid on for 5 minutes before serving.

Stuffed Tomatoes

SERVES 4 • PREPARATION TIME: 10 MINUTES
COOKING TIME: 25 MINUTES • DF V

We love these tomatoes so much that we'll sometimes have them for lunch on their own, with some sliced fennel. This is also a useful recipe if you have leftover baguettes.

4 large firm **tomatoes**
3 cups **fresh bread crumbs**
3 tablespoons good **olive oil**
2–4 cloves of **garlic**, chopped
(we like it really garlicky)
a handful of **fresh flat-leaf parsley**, chopped
salt and **freshly ground black pepper**

1. Heat the oven to 350°F.

2. Halve the tomatoes and carefully scoop out and discard the insides. In a separate bowl, mix together the bread crumbs, olive oil, garlic, parsley, salt, and black pepper.

3. Pack the bread crumb mixture into the tomato halves, making a nice little mound on top. Put the tomatoes in a roasting pan and bake in the oven for 20–25 minutes.

4. Serve immediately. But do be careful— they can be nuclear-hot inside.

TIPS

* Process any leftover bread in the blender and stick it in the freezer in bags until you need it.

* This often makes too much filling, depending on the size of your tomatoes. Toast any leftovers in a dry skillet for a few minutes until golden brown, then serve it with the tomatoes (or sprinkled over a salad) for extra crunch.

Sautéd Summer Vegetables

SERVES 4 • PREPARATION TIME: 10 MINUTES • COOKING TIME: 15 MINUTES • ♥ WF GF DF V

Perfect as an accompaniment to so many summer dishes, or just on its own as a light lunch.

2 tablespoons **olive oil**
2 cloves of **garlic**, chopped
½ a large **red chile**, seeded
  and chopped
1⅓ cups **peas**
3 small **zucchini**, sliced

12–16 **cherry tomatoes**, or 10–12 **small
  tomatoes**, halved
a few sprigs of **fresh thyme**
a good dash of **white wine**
salt and **freshly ground black pepper**

1. Heat 1 tablespoon of olive oil in a heavy saucepan over medium heat. Add the garlic and chile and cook for two minutes, just until the garlic begins to brown.

2. Now add the vegetables, tomatoes, thyme, salt, and black pepper. Cook for a couple of minutes, then add the wine. Bubble it up, stirring everything together in its steam, then turn down the heat and add the rest of the oil. Cook for another 7 minutes or so, stirring occasionally. Serve immediately.

Sautéd Radishes with Their Tops & Peas

SERVES 4 • PREPARATION TIME: 10 MINUTES • COOKING TIME: 10 MINUTES • ♥ WF GF DF V

There's something about the lovely peppery-ness of French radishes with the sweetness of English peas, so we suppose that this is the *entente cordiale* in a side dish. It tastes fresh and it uses everything.

14oz **radishes,** with their tops on
2 tablespoons good-quality **olive oil**
3 cloves of **garlic**, thickly sliced

1¾ cups **frozen peas**, thawed
a couple of big handfuls of **pea shoots**
salt and **freshly ground black pepper**

1. Remove the tops from the radishes and wash them thoroughly. Slice the radishes into fat ovals, about ¼ inch thick. Set aside.

2. Heat 1 tablespoon of the olive oil in a nonstick skillet over medium heat. Add the garlic and cook until it starts to brown.

3. Now add the radish tops. Cook until they start to wilt, then add the sliced radishes and the peas. Cook for another minute or so, then add the pea shoots. Keep everything moving around the skillet until the pea shoots are just wilting. Add the remaining olive oil and salt and pepper to dress. Serve promptly.

TIPS

* We think it's best to use frozen peas for this, unless you're growing your own, in which case you can pick them at their perfect sweetness. Sometimes those fresh peas in the supermarket are so old that they'd be better used as buckshot.

* You can whip up this dish quickly while a chop or a steak is resting. By the time you're done, the meat should be perfect.

Will's Onion Rice

SERVES 6–8 • PREPARATION TIME: 5–10 MINUTES •
COOKING TIME: 15 MINUTES • WF GF DF V

Well, this recipe has become Will's, but it started out as Katie and Put's. However, because Will doesn't have the largest of repertoires, and he cooks it so well, we are happy for him to claim it.

It is a simple way of making a tasty, oniony rice. But we invite you to add your own flourishes.

1 tablespoon **olive oil**
1 **onion**, chopped
4 mugs of **water**
2 mugs of **white basmati rice**
1 tablespoon **bouillon, chicken,**
   or **vegetable stock**
freshly ground black pepper

1. Heat the olive oil in a large saucepan. Add the chopped onion and sauté until it's translucent. Add the water and bring to a boil. Then add the rice.

2. Simmer with a lid on over low heat until it's cooked, around 10–12 minutes. The water should all be absorbed.

3. Add the bouillon or stock and stir it in. Season with a good grinding of freshly ground black pepper, then serve.

TIPS

* Try adding other things to the rice such as peas, fava beans, asparagus, or mushrooms.

* You can substitute brown or wild rice, but you'll need to double the cooking time.

HOW MANY SHEPHERDS DOES IT TAKE TO MAKE A PIE?

Hats off to Mrs Freeman, Eleanor's teacher. This year we went to Christmas Eve carols and Eleanor was able to answer all the questions about the angel and the shepherds that the vicar could throw at us.

Now, the fact that shepherd's pie is made of lamb is like zoo-keeper's pie being made of lion: I mean, aren't they meant to be looking after them? Either way, shepherd's pie and all related "pies" in this section are about goodness, comfort, and love. Something we explore a little in our Pie Fest video on our website, see www.leonrestaurants.co.uk.

JOHN

Alice's Vegetarian Shepherd's Pie

SERVES 4–6 • PREPARATION TIME: 20 MINUTES • COOKING TIME: 1 HOUR • V

This is based on a simple pumpkin gratin, the idea being to cook all those ingredients you might like to eat *with* your gratin *in* your gratin. It's a perfect fall dish.

1 small **pumpkin/butternut squash**, weighing about 2½ lbs
3 cloves of **garlic**
2 tablespoons **butter**
1 tablespoon **olive oil**
1 **onion**, finely sliced
10oz **mushrooms**, chopped (cremini, oyster, shiitake, are more flavorsome than button ones)
2 sprigs of **fresh thyme**
1 cup **sherry** (an amontillado or an oloroso)
2 x 15-oz **cans of navy beans** or **cannellini beans**, drained and rinsed
1 8-oz package **spinach leaves**
¼ cup **shredded cheddar, Gruyère, or other strong cheese**
½ cup fresh **bread crumbs**
salt and **freshly ground black pepper**

ALICE, OXFORDSHIRE, 1971

Alice is Kay's sister-in-law. She writes books. She lives in the country. If we say any more about her, she'll hunt us down.

1. Heat the oven to 400°F.

2. Peel and deseed the pumpkin/squash, then cut it into chunks. Place in a saucepan with salted water to cover and cook over low heat until the pumpkin is soft and mashable (about 15 minutes). Drain, then mash with a fork. Crush 1 clove of garlic and stir it in, then season with salt and pepper. Set aside to cool.

3. Meanwhile, heat the butter and oil in a skillet, then add the onion and sauté slowly until it's as browned as you like it. Chop the remaining cloves of garlic and add to the skillet with the mushrooms, thyme, sherry and beans. Season well with salt and black pepper and let the mixture simmer until the sherry has reduced—about 10 minutes or so (you don't want the filling to be too sloppy). At the last moment stir in the spinach leaves to wilt.

4. Place the filling in a casserole dish and spoon the mashed pumpkin on top. Mix the cheese with the bread crumbs and sprinkle on top, then give it a light drizzle of olive oil. Bake in the oven for 35–45 minutes, or until the topping is golden brown.

A SHORT PHOTO STORY

REAL SHEEP

A REAL VEGETARIAN (NOT A REAL SHEPHERD)

TIME TO GO HOME

THE BUS IS LATE

SHEPHERD'S PIE FOR THE LOCAL?

Mrs V's Shepherd's Pie

SERVES 8 • PREPARATION TIME: 1 HOUR • COOKING TIME: 55 MINUTES

Perfect English comfort food.

2¼ lb **potatoes**, peeled and cut into chunks
2 tablespoons **butter**, plus extra for glazing the top
2 tablespoons **milk**
1 large **onion**, finely chopped
2 tablespoons **vegetable oil**
1 lb **ground lamb**
1 large or 2 medium **carrots**, grated
1 stick of **celery**, finely chopped
2 cups **stock** (water and 1 tablespoon
   bouillon granules)
½ teaspoon **dried mixed herbs**
1 teaspoon **Worcestershire sauce**
2 teaspoons **tomato paste**
salt and **freshly ground black pepper**

1. Boil the potatoes and when they're cooked, mash together with the butter and the milk. Season with salt and pepper, then set aside and let cool.

2. Meanwhile, heat 1 tablespoon of the oil in a large, deep skillet. Add the onions and sauté gently until transparent and beginning to brown. Remove the onions with a slotted spoon and set aside.

3. Add the rest of the oil to the pan and add the lamb, using a wooden spoon to break it up. Once browned, add the carrot, celery and fried onion and season with salt and pepper.

4. In a separate saucepan slowly bring the stock to a boil. Add the herbs, Worcestershire sauce and tomato paste, then pour it into the skillet, mixing it well with the meat and vegetables.

5. Cover the pan and simmer gently over low heat for 45 minutes, stirring occasionally. If the mixture seems runny, raise the temperature to reduce it a little.

6. Heat the oven to 400°F. Tip the meat mixture into a deep enough ovenproof dish and spread the mashed potato over the meat. Brush the surface with a little melted butter and cook in the oven for 30 minutes, or until the top is brown and crispy.

JOHN AND HIS MOM MARION, 1973

My mom is sort of a shepherd. She is one of the best and most committed teachers I know, and there are many former pupils who will tell you so. She has spent many years tending her many flocks, while taking time to understand each one. This is the recipe I grew up with, and it saw me through many years of latenight homework and sports matches. Mom has always been very good at getting the potato nice and crispy. Thank you Mrs V aka Mom.
JOHN

Fisherman's Pie at 91a

SERVES 4–6 · PREPARATION TIME: 15 MINUTES · COOKING TIME: 1 HOUR 5 MINUTES ·

Kay is not a great lover of fish pie. Too many memories of dry, egg-ridden school meals. We however, are big fans of a really fishy fish pie. So she created one for us. Here it is.

12oz **pollock or cod fillets**, skinned
   and cut into chunks
12oz **smoked haddock**
2½ cups **whole milk**
¼ cup **heavy cream**
1 **bay leaf**
½ a small **onion**
10 **peppercorns**
1 clove of **garlic**
1 stick of **celery**
a pinch of **saffron**
5oz **hot-smoked salmon**,
   cut into chunks

1 heaping tablespoon **capers**, rinsed
1 tablespoon rinsed and
   chopped **cornichons or dill pickle**
a small bunch of **chervil**
   or **fresh flat-leaf parsley**, chopped
2¼ lbs **russet or Yukon gold**
   potatoes, peeled and cut into chunks
1 stick **butter**, plus extra to dot on top
1 heaping tablespoon **flour**
sea salt and **freshly ground**
   black pepper

1. Put the pollock and haddock into a skillet and pour the milk and cream over them. Add the bay leaf, onion half, peppercorns, garlic clove, celery, and saffron. Bring slowly to a boil, then simmer for 5 minutes, or until the fish is cooked.

2. Remove the fish from the skillet, reserving the milk, and flake into a lightly buttered casserole dish, peeling away any skin and checking for bones. Flake in the hot-smoked salmon now, too, and mix in well, along with the capers and cornichon and some chervil or parsley. Set aside to cool completely.

3. Strain the reserved poaching milk into a small dish and let cool.

4. Meanwhile, boil the potatoes in plenty of salted water until very tender and mashable. Drain them and put them back into the saucepan. Add 3 tablespoons of the poaching milk, ½ stick of the butter, some salt and black pepper, and mash well. Set aside.

5. Heat the oven to 400°F.

6. Now make the creamy sauce. Melt the remaining butter in a saucepan, then add the flour and cook for a minute or two. Add the remaining poaching milk and whisk well until combined and smooth. Put the pan back on the heat, bring to a boil and stir until the sauce has thickened.

7. Remove the sauce from the heat and pour it over the fish. Spread the mashed potatoes over the fish-and-sauce mixture and dot a little butter on top.

8. Put into the oven for 35–40 minutes, or until golden brown on top.

Cottage Pie

SERVES 4–6 • PREPARATION TIME: 15 MINUTES PLUS COOLING • COOKING TIME: 1 HOUR 10 MINUTES

When is a shepherd's pie not a shepherd's pie? When it's made of beef—then it's a cottage pie! We don't care what you call it.

2¼ lbs **russet or Yukon gold potatoes**, peeled and cut into chunks
¼ cup **milk**
½ stick **butter**
2 tablespoons **olive oil** or **vegetable oil**
1 **onion**, finely chopped
1 **carrot**, finely chopped
1 stick of **celery**, finely chopped
1 clove of **garlic**, finely chopped
1½ tablespoons finely chopped **fresh flat-leaf parsley**
1 lb **ground sirloin beef**
½ cup **red wine**
1 **beef stock cube**
1¼ cups **water**
1 tablespoon **tomato paste**
a few good dashes of **Worcestershire sauce**
salt and **freshly ground black pepper**

1. Bring a large saucepan of salted water to a rolling boil, add the potatoes, and cook until tender. When they're done, drain them and mash them with the milk, butter, and some salt and black pepper to taste. Set aside to cool.

2. In a sauté pan, heat 1 tablespoon of the oil over low to medium heat and gently cook the onion, carrot, and celery until they're soft and the onion has a golden, almost translucent quality. Add the garlic and parsley and cook for 2 minutes, until really fragrant. Then spoon all the vegetables out of the sauté pan into a bowl.

3. Increase the heat, return the sauté pan to the stove and add the remaining oil. Now brown the beef. When it's done, pour in the wine. Rapidly simmer to cook out the alcohol, then crumble in the bouillon cube, add the water, tomato paste and Worcestershire sauce, and stir them in well. Season with salt and pepper.

4. Add the vegetable mixture to the meat, stir it in well and cook on the stove for 5–7 minutes to reduce and to amalgamate all the flavors.

5. Heat the oven to 400°F. Tip the meat and vegetable mixture into your pie dish, then cover with the mashed potato and score it with a fork. Dot with a extra butter and bake in the oven for 45 minutes, or until brown and crispy on top.

TIPS

* Feel free to change the herbs—rosemary is wonderful, as is marjoram.
* Cut the potato with some boiled, mashed carrot or celeriac for a change.

(PIE IT YOURSELF)

The (humble) pie: it's the ultimate one-dish meal. Even in Thailand, we had pies. What's a classic curry puff if not a tiny, perfect pie? My mom, Betty, used to make a great steak and kidney pie, with golden pastry and a rich, meaty gravy. You can make a pie with just about anything, and I started early, by trying to sell mud pies to passersby. I thought they'd be particularly good with worms and extra baby mud crabs. There's no mud in these pies, but there's a good cross section, running from the simplest tomato and thyme to the richest tartiflette. All here to give you some *pie-deas*. Just omit the mud.

KAY

Swiss Chard & Bacon Tart

SERVES 6–8 • PREPARATION TIME: 25 MINUTES • COOKING TIME: 40–50 MINUTES

The marriage of cream, bacon, Swiss chard, and cheese sits happily-ever-after in a crisp pastry crust. One of our indulgent favorites. And you don't even need to roll out the pastry dough.

3oz **bacon**, chopped
1 tablespoon **olive oil**
1 clove of **garlic**, peeled and finely sliced
100g **shredded Swiss chard leaves**
2 **eggs**, lightly beaten
1 **egg yolk**
1 cup **heavy cream**
1–2 sprigs of **fresh thyme**, leaves picked

4oz **Gruyère or Swiss cheese**
salt and **freshly ground black pepper**

For the pastry dough:
2 cups **all-purpose flour**
1 stick **unsalted butter**, straight from the refrigerator, diced
a good pinch of **sea salt**
a small glass of **iced water**

1. Heat the oven to 400°F. Butter a 9-inch round, nonstick tart pan with a removable bottom.

2. First make your pastry dough. Measure out the flour into a large bowl and add the butter. Start rubbing the flour and butter together with your fingertips, lifting it and gently working it until you have what looks like fine bread crumbs.

3. Add the salt. Then add the iced water, a teaspoonful at a time, until the dough just comes together. Don't add too much water or you'll have a hard pastry.

4. Roll it into a loose ball and, using your fingertips, gently push the dough into the prepared tart pan, easing it around until it evenly covers the bottom and sides. Cover the whole thing with a sheet of wax paper and weigh it down with some pie weights or dried beans. Then bake it in the oven for 10 minutes.

5. Cook the chopped bacon in a skillet over medium heat for about 5 minutes, until cooked through. Remove with a slotted spoon and set aside.

6. Wipe out the skillet, then return it to the heat and add the olive oil. Add the garlic. Sauté for a minute—don't let it brown too much—then add the Swiss chard and a pinch of salt and cook until it is just wilted. Remove from the heat, set aside, and let drain in a colander. Then, when it's cool, squeeze out any excess liquid.

7. Take the tart crust out of the oven. Carefully remove the paper and weights, and put it back into the oven for another 5 minutes until crisp.

8. In a clean bowl, beat the eggs, egg yolk, cream, salt and pepper with an electric mixer. Stir in the Gruyère and the thyme leaves and season with salt and pepper.

9. Remove the tart crust from the oven. Sprinkle the Swiss chard across the bottom. Sprinkle the bacon bits over the top, then pour in the cream and the egg mixture.

10. Bake the tart in the oven for about 30–40 minutes, until the filling has puffed up and the pastry is a wonderful golden brown.

Tomato, Thyme & Goat Cheese Tart

SERVES 4–6 • PREPARATION TIME: 15 MINUTES • COOKING TIME: 20–25 MINUTES • V

You can whip this up in minutes, making it the perfect quick lunch or dinner.

1 sheet of **ready-to-bake puff pastry**
2 tablespoons **extra virgin olive oil**
3 cups halved **cherry tomatoes** or 4 **small tomatoes**, quartered
4 sprigs of **fresh thyme**, leaves picked
1 clove of **garlic**, peeled and chopped
3oz **soft goat cheese**
salt and **freshly ground black pepper**

1. Heat the oven to 425°F.

2. Lay out the puff pastry on a baking sheet lined with parchment paper. Then, using a sharp knife, score a line—not all the way through—down and across each side of the pastry, about ¾ inch in from the edges. This will give the tart a nice crusty raised edge.

3. Put the olive oil, cherry tomatoes, thyme leaves, and garlic into a bowl and mix until they are well coated. Season with salt and pepper and mix again.

4. Spread the tomato mixture evenly over the pastry, keeping it within the lines.

5. Crumble the goat cheese over the top among the pieces of tomato.

6. Add another quick dash of freshly ground pepper and put it into the oven for about 20 minutes, or until it's golden brown and puffy on the outside and the tomatoes are collapsing slightly and the cheese is melt-y, then serve.

TIPS

* For something a little sweeter, you could replace the tomatoes with sliced fresh figs. Keep everything else the same—just add a good drizzle of honey before serving.

Katie's Tartiflette

SERVES 8 • PREPARATION TIME: 20 MINUTES • COOKING TIME: 30 MINUTES • WF GF

Tartiflette is one of those skiing dishes that you shouldn't need to be above 10,000 feet to eat. It's completely indulgent and works well with a salad, or just on its own for lunch.

This recipe is inspired by our friend Charlie Tomlinson (a lady, and wife of lovely Patrick) who made this for us at the end of a long week of work, with a gorgeous steak. Can you think of a better way of reviving the spirits?

2¼ lb **potatoes**, peeled and thickly sliced
1 tablespoon **olive oil**
2 **onions**, chopped
6 slices of **smoked bacon**, cut into strips
1 whole **Reblochon cheese**, cut into cubes
1¾ cups **heavy cream** or **crème fraîche**
½ cup **white wine**
salt and **freshly ground black pepper**

1. Steam or parboil the potatoes for about 10 minutes until they're tender but not overcooked.

2. Heat the oven to 350°F.

3. Meanwhile, heat the olive oil in a skillet and cook the onions until they're translucent. Add the bacon to the onion and sauté until the bacon is cooked—you don't want the onion to burn.

4. Put a fat layer of potato into an ovenproof dish, season with salt and black pepper, add half the onion-and-bacon mixture and spread over half the cheese. Layer the rest of the sliced potato on top, with the rest of the bacon and onion, and top with the remaining cheese. Add some more seasoning.

5. Mix the heavy cream with the white wine and pour it over the whole shooting match. If you're using crème fraîche, warm it through in a saucepan with the wine to loosen it up for pouring.

6. Put the dish into the oven for 20 minutes or so, or until it's golden and bubbling. Check the potatoes really are cooked through. Then dive in.

FOOD FACT

Reblochon is a cow cheese from the Haute-Savoie region of France. Its name apparently comes from a fourteenth-century tax dodge. Back then, landowners would tax farmers according to the amount of milk their herds produced. So these canny farmers would not fully milk their cows until the landowners had measured their output. Hence "reblocher"—to pinch the cow's udder again. This retained milk is richer, creamier and sinfully delicious.

My best snowy memory is the message I got from John when I was struggling home in the snow one evening. "We're going to pretend we're on a skiing holiday," he said. "When you get home, get into your ski kit, our neighbours are coming over, we're going to walk around the garden in the snow and then come indoors and drink glühwein and eat tartiflette." And we did. It was a very silly evening and the tartiflette was just as delicious eaten at home as it is in the Alps. KATIE

A good burger is so easy to make. You can cook them just how you like them, and everyone can pick their own favorite garnishes. Hell, if you want to, you can even bake your own bun. At our place, they're just the thing for a live football game on the TV (but, at the stadium, I think you've got to have a hotdog.). So here're our burgers. Go on … you know you want to.

KAY

FRED'S CLASSIC HAMBURGER

Fred's Classic Hamburger

MAKES 4 • PREPARATION TIME: 10 MINUTES • COOKING TIME: 10–15 MINUTES • ✓ WF GF

This is about as simple as it gets: just beef, onion, salt, and black pepper. Fred says he used to mess around with it a lot more, but he made so many burgers for his pals during Euro 96, and this was the version everyone preferred.

1 **onion**, peeled and cut into chunks
1 lb **ground chuck beef**
1 tablespoon **olive oil** or **vegetable oil**
salt and **freshly ground pepper**

1. In a food processor, process the onion into tiny pieces. Add the ground beef and pulse just enough to mix the onion into it. You don't want to be overzealous, or you'll end up with a meat paste. We want it well blended, but with texture.

2. Turn the meat mixture out into a bowl and season well with salt and pepper, mixing it together thoroughly with your hands. Now divide it into 4 equal patties.

3. Heat a nonstick skillet over medium to high heat. Rub both sides of the patties with olive oil and season them again with salt and pepper. Then put them into the skillet. Cook for 10–15 minutes, turning once or twice, until they're cooked how you like them. Serve on a bun, with lettuce, cheese, ketchup, and mustard.

Kay's Hollywood Turkey Burger

SERVES 4 • PREPARATION TIME: 15 MINUTES • COOKING TIME: 15–20 MINUTES • ✓ ♥

A favorite among all our LA pals. Low in fat, big on flavor. Just the thing before you squeeze into your Oscar dress.

1 lb **ground turkey**
2 cloves of **garlic**, finely chopped
2 **scallions**, finely chopped
a large handful of **fresh cilantro**, finely chopped

½ a **serrano** or other **medium-hot chile**, finely chopped
1 tablespoon **olive oil**
salt and **freshly ground black pepper**

1. In a food processor, mix the turkey, garlic, scallions, cilantro and chile together in a series of short pulses. Turn the mixture out onto a board, and work it into 4 equal patties.

2. Heat the olive oil in a nonstick skillet over medium heat. Season the burgers on both sides with salt and black pepper, then cook for about 8–10 minutes each side until cooked through.

3. Serve in a whole wheat or gluten-free bun with a slice of tomato, lettuce, and a little chipotle mayonnaise.

"Ciao Bella" Italian Burger

SERVES 4 • PREPARATION TIME: 10 MINUTES • COOKING TIME: 15–20 MINUTES • ✓

Think Sophia Loren on a bun.

1 **onion**, cut into chunks
1 clove of **garlic**
1 sprig of **fresh rosemary**, leaves picked
3 sprigs of **fresh flat-leaf parsley**
6oz **ground veal**

6oz **ground pork**
6oz **ground beef**
1 tablespoon **olive oil**
salt and **freshly ground black pepper**

1. In a food processor, process the onion, garlic, and herb leaves. Add the meat and pulse to blend it together.

2. Turn the mixture out into a bowl and season with salt and pepper, working the seasonings in thoroughly with your hands. Now divide it into 4 equal patties.

3. Heat a nonstick skillet over medium high heat. Rub the patties on both sides with the olive oil and season with salt and pepper. Cook them for 15–20 minutes, turning once or twice, or until they're cooked to your liking.

4. Serve on ciabatta rolls, with lettuce, tomato, and maybe some *mostarda di frutta* or a spiky onion relish.

The Veggie Burger

SERVES 4 • PREPARATION TIME: 10 MINUTES • COOKING TIME: 15 MINUTES • ✓ ♥ V

This is not your usual veggie burger bulked up with beans, this is just veggies pure and simple.

2 tablespoons **olive oil** (more if you are cooking in 2 batches)
4 large **portabella mushrooms**, about 5oz each, trimmed and wiped
1 **red bell pepper**, seeded and cut into 8 rings
3–4 cloves of **garlic**, peeled and chopped
a good handful of fresh **parsley**, chopped
1 **avocado**, sliced
4 **whole wheat buns** (or buns of your choice), to serve
salt and **freshly ground black pepper**

1. Heat 1 tablespoon of the olive oil in a wide skillet. Add the mushrooms and gently sauté them, turning occasionally until they are just done—about 5–7 minutes in all. Remove the mushrooms from the skillet with a slotted spoon and set aside.

2. Heat the remaining tablespoon of olive oil. Sauté the red bell pepper rings until they start to brown, but are still crisp. Remove them from the skillet and set aside. Add the garlic and parsley and sauté until softened and fragrant—just a couple of minutes.

3. Return the mushrooms to the skillet, along with any juices that have come from them. Stir to mix everything thoroughly and season with salt and black pepper.

4. Place the mushrooms on the halved buns. Put two red bell pepper rings on top of each, a few slices of avocado, and top with mayo.

KAY'S HOLLYWOOD TURKEY BURGER   "CIAO BELLA" ITALIAN BURGER

Spicy Thai Pork Burger

SERVES 4 • PREPARATION TIME: 10 MINUTES • COOKING TIME: 15–20 MINUTES • ✓

We saw something similar to this served innovatively between two circles of sticky rice in northern Thailand. So we decided to create our own.

1½ tablespoons **white peppercorns**
a ¾-inch piece of **fresh ginger**, chopped
3 **cilantro roots** (from a coriander plant)
3 cloves of **garlic**, peeled
a pinch of **salt**

1 lb **ground pork**
1 tablespoon **Thai fish sauce**
1 tablespoon chopped **fresh cilantro**
2 tablespoons **vegetable oil**

1. Grind the peppercorns in a mortar and pestle. Then add the chopped ginger, cilantro roots, garlic, and a pinch of salt, and grind them into the peppercorns until you have a dry paste.

2. Put the paste into a bowl, add the ground pork, along with the fish sauce and the fresh cilantro, and work all the ingredients together. (You can do this in a food processor, just don't process it too hard.) Form into 4 equal patties.

3. Heat the oil in a nonstick skillet and cook the patties for about 15–20 minutes, turning them from time to time, until they're cooked through. Serve in a soft white bun, with mayonnaise, sriracha sauce, crisp lettuce, and a slice of cucumber or tomato.

TIPS

* White pepper is a key ingredient in Thai food. By all means, cut down the pepperiness if you like, but leave in at least half a tablespoonful or the burger will be very bland.

VEGGIE BURGER

SPICY THAI PORK BURGER

AFTER LIGHTS OUT

There is something magical about putting your kids to bed. Occasionally. At other times it is a nightmare. You end up at 10:30 p.m. having finally got them to sleep. You are exhausted, in need of caffeine, and you have to start on your work that needs to be done the next day.

These recipes are for those almost fairy-tale evenings where the kids say at 7:30 p.m. that they're tired and will go to bed. Where they get into their pajamas themselves, clean their teeth, pack everything for the next day, where the bedroom is tidy and smells of lavender, where they read one chapter of an enriching book, ask you a few life-enhancing questions to which you have good and pertinent and loving answers, and where the lights go out and you glide downstairs to enjoy a romantic dinner just like on TV.

If it ever happens, or if you ever get close, these recipes are for you.

Betty's Quick Shrimp Red Curry

SERVES 2 • PREPARATION TIME: 10–15 MINUTES • COOKING TIME: 10 MINUTES • ✓ WF GF DF

Here's a quick trip to Thailand in one very simple curry.

1 tablespoon **vegetable oil**
2 cloves of **garlic**, peeled and finely chopped
1 tablespoon **Thai red curry paste**
1 cup **coconut milk**
½ cup **water**
a ¾-inch piece of **fresh ginger**, peeled and slivered
12 **fresh basil leaves**, plus a few for garnish
3 **kaffir lime leaves**, slivered
1 tablespoon **roasted peanuts**, crushed
10oz large **shrimp tails**
a squeeze of **lime juice**
2 teaspoons **sugar**
2 teaspoons **Thai fish sauce**
1 large **red chile**, finely slivered

BETTY, BANGKOK, 1963

1. In a wok or a skillet heat the oil and sauté the garlic until it just begins to brown. Add the curry paste and stir in well, until you can really smell it.

2. Add ½ cup of the coconut milk and bring to a boil. Add the water and bring back to a boil, then add the rest of the coconut milk and bring to a boil again. Add the sugar and fish sauce and stir in well.

3. Add the ginger, basil, 2 of the lime leaves, and the peanuts, one ingredient at a time, stirring well after each addition. Then stir in the shrimp. They will turn pink when they are cooked through—in no more than a minute or two.

4. Add a squeeze of lime, then turn out onto a serving dish. Garnish with the slivered chile, the last lime leaf, and a few leaves of basil. Serve with jasmine rice (see page 272).

TIPS

* When you buy your curry paste, make sure you get a good one.

* Remember that chiles freeze really well, so don't worry if you have to buy a whole pack. Just freeze them for next time. The same goes for lime leaves—put them into a plastic bag and freeze them, too, and coconut milk: freeze it in an ice cube tray.

* Serve some of the *nam pla prik* on the side for extra punch (see tip on page 137).

My mom, Betty, had big blue eyes, dangerous curves, and cool pastry hands. She and my dad were childhood sweethearts. Engaged at sixteen, married at twenty-two, they embarked on a grand adventure together, a few years later, when they left south London for the bright lights of 1960s Bangkok. She immediately fell in love with the food and the country.

I found this recipe written on a scrap of paper in Mom's handwriting when I was going through some things in the kitchen. She was an amazing cook. She only ever had a handful of cookbooks—the classics: Marguerite Patten, Delia, Josceline Dimbleby, and a stack of *Aussie Women's Weekly*. And she would come up with incredibly delicious dishes that never failed.

I have a lot to thank her for. And I miss her terribly.

KAY

Perfect Pepper Steak

SERVES 2 • PREPARATION TIME: 10 MINUTES • COOKING TIME: 10–15 MINUTES • WF

Pepper steak, or steak au poivre, is a bistro classic that we all take for granted. And it's one which, because it's so simple, is all too often made really badly. We think this recipe gets it just about right, all the way down to the retro 70s whiskey cream sauce.

2 **steaks** of your choice
1 clove of **garlic**, halved
1 teaspoon **olive oil**
1 tablespoon **whole white peppercorns**, coarsely crushed
1 tablespoon **whole black peppercorns**, coarsely crushed
1 tablespoon **coarse sea salt**
scant ½ cup **whiskey** (optional)
½ cup **heavy cream** (optional)
1 tablespoon **green peppercorns**, rinsed (optional)

1. Pat the steaks dry and rub the cut side of the garlic liberally over both sides of each steak, then rub with the olive oil.

2. Pat the crushed pepper onto the steaks and let macerate for an hour. (If you're in a hurry, don't worry—the steaks just won't be as peppery.)

3. Heat a wide skillet as hot as you dare. Season the steaks with the sea salt, then slap the meat into the skillet. Now, here's the thing—every steak has its own time scale. We swear by the following test: Hold out your left hand. With your right hand, feel that fleshy part of palm under your thumb. You'll see it goes from soft and squishy to hard by your wrist. Keep touching the steaks with your finger. Soft and squishy = rare; medium = medium; hard = well done. It really is the best way.

4. When the steaks are cooked just how you like them, set them aside on a warm plate to rest for at least 5 minutes. This is very important. It lets the fibers of the meat relax and the flavors develop.

5. While the steaks are resting, deglaze the skillet with the whiskey, then pour in the cream. Let bubble so the cream thickens for about a minute, then add the green peppercorns. Pour the sauce over the steaks, and serve with a green salad, or a baked potato and spinach.

A SHORT PHOTO STORY...

PERFECT PEPPER STEAKS

OR SOME WILD MUSHROOMS...

READY TO PLAY 70S COP SHOW

KEEP YOUR EYE ON THE TARGET

John's Wild Mushroom Sauté

(A THEME AND VARIATIONS)

SERVES 4 • PREPARATION TIME: 15 MINUTES • COOKING TIME: 15–20 MINUTES • ✓ ♥ WF GF DF V

Genghis Khan was, apparently, so prolific in his "travels" that most of us are in some way related to him. In that spirit, I have tried here to give you a dish that can provide the grand-daddy from which many variations and related dishes can come.

⅓ cup **olive oil**—judge for yourself how much
1½ lb **mushrooms**, sliced—ideally a lot of different varieties,
   but if you only have button mushrooms, then that's cool
4 cloves of **garlic**, chopped
some **fresh herbs** you like (such as **thyme, tarragon**), chopped
a couple of tablespoons finely chopped **fresh parsley**
salt and **freshly ground black pepper**

1. Heat 2 tablespoons of the oil until hot (you know, until the steamy effect occurs). Cook the mushrooms until they're just sealed. You'll need to do this in batches: The idea here is to quickly cook the mushrooms and to keep the moisture in, so set each batch aside on a warm plate as you work. And add a little more oil, as needed, for each batch, too.

2. If your mushrooms release a little moisture into the skillet, spoon it out and keep cooking.

3. When all the mushrooms are cooked and set aside, add the chopped garlic, thyme, and tarragon to the pan. When the garlic is lightly brown, return the mushrooms to the skillet, season with salt and black pepper, and stir in the parsley. Serve immediately.

TIPS

Once you have mastered the basic dish, try:

* Adding blue cheese and melting it into the mushrooms.

* Putting on a poached egg.

* Adding strips of bacon.

* Cooking with dried porcini mushrooms (you'll need to soak these for half an hour before cooking).

* Adding truffle oil.

Or try your very own variation:

My variation is:

THE CHASE HAS BEGUN

COVER ME

QUICK SNACK

AND A SIT DOWN. TIME FOR TEA.

Butterflied Game Hens with Rosemary & Garlic

SERVES 2 • PREPARATION TIME: 15 MINUTES • COOKING TIME: 30 MINUTES • ✓ ♥ WF GF DF

At Leon, we love to butterfly. And with Cornish game hens, it really speeds up the cooking time, so this quick and healthy dish won't take too long to make after a hard day.

> 2 **Cornish game hens**, butterflied
> a bunch of **fresh rosemary**
> 2 cloves of **garlic**, chopped
> the zest of 1 **lemon**
> 2 tablespoons **olive oil**
> **salt** and **freshly ground black pepper**

1. Heat the oven to 425°F.

2. Clean and dry the hens. Then sprinkle all but one sprig of rosemary across the bottom of a roasting tray and lay the birds, skin side up, on top.

3. Strip the leaves off the remaining sprig of rosemary and chop them as finely as possible. You should end up with about a teaspoonful. Mix with the garlic, lemon zest, olive oil and some salt and black pepper, then spread the mixture evenly over the hens.

4. Roast in the oven for 25–30 minutes, or until cooked through, then serve with a green salad.

TIPS

* If you like it spicy, why not turn these into Deviled Game Hens by adding a teaspoon of dry mustard and plenty of black pepper to the olive oil mixture.

Moules Marinières

If you think 4½ lb of mussels seems a lot—don't! By the time you have lost the bad ones in the process then picked them out of the shell, it's a perfect amount. Just serve with a salad and some bread for dunking, or some boiled new potatoes.

4½ lb **mussels**
½ stick **butter**
2 tablespoons **olive oil**
2 **banana shallots**, finely chopped
2 sticks of **celery**, finely chopped

2 cloves of **garlic**, finely chopped
a large handful of **fresh flat-leaf parsley**, finely chopped
300ml **dry white wine**
salt and **freshly ground black pepper**

1. Wash and scrub the mussels under running water, debearding them as you work. The beard is, well, a beard-y thing sticking out the side of the shell. Just rip it off, discarding any mussels that won't close up.

2. Heat the butter and olive oil in a large, deep saucepan over medium heat. Add the shallots, celery, garlic, and half the parsley and cook for about 5–7 minutes, or until they are soft and fragrant, adding salt and black pepper to taste. Be careful with the salt at this stage—the mussels will bring some salt of their own.

3. Once the vegetables are soft and fragrant, add the wine and bring to a boil. Add the mussels and immediately put a lid on. Cook them for about 4–5 minutes, shaking the pot every minute or so. The mussels at the bottom will cook faster than the ones at the top, so make sure you shift them around.

4. Give it all a stir, adding the rest of the parsley. They're done when all the mussels are open. Any that remain closed were dead before you started—so don't even try opening those. Serve immediately.

Aioli

3 cloves of **garlic**
3 **egg yolks**
1 tablespoon **Dijon mustard**

⅔ cup **vegetable oil**
a squeeze of **lemon juice**
salt and **freshly ground black pepper**

1. Peel and coarsely chop the garlic and place in a food processor with the egg yolks, mustard, salt, and black pepper.

2. Process together, then slowly drizzle in the oil while the processor is still running.

3. Check the seasoning and add a squeeze of lemon juice.

Roasted Cod with Salsa Verde

SERVES 2 • PREPARATION TIME: 10 MINUTES • COOKING TIME: 10-15 MINUTES • ✓ ♥ WF GF DF

There's plenty of garlic in this one, so share it with the one you love/have to kiss.

½–1 tablespoon **olive oil**
2 skinless, boneless **cod steaks**,
    about 5–6oz each
salt and **freshly ground black pepper**

1. Heat the oven to 425°F.

2. Rub the oil over both sides of the fish and season with salt and black pepper. Place in a roasting pan and cook in the oven for 10–15 minutes, or until the fish is white and flaky.

3. Take the roasting pan out of the oven and transfer the fish to serving plates. Serve with Salsa Verde (see below), some new potatoes, and your favorite vegetable.

Salsa Verde

SERVES 4 • PREPARATION TIME: 6 MINUTES • COOKING TIME: NONE • ✓ ♥ WF GF DF

6–8 cloves of **garlic**,
    peeled and coarsely chopped
1 (2-oz) **can of anchovies**,
    drained and chopped
1 tablespoon **capers**,
    rinsed and chopped
a large handful of **fresh flat-leaf
parsley**, chopped
a large handful of **fresh mint**,
    chopped

a large handful of **fresh basil**,
    chopped
the juice of ½ a **lemon**
2 tablespoons **olive oil**
2 tablespoons **extra virgin olive oil**
salt and **freshly ground
    black pepper**

1. Mix together the garlic, anchovies, capers, parsley, mint, and basil. Then, using your mortar and pestle, pound them all gently together. If you have a small mortar and pestle, do this in batches. Add the lemon juice and both olive oils. Season to taste and set aside. It may look like a lot—but this is very ADDICTIVE!

TIPS

* Salsa verde also goes well with steaks, the Midweek Lamb on page 130, and the Roasted Chicken on page 265.

* If you have cod with the skin still on, roast it skin side down, then serve it skin side up.

* If you don't want to eat cod, or can't find any that has been caught sustainably, pollock or red snapper will serve you well.

FOOD FACT

COD
Our fish stocks are in crisis and we need to do our part to preserve our oceans' biodiversity. Please buy cod from sustainable fisheries. There are numerous websites that will help, if in doubt, or ask your fish dealer.

SOMETHING SWEET

Most of us cannot resist a tiny, or sometimes large, treat of sweetness. At the end of a dinner. As an afternoon snack.

The thing is, when it comes to sugar, our evolution works against us. Back when we were hunter-gatherers, most of our sugar came from the fruits and vegetables we foraged. For that supersweet hit that, even then, we craved, we had to find honey. Which, before beekeeping, came with the inherent risk of stings. Early humans evolved to cope with scarcity. When we found sweet, our bodies were programmed to gorge on it, storing the energy for the hard times that undoubtedly lay ahead. In our plentiful times, this evolutionary need to stuff our faces has become something of a problem.

Here at Leon, we're not preachers and we're not hypocrites: We love dessert as much as the next restaurant. But we say all things in moderation. We try to avoid processed sugars wherever possible. And we go easy on the cream.

That said … who's for dessert?

Lychees with Fresh Ginger & Sherry

SERVES 2–4 • PREPARATION TIME: 10 MINUTES • COOKING TIME: 5 MINUTES • WF GF DF V

We know—it's very simple. But how does that saying go again? Sometimes it's the simplest things that give the most pleasure. Here we have sweet, honey-ish lychees, spiky fresh ginger, and mellow sherry.

Try to make sure all three elements are well chilled …

> 1 (20-oz) **can of lychees**, drained but reserving the liquid
> ½ cup **medium sherry**
> a ½-inch piece of **fresh ginger**, peeled and julienned finely
> 4 **ice cubes**, crushed

1. Put the drained lychee liquid into a small bowl, cover, and refrigerate until needed. Pour the reserved lychee liquid, sherry, and ginger into a small saucepan. Bring to a boil, then reduce the heat and simmer for a few minutes, or until slightly reduced and thickened. Remove from the heat and let cool. When completely cold, cover and chill in the refrigerator.

2. Divide the chilled lychees among 4 glasses. Put a spoonful of crushed ice into each glass and stir quickly. Pour over the sherry/ginger mixture. Stir again. Serve.

TIPS

* Cans of lychee vary in size as do the size of the lychee within. Our 20-oz can yielded 14 large lychees.

Prosecco & Nectarines

SERVES 4 • PREPARATION TIME: 5–10 MINUTES • COOKING TIME: NONE • WF GF DF V

This dessert is superquick and supersimple—sort of a deconstructed Bellini. If you're feeling fancy, why not go the full Melba and toss in a few raspberries?

> 4 ripe **nectarines**, peeled, pitted and cut into cubes
> the juice of ½ a **lemon**
> 1–2 tablespoons **confectioners' sugar** (or to taste)
> 1 cup **prosecco**
> **raspberries**, to serve (optional)

1. Put the nectarines, lemon juice and sugar into a clean bowl, toss together, and let stand for 5 minutes.

2. Then divide them among 4 coupes and pour prosecco over each one. Top with fresh raspberries, if you desire. Make sure the fruit is at room temperature and that the wine is nice and cold.

Cheese, Pears & Honey

SERVES 2 • PREPARATION TIME: 10 MINUTES • COOKING TIME: NONE • WF GF V

This is not so much a recipe as a good idea. And it's not one of ours. When Kay went on her honeymoon, she and Fred arrived at their hotel in Rome late on a Sunday. There was no food. Until the kindly barman returned with two plates of cheese, honey, and pears, to be washed down with Sardinian *mirto*. Perfect.

It stands to reason that you want to buy the best pears you can find, and tip-top cheese.

> 2 **pears**
> 3oz **Taleggio**
> 3oz aged **Pecorino**
> 3oz **Gorgonzola**
> 2 tablespoons **honey**

1. Place the pears on a board plate beside the cheeses. You can slice them if you like.

2. Spoon the honey into 2 small dishes and put them on the plates, too. Serve with some good bread, and a knife to cut and smear.

TIPS

* Vary the cheeses to your liking; ricotta is wonderful, especially with a grating of orange zest.

* You know at Christmas, when you're left with hordes of panettone? No? Well, we do. Thinly sliced and toasted, panettone is heaven on a plate with cheese, pears, and honey.

Roasted Figs with Triple Sec

SERVES 4 • PREPARATION TIME: 10 MINUTES • COOKING TIME: 15–20 MINUTES
(BUT CHECK ON THEM, BECAUSE SOME FIGS COLLAPSE MORE QUICKLY) • WF V

Simple roasted figs, with a splash of liqueur.

> 8–12 ripe **black figs**
> 2 tablespoons **butter**
> the grated zest of ½ an **orange**
> ¼ cup **triple sec**
> 2 tablespoons **honey**
> a pinch of **salt**

1. Heat the oven to 350°F.

2. With a sharp knife, make a cross in the pointy end of each fig, cutting them about halfway through. Then squeeze the fat bottoms gently so that each fig opens up like a flower. Lay the figs in a roasting pan or ovenproof dish, and dot each one with a little butter.

3. Mix the orange zest and liqueur together in a bowl, and pour evenly over the figs. Drizzle with the honey and season with a pinch of salt. Put them into the oven for 15–20 minutes. Serve hot, with some of the sauce spooned over them and some good ice cream or yogurt.

TIPS

* Triple Sec is made from orange peel and crops up most frequently in cocktails. If you don't want to use the alcohol, replace it with orange juice and serve the figs accompanied by some good vanilla ice cream.

* These are delicious with the Spiced Honey & Orange Cake on page 96.

Hot Chocolate 5 Ways

Warming and reassuring, it's a hug in a mug. Here are our top five:

① The Building Block Choc

MAKES 1 • PREPARATION TIME: 2 MINUTES • COOKING TIME: 10 MINUTES • V

The basic hot chocolate from which all the others (in this book) descend.

> 1 mug of **milk**
> 1oz **good-quality semisweet chocolate**, grated

1. Heat the milk gently in a small saucepan. As soon as it reaches scalding point but before it boils, whisk in the grated chocolate until it has all melted thoroughly into the milk. (This has the added bonus of frothing everything up a little.)

2. Pour out into your mug and serve.

② Mexican Hot Chocolate

Add a stick of **cinnamon**, a good grating of **orange zest**, and a pinch of **chile powder** to give your chocolate a South of the Border feel. Arriba!

③ Swedish Hot Chocolate

Adults Only … well, you know what we mean … add a good slug of **vodka** and put an Abba track on the stereo.

④ Natasha & Eleanor's Hot Chocolate

Top the Building Block Choc with a good sprinkling of **miniature marshmallows** and plenty of **whipped cream**.

⑤ Jamaican Hot Chocolate

Stir it up with a good pinch of freshly **ground allspice** and a slug of **Jamaican rum**. Now we be chillin'.

TIPS

* We're using a good semisweet chocolate here so we can avoid all the added sugar, etc. you'll find in powdered cocoa mix.

* All recipes these days go on about "good-quality chocolate." They'll then go on to specify a minimum of cocoa solids in the chocolate, and so on. In this case, the flavor of the chocolate *absolutely* determines the flavor of your hot chocolate, so buy the brand you like. We love Original Beans—for their flavor, of course, but also for their fantastic work in the conservation of threatened rain forests and sustainable farming practices.

TOMORROW

Who says it never comes? Here it is. Tomorrow. The part of our book that is about things happening in a few days time, or weeks time, that are worth a little planning. For a few friends. For a larger family feast.

We cannot promise to eradicate completely the slight nervousness that comes when the doorbell rings and everything isn't perfect like in the movies, or like you had in mind, but we hope these recipes allow for a happy ending.

FOOD ON THE MOVE

These are edible messages of love. You send your kids, husband, wife, or grandchild off to school or work with a package, to be opened up hours later as a reminder of home and of how great you think they are.

So that's why a chocolate bar and a bag of potato chips doesn't do it for me.

At Chase Side school in Enfield, you were either a school meals kid or a lunch-bag kid. I was a lunch-bag kid and can remember very clearly where our table was and who sat there, and I can taste right now the ham and coleslaw sandwiches my mom used to make me. They used to give me the energy for kiss chase, football, or a fight with Matthew Skordis.

JOHN

Rachel McCormack's Tortilla Española

SERVES 2–4 • PREPARATION TIME: 15 MINUTES • COOKING TIME: 30 MINUTES • ✓ ♥ WF GF V

This is the basic recipe for a classic Spanish potato omelete. Rachel says the secret of a great tortilla lies in practice and a very good nonstick pan.

½ cup **olive oil**
1 **onion**, finely sliced
3 **potatoes**, peeled and cut into small even pieces
4 **eggs**
a good pinch of **salt**

1. Heat the olive oil in a nonstick omelete pan or small skillet over medium–low heat. Add the onion and then add the potatoes to the pan and let them poach in the oil for about 10–15 minutes. You're not deep-frying them—you don't want either of them to get crunchy; you want them to remain soft.

2. Meanwhile, beat the eggs in a large bowl.

3. Once the potatoes and onions are soft and cooked, strain off the oil into a heat-resistant bowl and set aside. Let the potatoes and onions cool a little, then stir them into the beaten eggs and season with salt.

4. Return the pan to a medium-high heat. Add a tablespoon of the potato/onion oil and, when it's hot, pour in the egg mixture. Cook for about 5–10 minutes, shaking occasionally to see if the bottom is cooked properly. (If the tortilla mixture is very thick, reduce the heat a little to make sure the middle cooks.) Use a spatula or a saucer to round off the omelete in the pan.

5. Now, if you want to be traditional, Rachel says you should turn the omelete by taking a dinner plate, putting it on top of the skillet, then flipping it over. Slide the omelete back into the pan, using the spatula or saucer to make sure it keeps a nice round shape as it goes back in. Cook for another 5 minutes, then turn out onto a plate.

6. However, if you find that daunting, you could finish the omelete off in the oven, preheated to 350°F, for 5–10 minutes. Just make sure you are using a pan with a metal or ovenproof handle.

7. Turn out onto a plate and serve hot or cold with a salad, bread, tomato sauce, mayonnaise… anything you like.

Rachel is a woman obsessed. To hear her talk about Catalan cooking is a joy to behold. She's a great teacher, a damn fine cook, and great company.

Rachel says: "The best Spanish omeletes I ever had were made by Paquita, who ran a small bar with her husband below my apartment on Carrer Bruniquer in Barcelona. They would have on the counter at least four huge, round heavenly visions of yellow. All of them contained potato, the rest of the ingredients limited only by season and Paquita's imagination."

RACHEL, PUERTO POLLENÇA, MALLORCA, 1981

Diamond Jubilee Chicken Sarnie

SERVES 4 • PREPARATION TIME: 15 MINUTES • COOKING TIME: NONE • ♥

This is based on a British classic: Rosemary Hume and Constance Spry's Coronation Chicken, created in 1953 for the Coronation of Queen Elizabeth II.

This is our updated Leon version, still using the same building blocks but, as an homage to the wonderful multicultural Caribbean, tweaked to make it a lighter, spikier sandwich.

2 tablespoons **thick yogurt**
1 tablespoon good **mayonnaise**
2 teaspoons **curry powder**
2 cups **shredded, cold roasted chicken**
4 slices from **your favorite bread**
salt and **freshly ground black pepper**

For the mango salsa:
2 ripe **mangoes**, peeled, pitted and cubed
a good squeeze of **fresh lime juice**
¼ of a **Scotch bonnet chile**, seeded and chopped
½ a **red onion**, finely diced
a good handful of **fresh cilantro**, finely chopped
salt and **freshly ground black pepper**

1. Gently mix together the yogurt, mayonnaise, curry powder, salt and pepper in a large bowl. Taste. Add more seasoning if needed.

2. Stir in the shredded roasted chicken and coat well. Put into a plastic container for travel.

3. To make the salsa, just mix all the ingredients together, taste for seasoning and place in a separate container.

4. To put the sandwich together, first put celebratory crowns on your heads.

5. Pile the curried chicken mixture onto your slices of bread.

6. Top with the mango salsa.

7. Salute the Queen and toast her heath with glass of bubbly. Huzzah!

TIPS

* We use Bolst's medium curry powder, but use whatever is your favorite.

* Homemade mayonnaise would be amazing in this.

"Rubies in the Sand" Salad

SERVES 4 • PREPARATION TIME: 25 MINUTES • COOKING TIME: 25 MINUTES • ✓ ♥ WF GF DF V

Quinoa is one of our great favorites. It contains no gluten and is a complete protein—ideal for vegetarians.

1 cup **dried quinoa**
2 **mixed bell peppers** (yellow, orange, red),
   seeded and halved
2–3 sprigs of **fresh thyme**
2 **cloves** of **garlic**, unpeeled, crushed
1 tablespoon **olive oil**
a good handful of **fresh cilantro**, chopped
½ cup **pomegranate seeds**

For the dressing:
2 tablespoons **extra virgin olive oil**
the juice of 1 **lime** or ½ **lemon**
2 teaspoons **ras el hanout**
salt and **freshly ground black pepper**

1. Wash the quinoa thoroughly, then cook it as per the directions on the package. Some quinoa is presoaked, some not, so you need to check. Once the quinoa is cooked, drain and set aside to cool.

2. Meanwhile, heat the oven to 350°F.

3. Put the bell peppers on to a roasting pan with the thyme, garlic, and olive oil. Roast in the oven for about 20–25 minutes, or until al dente. Remove from the oven, discard the garlic and thyme, then set aside to cool. Chop the bell peppers into ¾-inch squares.

4. Mix the cooled quinoa with the mixed bell peppers, the chopped cilantro, and the pomegranate seeds.

5. Mix all the dressing ingredients together thoroughly. Stir into the quinoa mix. Taste and season with salt and black pepper if needed.

TIPS

* Ras el hanout is a mixed spice available in some supermarkets and online. Moroccan in origin, it contains cardamom, cloves, chile, cumin and cinnamon, among other spices.

* Try this with about 3oz of gently fried crispy chorizo sprinkled on top.

Benny's Scotch Eggs

SERVES 6 • PREPARATION TIME: 30 MINUTES PLUS COOLING • COOKING TIME: 20 MINUTES • ✓ WF GF

Benny Peverelli was a key part of the Leon team for eight years, a lot of that time as Executive Head Chef or Chief Foodie Personage. We love him. And we love his Scotch eggs.

> 7 medium **eggs**, at room temperature
> 4–5 **rice cakes**
> **canola oil** for deep-frying (we reckon you'll need about 4 cups)
> 125g **rice flour**
> 2 tablespoons **milk**
> 6 **wheat-free**, **gluten-free pork sausages**

1. Make sure your eggs are at room temperature, then bring a medium saucepan of water to a boil. Gently lower 6 of the eggs into a boiling water and cook them for 6 minutes for soft centers, or 9 minutes for hard yolks.

2. Once the eggs are cooked, run them under cold water for 10 minutes to cool them down.

3. Gently tap the eggs all over to crack the shell, then peel them carefully because they will be soft. (Every time you take a piece of shell off, dip your fingers back into the water, otherwise they may become tacky and you could break the egg.)

4. To make the crumb, break the rice cakes into small pieces, then put them into a food processor and process for a minute or so.

5. Heat the canola oil to 350°C in a deep fryer. (You can do this in a heavy saucepan over medium heat, but be very VERY careful. You do so at your own risk.)

6. While the oil is heating up, prepare your crumbing station. Take 3 large-ish bowls and place your flour in one, your crumbed rice cakes in another, then break your final egg into the third bowl and whisk in the milk.

7. Cut out 2 large pieces of plastic wrap. Place one on your work surface and set aside the other for later.

8. Now take a sharp knife and run it down the length of one of the sausages. Squeeze the contents of the sausage into your hand and squash together to form a ball. Repeat with the remaining sausages. Then place each sausage ball on the plastic wrap. Put the other piece of plastic wrap over the top and squash down until you have 6 sausage ovals, about ¼ inch thick.

9. Next, dry your boiled eggs with paper towels and place one into the flour, coating it all over (this will help the sausagemeat stick). Peel a sausagemeat circle off the plastic wrap and lay it over the egg. Gently fold the sausagemeat around the egg and press the seam together. Put to one side. Repeat with the other eggs.

10. Now take a small bowl of water and dampen your hands. Use your damp hands to smooth the sausage-coated eggs and turn them into smooth egg shapes.

11. Take an egg shape and gently roll it all over in the flour. Then place it in the egg-and-milk mixture and coat fully. Now place it in the rice cake crumbs and cover all over, patting the egg to make sure it all sticks. Repeat this for each egg.

12. Check your oil is hot enough by dropping a small piece of bread into the oil—if it gently bubbles and fries, it's the right temperature. Using a slotted spoon, gently lower your egg into the oil, making sure you carefully keep splashing oil over it if it's not fully covered. Fry for 10 minutes (or 5 on each side if your egg is not fully covered), cooking up to 3 eggs at a time.

13. Once they're cooked, place the eggs on paper towels to drain.

14. Let stand for 10 minutes to cool, then tuck in with some ketchup.

SONNY AND HIS DOG COOPER

As soon as Sonny could stand, he had a place cooking with his daddy and he soon became the best potato-peeling three year old you have ever laid eyes on. Wherever Sonny went, you could guarantee Cooper would be right there by his side, enjoying the spoils of Sonny's riches.

Sadly Cooper said good-bye in January 2012, but he will never be out of our thoughts, a true family dog and the perfect cooking companion.
R.I.P. COOPER

Ploughman's in a Box

SERVES 2 • PREPARATION TIME: 15 MINUTES • COOKING TIME: NONE • ✓

This lunch dish is a great British pub staple—and a perfect portable feast.

8oz **cheddar cheese**
4 fat slices of good **ham**
2 large **pickled onions**
2 **crisp apples** (we love a Pippin)
2 slices of your favorite **bread**
½ stick **unsalted butter**
2 sticks of **celery**, trimmed
a splodge of **Branston pickle**, or homemade **chutney** or relish of your choice
salt and **freshly ground black pepper**
a bottle of **beer** (optional)

1. Find a beautiful box—something vintage would be great, but a large plastic food container or brown cardboard is just as good. Arrange everything, except the beer, snugly inside. Tie up with string.

2. Chill the beer.

3. Picnic.

TIPS

* Feel free to replace the cheddar with your favorite cheese: we are fans of Stilton or Gruyère.

* Add some scallions if you like, and some wedges of crisp lettuce or endive.

WEEKEND BLOWOUTS

I love get-togethers. With our extra time on the weekend, we can gather up friends, family, extended family for some old-style social networking. And I love to get everyone involved too. Back at my gran's house in London, she ruled her kitchen, but we all had our little jobs to help out while she created epic Sunday lunches on a grand scale.

I can see the whole layout of her house right now: the wartime utility cabinets on the wall, painted a buttery yellow; a door that opened onto the backyard path leading to the outside bathroom (my favorite—instead of a light, it had a flashlight hanging on the back of the door on a piece of string, which I thought was marvelous!); the serving hatch into the dining room. Those times around her table, with that old Tretchikoff print of the Chinese girl looking down on us from the dining room wall, make up some of my favorite memories.

Weekend blowouts don't have to be fancy. But wine should be poured. Kids should race around. Board games should be played. This is about fun. And love and generosity. And making memories.

KAY

Oven-fried Chicken with Collard Greens

SERVES 6 · MARINATING TIME: 2 HOURS–OVERNIGHT · PREPARATION TIME: 20 MINUTES
COOKING TIME: 1 HOUR 20 MINUTES · ✓ ♥

Fried chicken: What else is there to say, other than that this is finger-lickin' good.

1 cup **buttermilk**
½ tablespoon **English mustard**
½ tablespoon smooth **Dijon mustard**
1 clove of **garlic**, crushed
1 **bay leaf**
2 teaspoons **sea salt**
3 dashes of **Tabasco**

1 **chicken**, cut into 8 pieces
1 cup **buckwheat flour**, sifted
¾ cup **cornmeal**
1 tablespoon **Kay's Cajun Magic**
  (see page 57)
¼ cup **vegetable oil**, for frying
salt and **freshly ground black pepper**

1. Put the buttermilk and the mustards into a bowl and add the garlic, bay leaf, sea salt, and , Tabasco. Coat the chicken liberally with the mixture and let marinate for at least an hour or two, but preferably overnight.

2. When you're ready to cook, heat the oven to 350°F.

3. Mix together the sifted buckwheat flour, the cornmeal, and Kay's Cajun Magic with a little salt and a good few grindings of black pepper.

4. Remove the chicken from the marinade and shake off any excess. Thoroughly coat each piece in the seasoned flour and cornmeal.

5. Heat the oil in a large nonstick skillet until it's HOT. Fry the chicken—3 or 4 pieces at a time, until golden. When its ready, place each piece on a rack in a roasting pan. Put the roasting pan into the oven and bake for about 40 minutes, until cooked through. Serve with mashed potatoes and collard greens (see below).

Quick & Easy Collard Greens

SERVES 6 · PREPARATION TIME: 15 MINUTES · COOKING TIME: 8 MINUTES · ✓ WF GF

3oz **bacon**, chopped
vegetable oil (optional)
2 cloves of **garlic**, peeled and sliced
1 lb **collard greens**,
  sliced, with stems removed

salt and **freshly ground**
  black pepper
a few dashes of **hot sauce** (optional)

1. In a dry sauté pan with a lid, cook the bacon over low heat until golden and crispy. They should release about a tablespoon of fat, but if the pan's looking a little dry, add a dash of vegetable oil. Then add the garlic, and sauté until golden.

2. Increase the heat, add the greens, and toss them with the bacon and garlic. Season with salt and black pepper and the hot sauce, if using, then put the lid on, shake the pan to mix everything together, and cook for 3–4 minutes. Serve immediately.

Henry's Sunday Dinner

(ROAST PORK BELLY & LIMA BEANS)

SERVES 8 • PREPARATION TIME: 20 MINUTES • COOKING TIME: 3 HOURS 30 MINUTES • ✓ WF GF DF

This is a simple Sunday dinner that can be mostly prepared beforehand, leaving you time to enjoy the day (see picture on page 196–97). The spicy lemon kale (opposite) makes a great contrast to the rich pork. This fast, slow, fast method of cooking the pork is the key to perfect crackling every time.

4½ lb **pork belly**, skin scored in thin lines
a little **olive** or **sunflower oil**
2 x (15-oz) **cans of lima beans**
4 large **carrots**
3 **leeks**
1 tablespoon **coriander seed**
a large bunch of **fresh thyme**
1 bottle of **white wine** (see tips below)
sea salt and **freshly ground black pepper**

1. Heat the oven to 425°F.

2. Place the pork belly in a large roasting pan and smear it all over with the oil, salt, and black pepper, making sure to get a good amount of salt rubbed into the skin. Then put it into the oven.

3. Drain and rinse the beans. Chop the carrots and leeks into uneven, smallish pieces, then, in a bowl, mix the beans and vegetables with the rest of the ingredients.

4. After the pork has been in the oven for 25 minutes, if any fat's come out, baste it once. After another 20 minutes, remove the roasting pan from the oven. The pork skin should be going a little brown and bubbly.

5. Take the pork out of the roasting pan and pour out the fat. Then add the beans, vegetables, and wine. Place the pork belly on top and cover tightly with aluminum foil. Reduce the oven to 325°F and cook for another 2 hours.

6. When the time's up, remove the foil. If the vegetables at the bottom of the pan are drying out, add a touch of water. Turn the oven up to 400°F and roast the pork for another 15 minutes, or until it is fully crisped. Depending on your piece of pork, this could take another 30 minutes.

7. Transfer the meat to a board and carve at the table, and serve the vegetables and beans in a dish.

TIPS

* Play with the spices and herbs in the vegetables under the pork: bulb fennel and fennel seed work well.

* You can use pretty much any canned beans (or soak and cook your own).

* If you are being frugal, use ½ cup of white wine or cider vinegar and 2¾ cups of stock instead of the wine.

* Any leftover veg can be used for Frank's Bubble & Squeak (see page 261).

Spicy Lemon Kale

SERVES 8 • PREPARATION TIME: 20 MINUTES • COOKING TIME: 30 MINUTES • ✓ ♥ WF GF DF V

1½ lb **kale**, thick stems removed
2 tablespoons **olive oil**
2 cloves of **garlic**, sliced
1 long **red chile**, seeded and sliced
the juice of ½ a **lemon**
salt and **freshly ground black pepper**

1. Prepare the kale by peeling off the big stems and tearing any really big pieces of leaf into smaller pieces. Blanch in salted boiling water for about 5 minutes—it should still have a good bite to it, because everything else in the dish will be soft. Drain really well and set aside—you can do this the day before, and keep it in the refrigerator until the next day, if you desire.

2. In a sauté pan, gently heat the oil over low to medium heat and add the garlic and chile. When it is letting off a nice aroma—but hasn't browned at all—add the kale and warm through gently. Season with salt and black pepper, then add the lemon juice. Toss everything together off the heat and serve.

JOSEPH, LIZA, HENRY AND EDMUND, 1977

There are very few businesses or ventures that are the work of one person. Partly because one needs complementary skills and approaches, partly because, like wrestlers, one needs a tag team partner. Henry is mine and mine is Henry. We dream, argue, inspire each other, rescue each other, and eat together. Henry is a Viking (no, really). A Winston Churchill-esque bulldog who will not give up that bone. That dogged commitment, love and knowledge of food, love for hard work, his intelligence, his determination to build an excellent organization based on attention to detail and planning, his ability to build consensus, and his ability to not give up until a job is done would have not been out of place in the British Cabinet War Rooms.

JOHN

Butt Chicken with Cajun Spices

SERVES 6 • PREPARATION TIME: 20 MINUTES • COOKING TIME: 1½ HOURS • ✓ WF GF

This is chicken. With a can of beer up its butt. We're not kidding.

1 x (12-oz) **chicken**, about 3¼ lb
1 x 440ml **can of beer** or **lager**
3 **bay leaves**
a large sprig or two of **fresh thyme**
1 **scallion**
3 cloves of **garlic**, lightly crushed
½ a **red jalapeño chile**

2 tablespoons **light olive oil**
1 tablespoon **Kay's Cajun Magic**
   (see page 57)
½ teaspoon **ground cumin**
2 tablespoons **unsalted butter**
salt and **freshly ground black pepper**

1. Heat the oven to 400°F.

2. Season the chicken cavity with salt and black pepper. Open the beer can and take a sip. Then shove the bay leaves, thyme, scallion, garlic and jalapeño into the can. Stand it in a roasting pan, then push the chicken down onto the can. You should be able to fit most of it into the chicken and use the legs to help it balance.

3. Mix together the olive oil, Kay's Cajun Magic, and cumin. Brush it all over the chicken. Roast in the oven for about 1 hour and 15 minutes, basting two or three times with the olive oil mixture. The steam from the beer will cook the chicken faster than a usual roast. Be very careful not to spill the hot beer on yourself when you take it in and out of the oven.

4. When cooked, remove the chicken from the can and set aside. Transfer the contents of the can into the roasting pan and cook over high heat until the beer has reduced by two-thirds, then stir in the butter. Cut the chicken into 6–8 pieces and serve with a good splash of gravy and Almost-Philippe's Coleslaw (see below).

Almost-Philippe's Coleslaw

SERVES 6 • PREPARATION TIME: 20 MINUTES PLUS STANDING • COOKING TIME: NONE • ✓ WF GF V

Philippe's is one of our favorite places in Los Angeles. It's been open since 1908. This is our version of their delicious coleslaw.

¼ cup **buttermilk**
2 tablespoons **sour cream**
2 tablespoons **mayonnaise**
a good squeeze of **lemon juice**

1 tablespoon **celery seed**
½ head of a **pointed spring cabbage**,
   shredded
salt and **freshly ground black pepper**

1. Put the buttermilk, sour cream and mayonnaise into a small bowl. Stir in the lemon juice. Season with salt, black pepper, and the celery seed.

2. Put the cabbage into a large bowl, pour the dressing over it and toss all together. Let stand for at least 30 minutes, then serve.

Roast Beef

SERVES 6 • PREPARATION TIME: 5 MINUTES • COOKING TIME: I HOUR • RESTING TIME: 30 MINUTES • ✓ WF DF

Bottom round beef roasts surprisingly well for such a lean cut of meat, as long as you keep it rare. So we'll say it now, up front: If you prefer your meat more toward the medium or well-done side of things, this dish is not for you. Make sure you get a piece with a nice layer of fat on the top—it'll release some fantastic dripping and it will keep the meat deliciously moist.

> 3¼ lb piece of **bottom round beef**
> 1 tablespoon **olive oil**
> **salt** and **freshly ground black pepper**

1. Heat the oven to 425°F.

2. Rub the beef with the olive oil, then stand it in a roasting pan, fat side up, and season the fat well with salt and pepper. Put it into the oven for 25 minutes.

3. When the 25 minutes are up, baste the beef, then reduce the heat to 300°F and roast for another 30 minutes or so, basting once. (If you have a larger piece of meat, you might want to give it 30 minutes for its initial blast of heat, then figure on cooking it for 10 minutes per 1 lb).

4. When it's cooked, remove it from the oven and let rest for a good 30 minutes before carving. Make the gravy according to the recipe for Cheat's Demi-glace and serve with Celeriac Dauphinoise (see opposite).

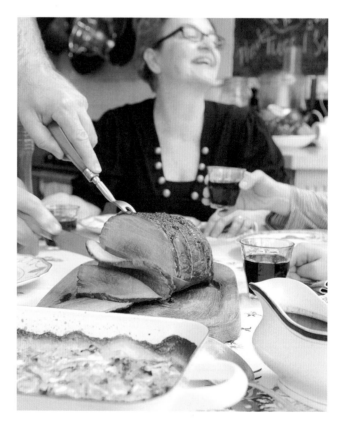

Cheat's Demi-glace

PREPARATION TIME: 10 MINUTES • COOKING TIME: 30 MINUTES • ✓ WF GF

This doesn't have an awful lot to do with a formal demi-glace, but it makes a great base for a gravy.

> 1 tablespoon **olive oil**
> 1 **banana shallot**, finely chopped
> 1 **beef bouillon cube**
> 1 cup **red wine**
> 1 **bay leaf**
> **salt** and **freshly ground black pepper**

1. Put the olive oil into a small saucepan over low to medium heat, then add the shallot and cook until soft and just taking a hint of color. Add ½ cup of water, then crumble in the bouillon cube. Stir everything together, add the wine and the bay leaf, and simmer until the sauce has reduced by at least half. Set aside to cool.

2. To make the gravy, pour off the fat from the roast. Put the roasting pan on medium heat and strain in the reduced sauce, discarding the shallot and bay leaf. Bubble it up, scraping up any bits from the bottom of the pan. Taste and season.

Celeriac Dauphinoise

SERVES 6 • PREPARATION TIME: 15 MINUTES • COOKING TIME: 45–60 MINUTES • ✓ ♥ V

This Dauphinoise tastes so luxurious that it seems as though it must have taken forever to make. But actually, it's a cinch, and its rich creaminess makes it the perfect foil for beef or game.

> 2 tablespoons **butter**, plus extra for greasing
> 1¼ lb **celeriac**, peeled and very thinly sliced
> ½ cup **shredded Gruyère cheese**
> a good grating of **nutmeg**
> ½ cup **milk**
> ⅔ cup **heavy cream**
> 1 clove of **garlic**, peeled and finely chopped
> **salt** and **freshly ground black pepper**

1. Heat the oven to 350°F.

2. Grease a baking pan, 11½ x 7½ inches, and fill it with layers of sliced celeriac. Season each layer with cheese, nutmeg, salt, and black pepper, until the celeriac is used up.

3. Melt the butter, then in a jug combine it with the milk, cream, and garlic. Stir and pour over the celeriac. Season the top layer with a final touch of cheese, nutmeg, salt and pepper, then bake in the oven for 1 hour. Check it after 45 minutes—when it's done, the celeriac should have a nice "give" to it and the sauce should be silky and rich.

Mom's Chicken Curry

(MURG KORMA)

SERVES 4 • PREPARATION TIME: 20 MINUTES • COOKING TIME: 40 MINUTES • ✓ ♥ WF GF DF

Our friend Mamta Gupta makes many different curries. This is the one her daughters request most often. It's always known at their house as Mom's Chicken Curry. It's a typical northern Indian-style dish, and is the one on which Leon's Mamta's Curry is based.

2 tablespoons **vegetable oil**
½ teaspoon **cumin seeds**
2 **onions**, chopped
a ¾-inch piece of **fresh ginger**, peeled and chopped
2–3 cloves of **garlic**, chopped
2–3 **tomatoes**, chopped, or
　2–3 tablespoons **tomato paste**
2 tablespoons **dried fenugreek** or **methi leaves** (optional)
1 lb **chicken thighs on the bone**, skinned
½ teaspoon **homemade garam masala** (see page 207)
a handful of **fresh cilantro leaves**, chopped
salt, to taste

The whole spices (see tip below):
1 **bay leaf**
1–2 pieces of **cinnamon stick** or **cassia bark**
2 large **cardamom pods**
3–4 small **green cardamom pods**
5–6 **black peppercorns**
4–5 **cloves**

The ground spices:
1 teaspoon **ground turmeric**
2 teaspoons **ground coriander**
1 teaspoon **paprika** (optional)
½ teaspoon **chili powder,** or to taste

1. Heat the oil in a heavy wok or sauté pan, and add the cumin seeds and the whole spices. Cook until the cumin seeds begin to sputter, being careful not to let them burn. Add the onion, ginger, and garlic, and sauté until browned and almost caramelized, stirring frequently so nothing sticks. Now stir in the ground spices, and cook for a few seconds to bring out their flavor.

2. Add the tomato and the fenugreek or methi leaves, if using, and cook, stirring frequently, until the oil separates. Finally, add the chicken and cook over medium to high heat, stirring frequently, until the chicken is well coated and sealed.

3. Cover the pan and cook over low to medium heat for about 15–20 minutes, or until tender. When the chicken is cooked, if the sauce looks a little thick, add some water to loosen. Turn off the heat, and stir in the garam masala and half of the cilantro. Season with salt to taste.

4. Finally, garnish with the remaining cilantro leaves and serve with rice, naan, roti, or chapati.

TIPS

* If you are short of one or more of the whole spices, leave them ALL out; use with 1½ teaspoons of homemade garam masala (see page 207) instead.

* Mamta says chili powders can vary greatly in strength, so get to know yours and use accordingly.

* Mamta says you can make this curry a day ahead of time, then reheat, garnish, and serve. This allows for the flavors to mingle nicely.

Eggplant Pickle-style Bhaji

(BAINGAN (BRINJAL) AACHARI)

SERVES 4 • PREPARATION TIME: 10 MINUTES • COOKING TIME: 20 MINUTES • ✓ ♥ WF GF DF V

Mamta says that, in the UK, the word "bhaji" is often used to refer to battered and deep-fried vegetables, which northern Indians call pakoras. Dry vegetable dishes are usually referred to as "sabji" or "bhaji', both words simply meaning "vegetable'. This dish is called a pickle-style bhaji because the whole panch pooran spices and mustard oil are often used in pickling.

> 2–3 tablespoons **mustard oil**
> 1½ tablespoons **panch pooran** (see tips below)
> a pinch of **asafotida** or **garlic powder**
> 1 whole **dried chile**, broken up
> 10 oz small, thin **eggplants**, cut in half lengthwise with stems left on
> 1 tablespoon peeled and grated or chopped **fresh ginger**
> ½ teaspoon **ground turmeric**
> ½ teaspoon **chili powder**, or to taste
> 1 teaspoon **salt**, or to taste
> the juice of ½ a **lemon**
> a small handful of **fresh cilantro**, leaves chopped

1. Heat the oil in a wok and, when it's hot, add the panch pooran and asafotida. When the seeds start to sputter, add the dried chile and stir for 10 seconds. Then stir in the eggplants, ginger, and all of the spices.

2. Season with salt and cook, covered, over low to medium heat for 5–10 minutes until the eggplants are tender. If you use a lower heat, you won't need to add any additional water.

3. Add the lemon juice, increase the heat, and stir gently, until all the liquid has been absorbed and the eggplants are shiny. They should not be mashed. Garnish with the chopped cilantro leaves and serve hot with chapatis or daal.

TIPS

* Panch pooran is a mix of five spices from the Bengal and Bihar regions of India and Bangladesh. To make it, mix together 1 teaspoon each of cumin seeds, black mustard seeds, fennel seeds, nigella seeds, and fenugreek seeds. Store them in an airtight jar. To use them in a recipe, heat some oil and add the spice mix—when the seeds sputter, add the onions or vegetables as your recipe requires.

* If you can't find small, thin eggplants, use large ones—just cut them into thick batons or sticks. With the smaller ones, Mamta prefers to leave the stems on when she halves them because it helps them keep their shape.

FOOD FACT

ASAFOTIDA

Asafotida is also known as the devil's dung because it doesn't smell so good when it's raw. But when it's cooked, it takes on a flavor a little like cooked leeks. It's often used as an aid to digestion in India and Thailand, or as an antiflatulent! And it's known in traditional medicine for its antimicrobial properties. Best of all, according to a report from the Kaohsiung Medical University in Taiwan, its roots may produce an antiviral compound that kills the H1N1 flu virus, confirming an idea floating around because asafotida was used to combat the Spanish flu epidemic of 1918. So there.

Garam Masala

MAKES ABOUT ⅓ CUP • PREPARATION TIME: 2–5 MINUTES • COOKING TIME: NONE • ✓ ♥ WF GF DF V

Garam means hot, and masala means spice mix. Since many store-bought versions are padded out with extra cumin or coriander, Mamta suggests you make your own for that proper punch.

1 tablespoon **black peppercorns**
1 teaspoon **cloves**
4–5 **brown cardamom pods**
4–5 **dried bay leaves**
a 2-inch piece of **cinnamon stick** or **cassia bark**
4–5 **green cardamom pods** (optional)
½ a **nutmeg**, freshly grated (optional)
1–2 tablespoons **cumin seeds** (optional)

1. Grind all the ingredients together finely in an electric coffee grinder or in a mortar and pestle. Then strain to remove any husks or fibers.

2. Store in an airtight container.

MAMTA WITH KAVITA, 1972

MAMTA WITH HER PARENTS, YASHODA AND SURESH, LONDON, 1972

TIPS

* Mamta does not recommend toasting the spices before you make your garam masala. Toasting releases the flavors, so they will be lost if you store the spices for any length of time. "Raw" ground spices will last much longer.

Mamta's daughter Kavita says, "Though Mom's Indian dishes are definitely our comfort food, my sister and I never learned to cook Indian food in any meaningful way—we didn't pick up the techniques, the instinctive use of spices, and wide repertoire of dishes that our cousins in India grew up with.

"When we left home, we missed Mom's Indian cooking the most and we'd frequently phone home for advice on making keema peas or chicken curry. We begged Mom to write her recipes down for us and so began the laborious process of handwriting a family cookbook.

"It wasn't long before the idea of a website version surfaced and Mom, my husband Pete, and I created Mamta's Kitchen (www.mamtaskitchen.com) back in 2001. We don't believe in secret family recipes. Today, we receive 2 million hits a year to our 1,500 recipes, discussion forum, menu tips, and festival page. Mom's recipes are at the core, but we also love sharing contributions from family, friends and readers who want to be part of our family cookbook on the web."

Rob Elliott Smith's Shrimp Creole

SERVES 4–6 • PREPARATION TIME: 25–30 MINUTES • COOKING TIME: 45 MINUTES • ✓ ♥ WF GF DF

Our American friend Rob makes a mean shrimp creole: spicy, sweet, and addictive. He would generally make a roux to thicken this, but here we have a lighter, just-as-delicious version.

2 **red bell peppers**, finely chopped
2 **onions**, finely chopped
4 sticks of **celery**, finely chopped
1 clove of **garlic**, peeled and chopped
2–6 **medium-hot red chiles**, seeded and chopped
3 tablespoons finely chopped **flat-leaf parsley**
2¾ lb **shrimp**, peeled, reserving the heads and shells
2–3 slices of **lemon**
2 tablespoons **vegetable oil**
6 **ripe tomatoes**, peeled and chopped
2 tablespoons **tomato paste**
3–4 sprigs of **fresh thyme** (optional)
salt and **freshly ground black pepper**

1. Heat the oven to 400°F.

2. Put the chopped bell peppers, onions, celery, garlic, chiles and parsley into a bowl and mix together thoroughly. Set aside.

3. Put the shrimp heads, legs, and shells into a saucepan. Pour in just enough water to cover, add the lemon slices, and season with salt and black pepper. Place the pan over medium to high heat and boil for 3–5 minutes, skimming off any scum that rises, to make a rich shrimp stock. Strain the stock and set aside.

4. Heat the oil in a large, wide skillet. Add the vegetable mixture and cook until softened but still retaining a little bite. Transfer to a large ovenproof casserole.

5. Add the tomatoes, 500ml of the shrimp stock and bring to a boil. Cook over medium heat until the tomatoes break down and release all their juices. Stir in the tomato paste and add the sprigs of thyme, if using. Season to taste with salt and black pepper.

6. Remove from the heat, add the raw shrimp, then put the casserole into the oven and bake for 25 minutes.

7. Serve on white rice, with cornbread (see page 210) and additional hot sauces for the brave.

TIPS | * If you can't buy shrimp with their clothes on, don't worry. Just buy 2½ lb of peeled shrimp and make 2 cups of fish stock with a good brand of cube or powder.

Cornbread

A Southern staple in the good old US of A. As well as making the perfect foil for Rob's Shrimp Creole (see page 209), you could also serve it with the Oven-fried Chicken on page 195. And it's a great alternative to bread with soup or salad.

a little **butter** or **bacon fat**, for greasing
1 cup **cornmeal**
1 cup **buckwheat flour**
¼ cup **sugar**
½ teaspoon **sea salt**
1 tablespoon **gluten-free baking powder**
¼ cup **vegetable oil**
½ cup **milk**
⅓ cup **buttermilk**
1 extra-large **egg**, lightly beaten

ROB WITH TWO BOOTLEGGERS,
ALABAMA, 1968

1. Heat the oven to 400°F. Grease an 8-inch square baking pan with butter or—better yet—bacon fat!

2. Combine the dry goods in a bowl. Then add the wet goods. Mix together thoroughly and pour into the prepared tin.

3. Bake in the oven for about 25 minutes, or until golden. To test that it's cooked, jab it in its thickest part with a toothpick. If it comes out clean, it's done. Serve warm with Prawn Creole.

TIPS

* Kay has a vintage cast-iron mold that makes cornbread shaped like corn cobs. Occasionally they show up for sale on eBay, and they're wonderful kitchenalia.

* For a change of pace, you could add a chopped, seeded jalapeño, or ⅔ cup of fresh or canned sweetcorn, or ¾ cup of cubed cheddar or Gruyère, or some chopped sage, to the batter. Rob, being a Southern gentleman of integrity, feels these additions are just plain wrong, but we love them.

* For a sweeter, more muffinlike cornbread, you can add an extra ½ cup of sugar with the dry ingredients.

Rob was born in Birmingham, Alabama. See the picture above? That's his grandpa taking him to visit the bootlegger ... which reminds me: Why not make a nice Mint Julep to sip while you're making this? Crush the leaves from a sprig of mint into a teaspoon of sugar. Pour over ¼ cup of bourbon. Stir together. Top up the glass with crushed ice. Most refreshing.

Rob's Shrimp Creole on page 209 is a version of his Daddy's traditional shrimp creole. Rob says: "Back home, shrimp creole is a special meal reserved for large family gatherings, probably in the summer. Something more intimate and traditional would be squirrel and dumplings. My great-grandmother—'Mom'—would prepare a batch of squirrels we'd shot; pan-fry them in a bit of flour, salt, and pepper, and stew with thick flour-and-lard dumplings. She'd serve the whole, ginormous bowl just for me. I'd always ask if she'd like some herself, but she invariably replied, 'I'll just gnaw on these,' presenting a plate of squirrel heads, deep-fried. Most people I meet prefer to stick with the creole."

Gardener John's Roasted Vegetables

SERVES 4 • PREPARATION TIME: 10 MINUTES • COOKING TIME: 50–60 MINUTES • WF GF DF V

John and Katie know a gardener called … John. He has been a gardener for a long time, and he leaves them gifts in the form of root vegetables. The trouble is he forgets to tell them when he's left them. So he will come around and say, "Did you cook those sweet potatoes I left at the end of the garden for you?" "Er, no, sorry, we didn't know they were there." Fortunately root vegetables are hardy and so most of the time they are still in good shape.

Roasting vegetables is easy—the trick is to learn which vegetables take longer to cook. As a general rule, if the vegetable's harder (like a parsnip), it will take longer to cook than a softer vegetable, say, a sweet potato or tomato. You can somewhat level the playing field by slicing the harder vegetables more thinly. Or, if you want to, you can experiment by adding the softer vegetables later on during the roasting.

That's all very nice, but the icing on the cake, kind of, is the tangy dressing you add at the end. Try the Salsa Verde on page 170, a balsamic dressing, or a mustard and honey vinaigrette. (Or cheat with a bottle of salad dressing. As long as you keep an eye on the ingredients in the bottle, you can do much worse.)

> 3–6 **parsnips**, cut into medium to thin strips
> 3–4 **onions**, red if you have them, cut thickly
>   (because these will cook quickly and can burn)
> 2–3 **sweet potatoes**
> **any other vegetables** you have in your arsenal that day
>   (**squash**, **eggplant**, etc.)
> plenty of **garlic** (to be trendy you can cut a whole head in half)
> a good handful of **fresh rosemary** and **fresh thyme**
> enough **olive oil** to make all the vegetables oily (maybe
>   ⅓ cup, maybe ½ a mug)
> the **tangy dressing** of your choice
> **salt** and **freshly ground black pepper**

1. Heat the oven to 400°F.

2. Put the chopped vegetables and the garlic and herbs into a roasting pan. Season with salt, and pepper, then pour on the olive oil and tumble the vegetables through it.

3. Put the pan of vegetables into the oven and roast for 50–60 minutes, taking it out halfway through for a little shake.

4. Once cooked, add your tangy dressing.

TIPS

* For meateaters who want to turn this into a feast, you can add chicken. Just sauté some sliced chicken in olive oil with a few herbs or spices, and add it to the veg.

Lamb Boulangère

SERVES 6 • PREPARATION TIME: 25 MINUTES • COOKING TIME: 1 HOUR 20–30 MINUTES • ✓ WF GF

A great piece of lamb, a bumper crop of potatoes, and a cool wind blowing the leaves in September: this is a classic, traditionally cooked in a baker's oven. We love it.

1 **leg of lamb** (weighing 3¼–4½ lb), bone in or partly boned
2 large sprigs of **fresh rosemary**, broken into small shards
4 cloves of **garlic**, cut into slivers
2 tablespoons **olive oil**
2 tablespoons **unsalted butter**
2¼ lb **red-skinned** or **white round potatoes**, peeled and thinly sliced
2 **onions**, thinly sliced
2 sprigs of **fresh lavender**, coarsely torn
1 cup **lamb stock**
½ cup **white wine**
1 x (15-oz) can of **great Northern beans**, drained and rinsed (optional)
a glass of **wine** or ½ cup **lamb stock** or **water**
an extra pat of cold **butter**
salt and **freshly ground black pepper**

1. Heat the oven to 400°F.

2. Pat the lamb dry with paper towels and make small incisions all over the lamb with the tip of a knife. Insert the shards of rosemary and the slivers of garlic into the incisions. Rub 1 tablespoon of the olive oil over the lamb and season generously with salt and black pepper.

3. Put the lamb into a large roasting pan and put it into the oven for 30 minutes.

4. Meanwhile, put the potatoes and onions in a bowl with the remaining tablespoon of olive oil, salt, black pepper, lavender, and any pieces of leftover garlic and rosemary.

5. After 30 minutes, remove the lamb from the oven and place it on a plate. Put the potato-and-onion mixture into the roasting pan and add the stock and wine. Dot the butter evenly over the surface of the potato, then put the pan back into the oven. Place the leg of lamb directly on the rack above the potatoes—the drip, drip effect will give you glorious potatoes.

6. Roast for another 40–50 minutes. Then remove the lamb from the oven and set aside on a plate or board to rest for 15–20 minutes. If the potatoes need more browning, leave them in the oven. When they are ready, transfer them to a serving dish with a slotted spoon, keeping as much goo in the pan as possible.

7. Once you have removed the potatoes, place the roasting pan over low heat and deglaze the pan with a glass of wine and let it bubble away, scraping down the sides until it's looking thick and smelling good. Add the (optional) beans and the pat of cold butter and heat through. Carve the lamb into slices and serve with a generous portion of the potatoes and a good dollop of gravy (and beans, if using).

Momma's Apple Pie

SERVES 6 • PREPARATION TIME: 20 MINUTES • COOKING TIME: 1 HOUR • V

"As American as Mom and Apple Pie," as the saying goes … This double-crust, old-fashioned pie reminds us of the pies we grew up seeing in the movies.

Serve it with cream, if you like. But to be really authentic, you should really have it *à la mode* with a scoop of excellent vanilla ice cream. God Bless America.

4 cups **all-purpose flour**
2¼ sticks **unsalted butter**, straight from the refrigerator
a large pinch of **sea salt**
2 tablespoons **superfine sugar**, plus an extra
   tablespoon for the top
1 small glass of **iced water**
1 **egg**, beaten, to glaze

For the filling:
2 lb **apples**, peeled, cored and sliced—we use
   a mixture of Braeburn and Cox's
½ cup **superfine sugar**
the juice of 1 **lemon**
½ teaspoon **ground cinnamon**
a good grating of **nutmeg**

1. First make your pastry dough: Measure out the flour into a large bowl. Cut the cold butter into small pieces and drop them into the flour. Coat them with flour, then start rubbing the flour and butter together with your fingertips, lifting it and gently working it until you have what looks like fine bread crumbs.

2. Add the salt. Then the sugar. Mix well. Now add the iced water, a teaspoonful at a time, working everything together with your hands until the dough just comes together. Don't add too much water, or you'll have a hard pastry. Roll it into 2 loose balls, cover with plastic wrap and refrigerate for at least 30 minutes.

3. Heat the oven to 350°F and grease a 9-inch pie plate.

4. Put the sliced apples into a large bowl. Sprinkle with the sugar, lemon juice, cinnamon, and nutmeg and mix well.

5. Take the dough balls out of the refrigerator and roll them out, one at a time, into circles the size of your pie plate. Line the bottom of the plate with one circle. Tip in the filling, then cover with the other circle and crimp the bottom and top together.

6. Bake the pie in the oven for 20 minutes. Then remove it from the oven and brush the top with the beaten egg. Sprinkle over the extra sugar and bake for another 40–50 minutes, or until golden brown and cooked through. Serve with vanilla ice cream.

Anna Hansen's Pumpkin & Miso Cheesecake

SERVES 8–12 • PREPARATION TIME: 1 HOUR • COOKING TIME: 1 HOUR 15 MINUTES
COOLING TIME: MINIMUM 4 HOURS • V

Anna is an extraordinary chef. At her restaurant, the Modern Pantry in Clerkenwell, London, she marries flavors that most of us would never dream of. As Kay has often said, Anna's palate is her playground. She designed this dessert just for us.

2 cups **cream cheese**
1 cup **superfine sugar**
2 tablespoons **confectioners' sugar**
¼ cup **miso paste**
the seeds of 1 **vanilla bean**
2 cups **roasted pumpkin puree** (see tip)
5 whole **eggs** and 2 **egg yolks**

For the crust:
20 **gingersnaps**
18 **graham crackers**
1 tablespoon **packed light brown sugar**
1 stick **butter**, plus extra for greasing
1¼ cups **heavy cream**, whipped, to serve

TIPS

* Pumpkin puree is very easy to make yourself, and the superior flavor of your cheesecake will be your reward. Simply roast 1¾ lb of pumpkin or butternut squash, skin on, in chunks, covered in aluminum foil, in a preheated oven, 400°F, for about 40 minutes to 1 hour—the time will depend on your pumpkin. When it's cooked, allow it to cool for a little while, then peel off the skin and process the flesh in a food processor. However, if you're feeling lazy, you can simply buy it in a can!

* Sometimes cheesecakes will "crack" when cooked—it depends on your oven. Don't worry if this happens—it won't affect the flavor of the finished product.

1. Heat your oven to 325°F. Line the base of a 9-inch spring-form cake pan with parchment paper and thoroughly grease the sides.

2. Start by making the crust: Process all the cookies and the sugar to a medium fine crumb in a food processor. Melt the butter, add to the cookie crumbs, and pulse until just mixed. Tip the mixture in the lined cake pan, then press it evenly into the bottom of the pan. Bake for 10 minutes, then remove from the oven and let cool.

3. Increase the oven temperature to 350°F. Wipe out the bowl of the processor, then add the cream cheese, sugars, miso paste, and vanilla seeds. Blend for a minute or so until smooth, scraping down the sides of the bowl. Add the pumpkin puree, eggs, and yolks and blend again until smooth, making sure you scrape down the sides of the bowl once more.

4. Transfer the batter into the cake pan and bake for 15 minutes, then reduce the heat to 225°F and bake for another 50 minutes to 1 hour and 10 minutes. It's ready when set around the edges and still slightly wobbly in the center.

5. Remove from the oven and let the cheesecake cool in its pan on a wire rack for an hour or so. Then run a knife around the edges of the pan, carefully remove the ring, and slide the cheesecake onto a plate. Let cool completely before serving— at least 4 hours, if not overnight in the refrigerator.

6. Serve with whipped cream.

ANNA WITH HER FRIENDS, NGATEA,
NEW ZEALAND, 1975

Banana & Chocolate Ice Cream Surprise

Katie says: "Like so many of us, I'm keen to please and yet have precious little time for faffing around. This dessert, which comes from an idea from my friend Julia Parker, falls into the winning category of being (a) popular with all ages, (b) phenomenally straightforward and cheap, and yet (c) looks really rather snazzy.'

    a container of inexpensive **vanilla ice cream**
    2 **bananas**
    2 **crumbly chocolate candy bars**

1. Empty the ice cream into a bowl that you can put into the freezer.
   Let it warm up just a little so that you can work with it and mix it around a little.
   Mash the bananas and stir them into the ice cream. Smooth it all over.

2. Bash up the chocolate and sprinkle it generously on top. Put in the freezer until you're ready to serve. (We told you it was easy.)

TIPS

* We've yet to meet a kid (or adult, for that matter) who doesn't love this. We're sure you can think of a whole host of additional surprises to mix into the ice cream (crumbled cookies, perhaps? Raspberries?). Katie tends to hand the whole affair over to the kids who are going to eat it, and lets them get on with it.

Eleanor's Eating Mess

SERVES 6 • PREPARATION TIME: 10 MINUTES • COOKING TIME (MAKING THE MERINGUES): 2 HOURS
COOKING TIME (BUYING THE MERINGUES): NONE • WF GF V

Eleanor, John and Katie's daughter, age six, came to the (mistaken) conclusion that Eton Mess is actually called Eating Mess. So in their house it has become such. (Hayward's Heath also inadvertently became Famous Thief.) Eleanor has become a really special cook and likes to make this simple but calorific concoction as a variation on the classic.

2 cups **heavy cream**, whipped
1 lb **strawberries**, hulled and halved

For the meringue:
3 **egg whites**
¾ cup **superfine sugar**

1. First make your meringues. Heat the oven to 250°F. Whisk the egg whites into stiff peaks. Then beat in a tablespoon of sugar, until the mixture looks like satin. Wait for about a minute, then fold in the remaining sugar in 2 batches.

2. Line a baking sheet with parchment paper, scoop the egg white onto it, and, with a spoon, spread it into a 5½–6-inch disk. Put it into the oven for about 1½ hours, until the meringue is golden on the outside and slightly gooey in the middle. Remove from the oven and let cool on a wire rack.

3. To make the mess, break up the cooled meringue into a bowl. Add the cream, and then the strawberries. Stir all the ingredients gently together. It should look as though a pavlova has slid off the shelf in the back of the car and splatted onto the windshield. Serve at room temperature.

TIPS

* Egg whites freeze wonderfully. So you can use the two you'll have leftover from Anna Hansen's Pumpkin & Miso Cheesecake on page 216.

* If you don't have time to make your own meringues, you can always buy them. We won't tell on you. You'll need 6 meringue nests for this recipe.

Giancarlo Caldesi and his wife Katie run Caffè Caldesi and
La Cucina Caldesi, London's only Italian cooking school.
Giancarlo is an amazing cook with an infectious passion
for his native Tuscany.

GIANCARLO CALDESI'S
PIZZA & PASTA MAKING CLASS

We asked Giancarlo Caldesi to show a bunch of Leon-flavored kids how to make pizza and pasta. These recipes are not dumbed down for children. They're the real deal and great fun to make.

Impasto per la Pizza
(PIZZA DOUGH)

MAKES 4 PIZZAS • PREPARATION TIME: 25 MINUTES PLUS RISING
COOKING TIME: 4–7 MINUTES • V

4 cups **all-purpose white flour**
2 teaspoons **salt**
1 heaping teaspoon **active dry yeast**
1⅓ cups lukewarm **water**

1. Place the flour and the salt into a large bowl. In a separate small bowl, add the yeast to the lukewarm water and mix until thoroughly combined. Add the yeast mixture to the flour and salt and mix together to make a dough.

2. Place the dough onto a lightly floured surface and knead for 8–10 minutes, until smooth and elastic. Cut into four and shape into balls. Cover each ball with a little oil to stop them from forming a crust and let rest on a floured surface. Cover the balls with an upturned bowl or a dish cloth and let rise until they have doubled in size.

3. Meanwhile, heat the oven to its maximum temperature.

4. On a lightly floured surface, roll out each ball until you have a circle of pizza dough about ¾ inch in thickness.

5. Now put two inverted baking pans into the oven to heat through—these will be your substitutes for a pizza stone.

6. Top the pizza dough with whatever you prefer (we used tomato-based sauce—see pages 40–1—cheese, salami and olives) and transfer to the oven immediately, before it turns soggy, using a floured board or a paddle to shunt it onto your heated baking pans. Bake for 4–7 minutes, or until crispy around the edges and hot and bubbling on top.

Pasta Fresca

(FRESH PASTA)

MAKES ENOUGH PASTA FOR 4 AS A MAIN DISH OR 6 FOR AN APPETIZER
PREPARATION TIME: 1 HOUR • COOKING TIME: 2 MINUTES • V

This is the general guide to pasta—1 egg to scant 1 cup of flour. However, because egg sizes differ, a little bending of the rules is sometimes necessary. Ideally, pasta is made on a wooden surface, because the tiny particles of wood that project from the surface add texture, helping the pasta absorb the sauce that eventually coats it. Italians use a tablecloth for the same purpose.

The surface of pasta rolled on a metal surface, or a work surface, or through a pasta machine is completely smooth and not so absorbent. This means that dried pasta, which is normally made through metal rollers, has a smooth, harder exterior better designed for liquid sauces, such as seafood or tomato. Its lack of absorbency prevents it from becoming soggy.

> 1⅔ cups **all-purpose flour,** plus a little extra for dusting
> 2 **eggs**

1. Put the flour into a bowl and make a well in the middle. The walls around the edge of the mound of flour should be high enough to contain the eggs. Crack the eggs into the well.

2. Using a table knife, mix the egg and flour together. Keep mixing the until they form a thick paste, using the fingertips of one hand to incorporate the rest of the flour.

3. The dough should form a soft, but firm flexible ball. If it still sticks to the palm of your hand, add a little more flour, but be cautious and stop adding flour as soon as it stops feeling sticky. If it's really dry and starts to crack, add a tablespoon of water.

4. Remove the dough to a lightly floured surface and knead it for 5–10 minutes, or until it springs back to the touch. Don't overwork it, or the result will be tough pasta. If you cut the ball of dough open at this stage, it should be full of small air bubbles—this means you have kneaded it for long enough.

5. Lightly dust the dough with flour and wrap it in plastic wrap to prevent it from drying out, then let it rest at room temperature for 20 minutes. Meanwhile, clean your work surface.

6. Lightly flour your work surface, flatten out your pasta dough, and, following the instructions on your pasta machine, start feeding the dough through it, rolling it thinner each time. DON'T ROLL IT THROUGH MORE THAN 6 TIMES—this will be the difference between a silky pasta and one with the texture of leather. Add the cutting attachment of your choice, depending on what shape pasta you want, then roll it through the machine a final time to cut.

7. Bring a large saucepan of salted water to a rolling boil. Add your pasta and boil for 2 minutes. Remove the pasta from the pan with a slotted spoon and place on to a warmed plate or tray. Serve immediately with a sauce of your choice (see pages 40–41 for some ideas).

BIRTHDAYS

OK, I'll admit it.

I LOVE birthdays.

I LOVE gifts.

I LOVE sausages on sticks.

Birthdays should be celebrated. I don't care how old you are. All this nonsense about not wanting to share your age with the world is silly! Every day is an achievement.

HAPPY BIRTHDAY!

KAY

The Spritz

SERVES 2 • PREPARATION TIME: 2 MINUTES • COOKING TIME: NONE • WF GF V

The Venetian drink of choice. It's cool, bittersweet, and colorful—just what you need for a party.

> a dash of **Aperol** or **Campari** per glass
> 1–1¼ cups **prosecco** (or white wine and sparkling water)
> a small bowl of **ice**
> 2 chunks of **orange** (preferably blood orange)
> 2 **green olives** in brine, rinsed

1. Pour a dash of Aperol or Campari into each glass.

2. Top up to about halfway with the prosecco or white wine and sparkling water. Add an ice cube.

3. Spear an orange chunk and an olive on each of 2 long toothpicks and place one in each glass. Serve with the bowl of ice on the side.

Vince Jung's Margarita

MAKES 1 • PREPARATION TIME: 2 MINUTES • COOKING TIME: NONE • WF GF V

Kay's friend Vince is the third-generation owner of the landmark Hollywood bar the Formosa Café, which has been serving everyone from movie stars to hoodlums since ... well... it depends on who you talk to, but no one's really sure. Vince's margaritas are the business.

> ¼ cup **silver tequila**
> 2 tablespoons **Cointreau**
> the juice from 1½ **limes**
> 3 tablespoons **simple syrup** (see opposite)

1. Fill a metal cocktail shaker with ice and add all the ingredients. Shake briskly. Serve on the rocks or straight up in a salt-rimmed glass, and garnish with a wedge of lime.

FORMOSA CAFÉ, 1956

If you ask Vince about the Formosa's past, most likely he'll ask you if you want the clean or dirty version. You definitely want the dirty version. Vince's grandfather's business partner Jimmy Bernstein, won the restaurant in a bet. Before that, it had supposedly been owned by the mob. Vince says: "This place was a one-stop shop. Back in the day, you could come in here, cash a check, get a drink, place a bet, have your lunch, and get a date." Vince has been in charge since 1993 and, while there aren't any mobsters anymore, it's one of the few places in town with that old Hollywood vibe where you can still rub shoulders with a movie star on their day off.

VINCE, LOS ANGELES, 1966

The Rude Boi

MAKES 1 • PREPARATION TIME: 2 MINUTES • COOKING TIME: NONE • WF GF V

Here's a tropical-inspired nonalcoholic cocktail for the kids, which we invented for Kay's nephews Alex and Alastair when they were younger. The high point in its genesis was the time Alastair discovered the cocktail shaker, and that carbonated drinks don't respond well to shaking, all in the same afternoon.

ice
store-bought mango and passion fruit smoothie
ginger beer

1. Fill a Collins glass with ice. Pour in 1 measure of the mango and passion fruit smoothie. Top up with ginger beer. Stir to blend and serve immediately.

ALEX & ALASTAIR, GOZO, 2002

TIPS

* You can substitute the ginger beer with sparkling pineapple and grapefruit drink. if you prefer.

Simple Syrup

A cocktail staple, this is supereasy to make and will see you through countless margaritas and other cocktails.

½ cup **superfine sugar**
½ cup **water**

1. Over low to medium heat, mix the sugar and water together in a saucepan until the sugar has completely dissolved. Don't boil.

2. Once it's all dissolved, set the pan aside to cool, then decant the syrup into a screw-top jar or bottle with a good fitting lid and store until you need it.

TIPS

* Be sure to frst sterilize your jar or bottle first.

* Simple syrup is also now available to buy in bottles at some supermarkets.

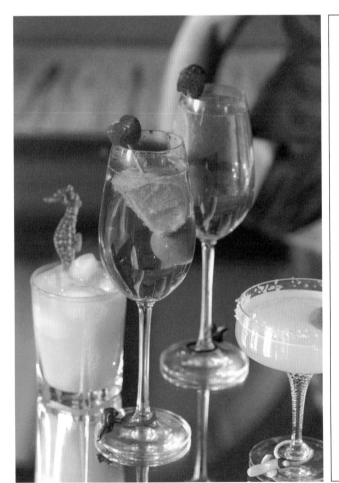

LEFT TO RIGHT: THE RUDE BOI; THE SPRITZ; VINCE JUNG'S MARGARITA

Devilish Chicken Drumsticks

MAKES 12 • PREPARATION TIME: 15 MINUTES PLUS MARINATING • COOKING TIME: 40 MINUTES • ✓ ♥

Chicken drumsticks are a party food staple. It's not just that they taste great. They're also really good for waving around when you're a bit tipsy and in the middle of an anecdote. These ones are "devilish" because they're based on a *pollo alla diavolo*, so they're real fiery.

1 teaspoon crushed **dried chile**
½ tablespoon **black peppercorns**, cracked
½ tablespoon **white peppercorns**, cracked
2 tablespoons **olive oil**
1 tablespoon **English mustard**
the leaves from 1 sprig of **fresh rosemary**
the juice of 1 **lemon**
a good pinch of **sea salt**
12 **chicken drumsticks**

1. In a large bowl, mix the chile and peppercorns with the oil, mustard, rosemary, and lemon juice.

2. Clean and dry the chicken drumsticks and cut some slashes into the meat. Add them to the bowl with a good pinch of salt and mix together well. Let marinate for at least an hour.

3. Heat the oven to 400°F. Lay the drumsticks in a roasting pan, making sure not to overcrowd the pan, and roast them for 40 minutes, or until crispy and cooked through.

4. Serve with something cool to put out the fire.

TIPS

* These are terrific for a barbecue. Just grill over medium coals until they're done. For an extra twist, soak the sticks from some old rosemary prunings in cold water for a few hours and throw them onto the coals before you put on the chicken. The rosemary smoke will add a superb flavor.

POPPY, MADDIE, JAMES, SARAH & DAISY, 2012

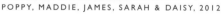

Annette's Sweet & Sour Chicken Drumsticks

MAKES 12 • PREPARATION TIME: 15 MINUTES PLUS MARINATING • COOKING TIME: 40 MINUTES • ✓ ♥

We first had this at Margaret Morris's place in Jamaica, then promptly lost the notebook with the recipe in it. So it's very much a re-creation. But it's a great dish for a party, especially one where everyone's expected to eat with their hands.

1 chicken **bouillon cube**
1 tablespoon **vegetable oil**
1 tablespoon **light soy sauce**
2 tablespoons good **mango chutney**,
   plus an extra 1½ tablespoons for a final glaze
1 clove of **garlic**, crushed
the zest and juice of ½ a **lemon**
1 tablespoon picked **thyme leaves**
12 **chicken drumsticks**
salt and **freshly ground black pepper**

1. Put the bouillon cube and the oil into a bowl and crush together into a paste. Add the soy sauce, chutney, garlic, lemon zest, and thyme, and stir everything together well.

2. Clean and dry the chicken drumsticks, then cut shallow slashes into the meat. Add them to the marinade, season with salt and pepper, and mix everything thoroughly, working the marinade into the cuts in the chicken legs. Let stand for a good hour.

3. Heat the oven to 400°F.

4. Lay the chicken drumsticks in a roasting pan, making sure not to crowd them too closely together. Roast them in the oven for 40 minutes, or until the chicken's cooked through and the marinade has become like sticky-sweet pants on the drumsticks.

5. In the last 5 minutes, stir in the final 1½ tablespoons of mango chutney to complete the glaze.

6. Sprinkle a little lemon juice over the top and serve piping hot.

TIPS

  * For an extra Jamaican kick, why not add a tablespoon of Pickapeppa hot sauce to the marinade?

THINGS ON STICKS!

The Italian Job

✓ ♥ WF GF V

Have a bowl of ripe **cherry tomatoes** ready. Oh, and a bowl of **baby mozzarella** (*bocconcini*) or just regular mozzarella chopped into bite-size pieces, and bathed in some **extra virgin olive oil**, **salt** and **black pepper**, and a crushed clove of **garlic**. Some nice **fresh basil** leaves, too. And a small bowl of mixed sea salt and freshly ground black pepper. Some sticks. You do the math.

Henley Regatta Smoked Trout & Cucumber Club

Toast as many pieces of **white AND whole wheat bread** as you want. Lightly butter each piece. Peel and slice a **cucumber** thinly.

Lay liberal slices of **smoked trout** on a piece of whole wheat toast. Season with **lemon juice** and **freshly ground black pepper**. Top with a piece of white toast. Liberally layer that with slices of cucumber. Season with **salt** and black pepper. Lay another slice of whole wheat toast on and again layer with smoked trout. Season with a dash more lemon juice and some black pepper. Finish off with a slice of white toast.

Cut into squares and spear.

Porchetta on a Stick

✓ WF GF DF

Cube some **pork cutlets**. Crush some **toasted fennel seeds** and some stripped **rosemary leaves** together. Mix with a good amount of **olive oil**. Marinate the pork for as long as you can. Season with **salt** and **black pepper**, then pan-fry for 7–10 minutes, or until cooked. Just before you take the pork out of the pan, add a crushed clove of **garlic** and stir it around—you want it to stick to the meat, but not to burn. Spear. Be careful not to burn your fingers.

TIPS

* If you are making BIG STICKS and putting them on the grill, remember to soak the sticks in water first.

What's a party without things on sticks? Our friend Zack says: "There's no foodstuff that can't be improved by putting it on a stick." We quite agree with you, Zack. Here are a few of our favorites:

Samurai on Horseback

✓ WF GF

You've heard of Devils on Horseback. You've heard of Angels on Horseback. Now, new and exclusive to Leon we give you Samurai on Horseback!!

Stretch some **bacon slices** with the back of a blunt knife. Cut them in two. Open a can of **water chestnuts** and drain them. Wrap each water chestnut in half a bacon slice and secure with a stick.

Put them on a baking pan, and into the oven at 400°F for about 20–25 minutes, or until the bacon is crisp.

Remove from the oven and serve. But be careful—the water chestnuts retain a furious heat! Serve with a bowl of spicy **Sriracha Sauce** or some good **mango chutney**.

Cold Roast Beef, Blue Cheese & Grapes

✓ WF GF

Stack a thin slice of **rare roast beef** on top of a chunk of **blue cheese** and a **grape**. Spike it. Eat it and weep.

Grilled Cheese

v

Spread 2 slices of **white bread** with **butter** on one side. Place a dry skillet over medium heat.

Slice some **cheese**. Have some **ham**, if you prefer.

Place the first slice of bread, butter-side-down in the skillet. Immediately place the cheese slice(s) on top. (Add the ham in if you prefer.) Slap the second piece of bread on top, butter side UP. Press down gently with a spatula. Flip the sandwich. The underside should be golden brown. Cook the other side until it is just as golden brown, and the cheese is melt-y.

Remove from the skillet. Cut into 4 squares. Stab with sticks. Serve **mustard** to dip. And some sharp **pickles** on the side.

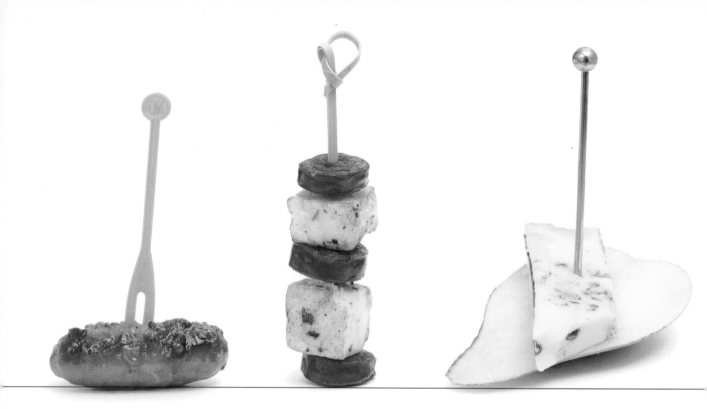

Honey Mustard Sausages

✓

An oldie, but a goodie! Buy some **good-quality (preferably gluten-free) cocktail sausages**. Put them in a roasting pan and into the oven at 400°F for about 20 minutes. Meanwhile, mix together 1–2 tablespoons of **honey** and 1–2 tablespoons of **grainy Dijon mustard**—depending on how many sausages you have. Take the sausages out of the oven and baste them liberally with the honey/mustard mixture.

Return them to the oven for about 5–10 minutes, or until sticky and golden brown.

Stab them with toothpicks.

Chorizo & Cheese Skewers

✓

Cube some **mozzarella** or **Muenster cheese** and marinate it in **olive oil** with a crushed clove of **garlic** and some fresh or dried **oregano**. Cook an ample amount of sliced **chorizo** in a saucepan until just oozing red oil and slightly cooked. Spear the chorizo and cheese together. Grill over medium heat for about 5 minutes, then serve immediately.

KAY, BANGKOK, 1968

Fig or Pear & Cheese

✓ WF GF V

Chunk up a ripe **pear** in the winter, or a ripe **fig** in the summer. Spear it together with your favorite **cheese**: blue cheeses go particularly well. So does a gooey Taleggio.

Layer Cake Squares

V

Who says stick-y snacks can't be sweet? Make a classic **layer sponge cake**—we like the recipe in *LEON: Baking & Desserts*. Fill with the **preserve** or **jam** of your choice (we love a little rose petal jam and some Greek yogurt or the classic combination of strawberry jam and whipped cream). Cut into small squares or wedges, dust with confectioners' sugar and SPEAR.

Cake Pop

V

Really? Our gorgeous friend Bumble guiltily admits she loves these ... it's simply your favorite cake... on a stick.

Make your absolute favorite **cake**. Maybe the gluten-free Flatplanet Brownies on page 80? Or any cake you like. Cut up and stick on a stick. Now the naughty part. DUNK it in:

- **Creamy buttercream**: use ¼ cup of sugar to every 1 stck of butter, with an added vanilla or chocolate or caramel hit. And a splash of liquid. Milk or booze. Your call.

- **Whipped cream**. Yes. Whipped cream. It is a birthday after all.

- **Low-fat yogurt, honey, and toasted flaxseed**—because you are GOOD.

- **Strawberries** or **raspberries** whooshed with a dash of **lemon juice** and a dash of **confectioners' sugar**. And for the grown-ups—a dash of **kirsch** or **Cointreau**.

Natasha's Buttered Toffee Apple Ice Cream

SERVES: 6–8 • PREPARATION TIME: 1 HOUR PLUS FREEZING • COOKING TIME: NONE • WF GF V

John's daughter Natasha loves apples and she loves ice cream. So Kay made this up for her.

1¾ cups **milk**
4 **egg yolks**
1 cup **superfine sugar**
¾ stick **unsalted butter**, softened
the zest and juice of ½ a **lemon**
1 teaspoon **sea salt**
8 **apples** (about 2 lb), peeled, cored, and
 chopped—we like to use Cox's or Pippins
1¾ cups **heavy** cream

1. Bring the milk up to a boil but DO NOT let it boil. Then take the saucepan off the heat and set aside.

2. In a large bowl, using an electric mixer beat the egg yolks with ¼ cup of the sugar.

3. Add the milk to the egg yolks and stir to combine. Pour the mixture back into the pan and put back on the stove to heat gently, stirring all the time. DO NOT let it boil. When you have a nice coating of custard forming over your spoon, remove from the heat. Set aside and let cool.

4. Meanwhile, spread the butter in the bottom of a smallish saucepan about 8–9 inches in diameter. Squash it down evenly with your fingers. Mix the rest of the sugar, the lemon zest, and salt together and sprinkle it over the butter. Put the apple pieces into the pan and try to keep them all in one layer. Pour the lemon juice over the apples. Then put the pan over low heat and melt the butter and sugar slowly.

5. Once it has melted, start gently flicking and spooning the mixture over the apples, making sure you shake the pan to move things around so that nothing burns or sticks to the bottom. Keep gently turning the apple pieces in the hot buttered toffee for about 20 minutes, or until the apples are soft and the mixture has a beautiful golden amber color. Remove from the heat and let the apple mixture cool completely.

6. When it's cold, mash the toffee-apple mixture and stir it into the custard. Don't worry if it's not smooth—the chunky pieces turn nice and chewy once they're frozen.

7. Stir in the heavy cream. Then pour into your ice cream maker and churn as per its instructions. Serve.

TIPS

* Make a quick batch of crumble topping with 1 cup of all-purpose flour, ½ stick of unsalted butter, ¼ cup of packed brown sugar, and a pinch of salt. Heat the oven to 375°F. Rub the butter and flour together until it resembles bread crumbs. Stir in the sugar and salt. Transfer onto a lightly greased baking pan and put into the oven for 15–20 minutes, until nice and crunchy. Serve sprinkled onto the ice cream.

* Homemade ice cream has a different texture to store-bought. If it seems a little soft, just put it into a lidded container and freeze for a bit. And remember, if it has been in the freezer for more than a few hours, you may have to soften it by putting it into the refrigerator for 30 minutes or so before serving.

Saffron, Honey & Orange Blossom Ice Cream

SERVES 4 • PREPARATION TIME: 10 MINUTES PLUS FREEZING • COOKING TIME: 15 MINUTES • ✓ WF GF V

This really is sunshine-chilled-on-a-plate—one of our favorite summer creations. Serve with a slab of the clementine cornmeal cake from *Leon: Baking & Desserts*, and with a hunk of honeycomb toffee sliding down the side …

> 1 teaspoon **orange flower water**
> a large pinch of **saffron**
> 1¼ cups **milk**
> 4 **egg yolks**
> ¼ cup good **honey**
> 1¼ cups **heavy cream**

1. Infuse the orange flower water with the saffron and set aside.

2. Bring the milk to a boil, but DO NOT let it boil. Take it off the heat, add the saffron and orange flower water, and set aside for 30 minutes.

3. In a large bowl, beat the egg yolks with the honey until combined and creamy. Add the milk mixture to the egg yolks and stir.

4. Pour the mixture back into the saucepan and heat gently, stirring. Again, DO NOT let it boil. When it coats the back of your spoon remove from the heat. Let cool.

5. When it's cold, stir in the heavy cream. Pour into your ice cream maker, and churn as per its instructions.

Apple's Easy Chocolate Birthday Cake

SERVES: 6–8 • PREPARATION TIME: 15–20 MINUTES PLUS COOLING • COOKING TIME: 50 MINUTES • V

Let's face it, you cannot have a good birthday without cake. We think that, for birthdays, the cake's got to be chocolate. This one, from Katie's cousin's wife Apple, a perennial Leon favorite cook, never fails with kids and adults alike.

For the cake:
1 stick **unsalted butter**
1 cup packed **light brown sugar**
¼ cup **sunflower oil**
¼ cup **unsweetened cocoa powder**
2 teaspoons **vanilla extract**
4 **eggs**
⅓ cup **milk**
½ cup **heavy cream**
2⅓ cups **all-purpose flour**
3 teaspoons **baking powder**

For the frosting:
½ stick **unsalted butter**
2⅓ cups **confectioners' sugar**
¼ cup **heavy cream**
¼ cup **unsweetened cocoa powder**

1. Preheat the oven to 350°F and grease an 8-inch cake pan.

2. Over low heat, melt the butter in a small saucepan. While it's on the stove, put the sugar, oil, cocoa powder, and vanilla extract into a bowl. Then, when the butter has melted, add it to the bowl and beat the mixture together until it's smooth.

3. Add the eggs, milk, and cream and mix until smooth. Sift the flour and baking powder together, and beat them into the chocolate mixture.

4. Pour the cake batter into the greased cake pan, cover it with aluminum foil, and bake it in the oven for 30 minutes. Then remove the foil and bake for another 20 minutes, or until it's cooked. You can test it by stabbing the thickest part of the cake with a fork. When it's done, the fork will come out clean.

5. Let the cake cool in its pan for about 10 minutes or so. Then remove, and set it aside on a wire rack to cool completely.

6. When the cake is cold, you can frost it as follows: Melt the butter over low heat. Then pour it into a bowl with the confectioners' sugar, cream, and cocoa, and beat until smooth. If it's looking too thick, add a little water to loosen. Smear it liberally over the cake, then decorate to suit its lucky recipient.

CHRISTMAS HOLIDAYS

Christmases in Bangkok as a child were quite something. It would be 90°F in the shade, but we still insisted on having the full roasted turkey and all the trimmings, with the caveat that we had the air-conditioning turned up to max, and plenty of fake snow sprayed on the windows. Outside, it was sweltering. Inside, it was a winter wonderland, complete with pine-cone-people skiing down fiberglass slopes on the sideboard!

Our regular treat was a frozen turkey imported from the United States which, much to my fascination, had a thermometer that popped out of the bird when it was done. What technology!

Christmas remains my favorite time of the year. While the food is a key component, it's more important to enjoy it. Really, you're just making a bumper-big Sunday lunch. So don't stress. It'll all come together just fine. Merry Christmas to you all!

KAY

Roasted Turkey with Scarborough Fair Butter

PREPARATION TIME: 30 MINUTES PLUS RESTING • COOKING TIME: SEE CHART • ✓ ♥ WF GF

Christmas lunch, Christmas dinner: we don't mind when you eat it. But when it comes down to it, we're turkey people. A great turkey, cooked just right, is a joy to behold. A real feast. Of course, this requires a good turkey. We work hard to source meat from the best farms we can. And when it comes to turkeys, we're huge fans of the Kellys' KellyBronze.

The Kellys have been farming turkeys since the 70s, and they're dedicated to the flavor of their free-range birds. The cooking times in this recipe are based on their recommendations. Guideline timings (for **unstuffed turkeys**):

OVEN READY ROASTING WEIGHT	TIME (WITHOUT STUFFING)	SERVES	OVEN READY ROASTING WEIGHT	TIME (WITHOUT STUFFING)	SERVES
9 LB	2 HOURS	8–9	17½ LB	3 HOURS	16–17
11 LB	2¼ HOURS	10–11	20 LB	3¼ HOURS	18–19
13 LB	2½ HOURS	12–13	22 LB	3½ HOURS	20–22
15 LB	2¾ HOURS	14–15	24 LB	3¾ HOURS	23–25

In case you think these timings seem short, don't worry, they work. The important part is to ensure your bird is a.) properly thawed if frozen, and b.) at room temperature—get it out of the refrigerator a good 2 hours before you want to cook it. Let's go:

1 **turkey**
1 large **onion**, coarsely chopped
1 sprig of **fresh thyme**
1 **bay leaf**
salt and **freshly ground black pepper**

For the Scarborough Fair butter
(makes enough to stuff up to a 15lb bird—double it if you are going bigger):
1 stick **unsalted butter**, softened
2–3 tablespoons chopped **fresh parsley**
3 big leaves of **fresh sage**
the leaves from 1 good sprig of **fresh rosemary**
the leaves from 4 sprigs of **fresh thyme**
the zest of ½ a **lemon**

For the gravy:
the **turkey giblets**
1 **onion**, coarsely chopped
1 sprig of **fresh thyme**
1 sprig of **fresh parsley**
1 **bay leaf**
4 cups **water**
1½ cups **Madeira**
¼–½ stick **unsalted butter**

TIPS

* We recommend using a meat thermometer if you are unsure about your turkey's "doneness." Remember, each turkey and each oven is different.

1. Heat the oven to 350°F.

2. First, make the Scarborough Fair butter to push up under the turkey's skin before roasting. It adds moisture and gives the skin a lovely St. Tropez tan… Put all the ingredients into a blender or food processor and blend them together.

3. Now—CAREFULLY—slip your hand (or the smallest family member's hand) up and under the turkey skin, gently prying it away from the flesh (there is a fine membrane holding them together). Try not to rip the skin. Gently push your way through (you can even, if your hands are small enough, loosen the skin that encloses the dark thigh meat, which really adds juiciness to these somewhat drier parts), and push the butter up and under the "glove" you've created, pushing and smoothing as gently as possible until you have worked the butter as far in as you can. Rub any excess butter over the bird, paying particular attention to the legs and thighs.

4. Season the cavity of the bird with salt and black pepper, and put the coarsely chopped onion and the herbs inside.

5. Roast the turkey in the oven breast side down for all but 30 minutes of its cooking time. The turkey's fat lies in its thighs and back. So it will trickle gently down basting the meat throughout the cooking time.

6. Half an hour before the end of cooking, turn the bird onto its back. Baste the breast and return it to the oven for the last half hour.

7. When the time's up check it's cooked by using a meat thermometer or by stabbing the tip of a sharp knife into the thickest part of the thigh. The juices should run clear. If not, baste it again and roast a little longer until they do.

8. Let the turkey rest for 30–60 minutes before carving. This is really important. It gives the juices time to spread back through the meat, and gives you the time to finish preparing the rest of the meal.

9. While the turkey's in the oven make a giblet stock. Reserve the liver and put the rest of the giblets into a saucepan with the coarsely chopped onion, the herbs, and the water, and bring it to a boil. As it bubbles up it will release a grayish scum to the surface. Skim this off and reduce the liquid by half. Season with salt and black pepper and set aside to cool. Chop the liver into ½-inch cubes.

10. When the turkey's resting, pour all the cooking juices into a heatproof bowl. Pour 2 tablespoons of the turkey fat (from the top of the cooking juices) back into the roasting pan. Then skim off the rest of the fat.

11. Heat the 2 tablespoons of fat in the roasting pan and sauté the turkey liver until it's sealed on all sides. It should take no more than a couple of minutes. Deglaze the pan with the Madeira. Simmer rapidly to cook out the alcohol, then add the giblet stock and the skimmed roasting juices. Stir it all together and reduce by between a third and a half. Taste and adjust the seasoning, then whisk in the butter to enrich it.

12. Carve the turkey and serve with all the yummy trimmings.

Three Ways to Get Stuffed

We love stuffing … but we prefer to cook it OUTSIDE the bird—the texture is better, it creates a nice crunchy top, and the turkey takes much less time to cook. Here are three options.

Sausage & Wild Rice Stuffing

SERVES 6–8 • PREPARATION TIME: 25 MINUTES • COOKING TIME: I HOUR 10 MINUTES • ✓ WF GF

1 cup **wild rice**
1 tablespoon **olive oil**
1 lb **gluten-free bulk sausage** or **sausage meat**
1 **onion**, peeled and chopped
½ a **red bell pepper**, chopped
½ a **green bell pepper**, chopped
1 clove of **garlic**, peeled and chopped

2 sticks of **celery**, chopped
2–3 sprigs of **fresh thyme**, leaves picked
a small handful of **fresh parsley**, chopped
2 teaspoons **Kay's Cajun Magic** (see page 57)
½ cup **white wine** or **stock**
salt and **freshly ground black pepper**

1. Bring 4 cups of salted water to a boil. Add the wild rice and bring back to a boil. Turn down the heat, cover, and simmer for 40 minutes, or until the rice grains split open. Strain the rice, then rinse under cold running water to stop it from cooking. Set aside.

2. Heat the olive oil in a skillet and sauté the sausage meat until it is cooked through. Remove with a slotted spoon and set aside. If there is too much liquid or oil remaining in the pan, drain some off. You may need to drain it all and add about a tablespoonful of olive oil—it will depend on how much liquid has been released by your sausagemeat.

3. Add the onion, bell peppers, garlic and celery to the skillet and cook over low heat for 4–5 minutes, or until just softened. Stir in the thyme and parsley. Tip into a clean bowl and mix with the sausagemeat and the cooked wild rice. Add the Kay's Cajun Magic and mix in well. Season with salt and black pepper, then taste and adjust the seasoning. Add the wine or stock and mix again. Spoon into a greased ovenproof dish and cook in a preheated oven at 375°F for 30–35 minutes, or until crisp on top and fragrant.

Herby Sausage & Apple Stuffing

SERVES 6–8 • PREPARATION TIME: 25 MINUTES • COOKING TIME: 55 MINUTES • ✓ ♥ WF GF

1 tablespoon **olive oil**
1 lb **gluten-free bulk sausage**
  or sausagemeat
the **turkey liver**, chopped (optional)
1 **onion**, chopped
2 **apples**, peeled, cored, and chopped
1 cup **chopped cooked chestnuts**

2 cups **fresh gluten-free bread crumbs**
8 small leaves of **fresh sage**, chopped
8 sprigs of **fresh thyme**, leaves picked
a pinch of **ground allspice**
½ cup good **hard cider** or **apple juice**
¼ cup **water**
salt and **freshly ground black pepper**

1. Heat the olive oil in a saucepan and sauté the sausage meat until cooked. Remove with a slotted spoon and set aside. If there is a lot of fat left in the pan, drain some off.

2. If using, add the turkey liver to the pan and sauté until cooked. Remove and set aside. Add the onions and apple to the pan and sauté until slightly soft.

3. Put everything into a large bowl and mix together thoroughly, adding the cider and water. Drink the rest of the cider while greasing an ovenproof dish. Spoon the stuffing into the dish and put into a preheated oven at 375°F for 30–35 minutes, or until crispy on top.

Polenta Stuffing

SERVES 4–6 • PREPARATION TIME: 20 MINUTES • COOKING TIME: 1 HOUR 5 MINUTES • WF GF V

1½ cups **polenta** or **cornmeal**
a good grating of **nutmeg**
1 tablespoon **olive oil**
½ cup **golden raisins**
40g **pine nuts**, toasted
1 teaspoon **dried sage**

1 **egg**, lightly beaten
2 tablespoons **Marsala**
½ cup **vegetable stock**
½ stick **butter** (optional)
salt and **freshly ground black pepper**

1. First make the polenta according to the package instructions, adding a pat of butter, a grating of nutmeg and salt and pepper to taste.

2. Pour the polenta into a greased roasting pan and let it cool completely. You can do this any time on Christmas Eve if you like, just to make things easier.

3. Slice the polenta into fat strips. Brush the olive oil all over the strips of polenta to coat, then broil for about 5–8 minutes, turning once, until they're crisp and golden. Remove from the heat and set aside on paper towels to cool slightly.

4. When cool enough to handle, coarsely crumble the polenta into a bowl. Add the remaining ingredients, except the optional butter, and mix well, without breaking the polenta up TOO much more. Put it all into a greased ovenproof dish, and, if you desire, finish with a few pats of butter on the top. Bake in a preheated oven at 375°F for 35–45 minutes, or until golden and crispy on top.

Perfect Roasted Potatoes

Crisp on the outside, fluffy within, this is just the best way to roast a potato. (And who says they're just for Christmas? These potatoes will brighten up any day you like!)

> as many **starchy potatoes** as you need
> 3 tablespoons **goose** or **duck fat** per roasting pan
> **sea salt**

1. Peel the potatoes and cut them into about 2-inch pieces. Put them into salted water and parboil them for 10–15 minutes, or until soft but not completely cooked through. Drain them in a colander. If they don't look fluffed up on the outside, pour them back and forth between the colander and the pan a few times, just to break up the outside. let them to dry and cool. (You can do this step quite a way in advance, if you desire.)

2. When you're ready to cook them, heat the oven to 400°F.

3. Heat the fat in a large roasting pan. When it's hot, carefully put in the potatoes. Make sure not to overcrowd the pan—if you're feeding a lot of people, do 2 pans and baste the potatoes with the hot fat. Season with salt, then put them into the oven. Roast the potatoes for 1 hour, turning them every 20 minutes or so, until they're crispy and golden brown.

TIPS

* Generally speaking, roasted potatoes like a hot oven (up to 425°F). But if you've only got one oven and the turkey's in it, you have to make do initially with the temperature the turkey needs. Don't worry. Put them in anyway, then turn up the heat to 400°F or 425°F (depending on what you need for your stuffings) when you pull out the turkey to let it rest.

* To get the proper crispiness, you must use a starchy variety of potato such as Yukon gold, rather than a waxy variety. Otherwise you're doomed to disappointment.

Spiced Red Cabbage with Dates

SERVES 6–8 • PREPARATION TIME: 15 MINUTES • COOKING TIME: 40 MINUTES • WF GF V

Instead of those long, slow braises, this is a quicker way of cooking red cabbage, and thanks to the dates there's no added sugar.

2 tablespoons **unsalted butter**
1 **onion**, finely sliced
1 **small red cabbage** (about 1¾ lb),
   halved, cored, and finely sliced
1 **apple** or **pear**, peeled, cored, and sliced
2 tablespoons **Somerset Pomona** or **apple liqueur**
½ cup **red wine vinegar**
½ cup **water**
20 **dates**, pitted and chopped
10 **cardamom pods**, gently crushed
a large pinch of freshly ground **Jamaican allspice**
salt and **freshly ground black pepper**

1. Melt the butter in a large, solid saucepan or casserole—one that has a good lid. Add the onion and sauté until just soft. Add the red cabbage and the apple or pear, and mix together well.

2. Add the Somerset Pomona, red wine vinegar, water, dates and spices. Bring to a boil. Then turn the heat right down, cover, and simmer gently for about 30 minutes.

3. Season with salt and black pepper, then serve.

TIPS

* You can make this the day before—even two days before. Keep it refrigerated and just heat it up when you need it. You may need to add a couple of tablespoons of water when you reheat.

* Add a handful or two of golden raisins or raisins too, if you desire.

* If you can't find the Somerset Pomona, you can substitute a mix of hard cider and Marsala wine or amontillado sherry.

FOOD FACT

Somerset Pomona is made by the great Somerset Distillery, whose apple brandies are extraordinary. It's an aged blend of apple juice and cider brandy—kind of a fortified apple juice, if you will. It's delicious with cheese and great to cook with.

Brussels Sprouts Three Ways

Brussels sprouts are a force for good … promise! Here are three surefire sprout recipes that have, so far, never failed to convert the doubters.

Sautéed Brussels Sprouts
WITH CANDIED WALNUTS

SERVES 4–6 • PREPARATION TIME: 10 MINUTES • COOKING TIME: 25 MINUTES • ✓ WF GF V

Thanks to Kay's lovely friend Sue McNamara for introducing us to these delicious walnuts.

1 lb **Brussels sprouts**, trimmed and halved
2 tablespoons **butter**
1 tablespoon **olive oil**
salt and **freshly ground black pepper**

For the candied walnuts:
½ cup **walnut halves**
2 tablespoons **brown sugar**
a good pinch of **salt**
a pinch of **chili powder** or **cayenne pepper**
a dash of **olive oil** or **walnut oil**

1. To make the candied walnuts, put all the ingredients into a wide skillet over medium heat. Keep stirring the nuts and sugar in the oil so that nothing gets too stuck together as the sugar begins to caramelize and coat the nuts. This should take about 3–5 minutes. Keep your eye on them, because they can burn quite easily. Tip them out onto some parchment paper and set aside until needed.

2. To cook the sprouts, bring a large saucepan of salted water to a boil. Plunge the sprouts in for a minute or two, just to blanch them. Drain them, then plunge them into a bowl of cold water to stop them from cooking. You want them a little tender, but still with some bite to them. Dry them well.

3. Now heat the butter and olive oil in a wide skillet or casserole dish. Add the sprouts and sauté them for about 5–7 minutes, until they are catching and browning on some parts. (You may need to do this in two batches—you don't want to overcrowd the skillet.) Season them with salt and black pepper.

4. To assemble the dish, transfer the sprouts to a serving bowl and gently stir in the candied walnuts, saving some to sprinkle over the top.

Pureed Brussels Sprouts

WITH ALLSPICE

SERVES 6–8 • PREPARATION TIME: 25 MINUTES • COOKING TIME: 15 MINUTES • WF GF V

This is heavenly, but very rich—a little goes a long way!

1 lb **Brussels sprouts**, trimmed
½ cup **crème fraîche** or **heavy cream**
2 tablespoons **unsalted butter**
a pinch of **ground allspice**
salt and **freshly ground black pepper**
a good grating of **nutmeg**, to serve

1. Bring a large saucepan of salted water to a boil. Toss in the Brussels sprouts and cook until just tender.

2. Drain the sprouts and put them into a food processor or blender. Add the crème fraîche or cream, the butter, allspice, salt, and black pepper, and process until you have a gorgeous creamy green purée.

3. Serve sprinkled with a grating of nutmeg.

Shredded Brussels Sprouts

WITH CHESTNUTS, CHILE & PANCETTA

SERVES 6–8 • PREPARATION TIME: 20 MINUTES • COOKING TIME: 10 MINUTES • ✓ WF GF

2 tablespoons **olive oil**
3oz **pancetta cubes**
2 cloves of **garlic**, sliced
1 **red serrano** or other **medium-hot chile**, seeded and sliced
¾ cup **chopped cooked chestnuts***
1 lb **Brussels sprouts**, trimmed, shredded and washed
salt and **freshly ground black pepper**

1. Heat 1 tablespoon of the olive oil and sauté the pancetta over a low to medium heat until it's crispy.

2. Now add the remaining oil, followed by the garlic and chile, and sauté until the garlic turns translucent, but hasn't begun to brown. Add the chestnuts and sauté for another minute or so.

3. Turn up the heat and add the Brussels sprouts. If they're still damp from washing, so much the better. If not, you may need to add a dash of water, just to get that steam into the saucepan to help them along. Sauté the sprouts for about 3–4 minutes. Season with salt and a few grinds of black pepper, and serve.

* YOU CAN BUY THESE VACUUM-SEALED. WE THINK THEY HAVE A TERRIFIC FLAVOR, AND THEY CRUMBLE WELL INTO THE SAUCEPAN.

Bryn Williams's Bread Sauce

SERVES 6–8 • PREPARATION TIME: 10 MINUTES • COOKING TIME: 15 MINUTES • V

Kay was never a huge fan of bread sauce until she worked with Bryn Williams on his book *Bryn's Kitchen: 5 Brilliant Ways To Cook 20 Great Ingredients*. This is his version, based on his gran's recipe.

> 6 thick slices of **white bread**
> 1 **onion**, cut in half
> 1 **bay leaf**
> 1 **clove**
> 2 cups **milk**
> ½ stick **butter**
> a pinch of grated **nutmeg**
> **sea salt** and **freshly ground black pepper**

1. Cut the crusts off the bread and discard. Then cut the slices into ¾-inch squares.

2. Chop one half of the onion as finely as you can and leave the other half intact. Place the half onion, the bay leaf, and clove in a small saucepan with the milk and bring to a boil. Simmer gently for about 2 minutes. Take off the heat and set aside to cool.

3. In a heavy saucepan, melt the butter and sauté the chopped onion. Cook gently for about 2 minutes until the onion is soft, but not browned.

4. Strain the milk through a strainer and pour on to the chopped onions and butter. Now bring to a boil. Once it reaches boiling point, remove from the heat and add the diced bread. Stir the mixture until combined and slightly softened—you still want some texture.

5. Season to taste with salt, black pepper and nutmeg. Cover the pan with a lid and keep the sauce warm until needed.

Cranberry Sauce

SERVES 6–8 • PREPARATION TIME: 5 MINUTES • COOKING TIME: 10 MINUTES • ♥ WF GF DF V

Of all the sauces you can serve with a turkey, nothing goes better than a tart cranberry sauce. This one's so simple to make. Best of all, you get to control the amount of sugar that goes into it.

> 3 cups **fresh cranberries**
> 1–2 tablespoons **sugar**, to taste
> the juice and zest of 1 **orange**
> ½ cup **water**
> 1 stick of **cinnamon**, broken in half

1. Place all the ingredients in a small saucepan and bring to a boil over medium heat. Turn down the heat and simmer until the berries start to burst. This should take about 8–10 minutes.

2. Remove from the heat, spoon into another container, and let cool to room temperature. Done. (We prefer the berries to retain a little bite, so we cook this for as little time as possible, just until everything's combined.)

TIPS

* Kay prefers her cranberry sauce to be very tart. Feel free to add an extra tablespoon of sugar, if you desire.

* For an extra kick, add a little grated fresh ginger just before you take it off the heat.

* You can also add a plethora of other, festive ingredients— throw in some currants or raisins, or add a grating or two of nutmeg. We've had blueberries in it before now.

* For a more adult sauce, why not add a slug of Grand Marnier or kirsch?

Spiced Cranberry & Apple Crumble

SERVES 4–6 • PREPARATION TIME: 30 MINUTES • COOKING TIME: 35 MINUTES • V

An English Apple crisp with a seasonal twist: the only decision is cream or ice cream?

1½ cups **all-purpose flour**
1 stick **unsalted butter**, chilled
¼ cup **packed light brown sugar**, plus an
   extra 2–3 tablespoons
a pinch of **salt**
5 **Granny Smith apples** or other
   sharp cooking apples (about 1¾ lb)
2 cups **fresh** or **frozen cranberries**
the juice and zest of 1 **orange**
½ teaspoon **ground cinnamon**
½ teaspoon **ground allspice**
a good grating of **nutmeg**

1. Heat the oven to 400°F.

2. Sift the flour and put it into a bowl. Cut in the butter, and using the tips of your fingers rub it together with the flour, lifting it high out of the bowl every now and again, until you have what looks like coarse bread crumbs. The coarser the crumb, the crumblier the crumble on top.

3. Mix in ¼ cup of the brown sugar and a pinch of salt with your hands, then set aside.

4. Peel, core, and slice the apples, and put the pieces into another bowl. Add the cranberries, orange zest and juice, the spices, and the remaining brown sugar. Mix together well and place in a lightly buttered ovenproof dish.

5. Cover with the crumble mixture and cook in the oven for 35 minutes. Serve crisp and bubblin'.

TIPS

* You could use a Magimix or blender to make your crumble topping. Kay prefers the texture and feel of the fingertip method.

Steamed Spiced Marmalade Pudding

WITH CRÈME JAMAIQUE

SERVES: 6–8 • PREPARATION TIME: 20 MINUTES • COOKING TIME: 2 HOURS • V

This is a great alternative to a traditional Christmas pudding. It still has all those festive spices, but none of the heavy fruit.

½ cup good **marmalade**
1½ sticks **unsalted butter**, softened
2 cups **granulated sugar**
2 teaspoons **ground ginger**
a really good grating of **nutmeg**
½ teaspoon **vanilla extract**
the zest of 1 **orange**
a pinch of **salt**
6–8 grinds of **black pepper**
1½ cups **all-purpose flour**
1 tablespoon **gluten-free baking powder**
1 tablespoon **orange juice**
3 **eggs**

1. First grease a deep, round, ovenproof dish with a little butter, then spoon the marmalade into the bottom of it.

2. Now cream the butter and sugar together thoroughly. Add the ground ginger, nutmeg, vanilla, orange zest, salt, and black pepper, and mix them in well.

3. Sift the flour and baking powder together. Add a spoonful of the flour into the butter and sugar. Add one egg, then the orange juice. Then add the remaining eggs one at a time and fold in the rest of the flour until you have a smooth batter. Pour the batter onto the marmalade. Your dish should now be about three-quarters full.

4. Cover the dish with wax paper into which you've folded a pleat and tie it on securely with string.

5. Steam in a tiered steamer for about 2 hours, or until the pudding has risen and it's light and airy. (To test it's cooked, remove the wax paper and stab the pudding with a toothpick, right to its middle. If it comes out clean, the pudding's cooked. Just so you know, if it's not cooked, you'll need to re-paper it and carry on steaming. So if in doubt, let it go a little longer. Unlike a cake, it's not going to burn, and these puddings resteam well. So an extra 15 minutes isn't going to hurt.)

6. Turn the cooked pudding out onto a serving plate. Spoon any marmalade that's stayed in the bowl over the top, and serve with Crème Jamaique (see opposite).

TIPS

* If you want more marmalade, don't put any more into the ovenproof bowl. It's best to melt a little in a saucepan and then pour it over the pudding once it's cooked.

Crème Jamaique

SERVES 6–8 • PREPARATION TIME: 5 MINUTES • COOKING TIME: 20 MINUTES • WF GF V

This is an allspice-and-rum-infused take on a classic crème Anglaise that'll put sunshine into the most wintry dessert.

1 tablespoon **allspice berries**
1 cup **whole milk**
4 **egg yolks**
¼ cup **superfine sugar**
1 tablespoon good **rum**—we prefer Appleton's
   for that proper Jamaican flavor

1. Bring a saucepan of water to a boil on the back of your stove.

2. In a dry, nonstick saucepan, toast the allspice berries over medium heat for about a minute, just to bring out their flavor. Crack them open in a mortar and pestle or with the back of a knife, then put them into a heavy-based pan with the milk.

3. Put the pan of milk and allspice over low heat. While the milk comes up to scalding point, beat the egg yolks, sugar, and rum together in a bowl big enough to sit over your pan of boiling water.

4. When the milk reaches scalding point, strain through a strainer onto the egg yolks, whisking them together. Heat the mixture in its bowl over a boiling water making sure the bottom of the bowl doesn't touch the water below and stirring all the time until it reaches your preferred thickness. (We don't think you want it too thick, just nicely glossy and silky.)

Glögg

SERVES 10–12 • STEEPING TIME: 2–4 HOURS • HEATING TIME: 20 MINUTES • V

Kay got this recipe from her mom and dad, who in turn got it from Scandinavian friends in Bangkok back in the day … It will certainly make a Christmas party go with a swing!

1 bottle of **vodka**
1 bottle of **red wine**
5 **cardamom pods**, cracked open
5 **cloves**
1 stick of **cinnamon**

1 piece of **orange rind**
1 piece of **fresh ginger**
1–1½ cups **sugar** (or to taste)
peeled almonds and **raisins**—a big
   handful of each (to serve)

1. Mix all the ingredients and let stand for 2–4 hours.

2. Heat the Glögg slowly. Do not boil.

3. Add the almonds and raisins just before serving.

BOXING DAY

Traditionally, British servants were given gifts by their emplyers on Boxing Day, the day after Christmas. These days, it is now seen as another day to relax at home.

Katie's family has a Boxing Day routine that is very established and also very dear to them. At the heart of that is Put Derham's potato cakes with red currant jelly. Miggy, aka Liz, Katie's sister, is very particular about having her red currant jelly, and they are all very particular about their ham. Boxing Day lunch is always a full, plated affair, and often a chance to do Christmas Day lunch again, maybe without the argument about how to cut and serve the Turkey.

JOHN

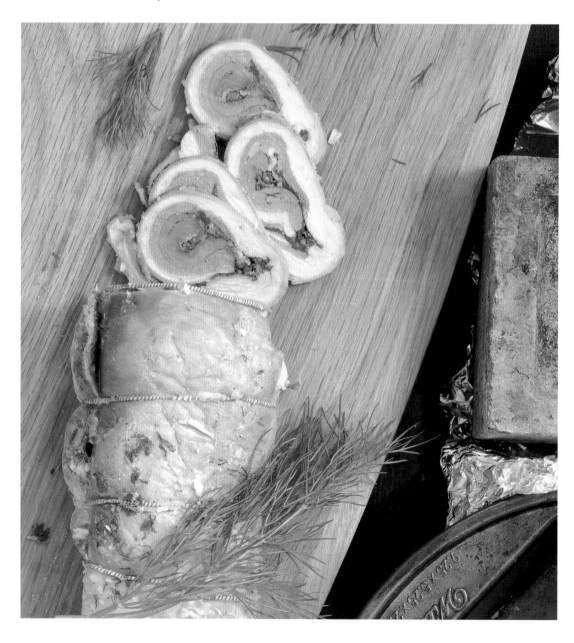

Rulle Pulse

SERVES: 6–8 • PREPARATION TIME: 25 MINUTES • COOKING TIME: 2 HOURS 30 MINUTES • ✓ WF GF

John says: "We have a friend called Christina. She is one of the best advertisements for Denmark one can imagine. She is the reason why many dads like taking their kids to school for the drop-off. Toby is good at darts. But I guess there must be more to why he ended up with such a lovely wife. This is Christina's mom's creation, and much cooked by her daughter. It's good Viking food, which makes something a little bit special from a cheap cut of meat. In Danish, its name means 'rolled sausage', but it's so much more. You can serve it thinly sliced as an hors d'oeuvre; it's good for an appetizer served with a little salsa or salad; or simply eat it on an open sandwich as the perfect lunch meat."

about 1¾ lb **lean lamb** or **pork belly**
   (which can be bought from supermarkets pre-rolled and tied)
a generous bunch of **fresh dill** and **parsley**, chopped
2 cloves of **garlic**, crushed
8 **whole anchovies** in pure olive oil (can be bought in small glass jars)
1 cup **stock** of your choice
salt and **freshly ground black pepper** or **chili pepper**

* You will also need a clean brick, wrapped in kitchen foil, to act as a compress

1. Heat the oven to 250°F.

2. Remove the ties from the meat (if elastic, set aside because they'll be useful to retie the meat). Unravel, remove any excess fat, and partly lift open the layers of meat. Sandwich in the rest of the ingredients, apart from the stock, laying the anchovies flat. Make sure that all the surface area is covered with the herbs, especially the side that you will start rolling up the meat from, so that you will see a complete spiral of green when you come to cut the finished pulse. Roll up the meat as tightly as possible, then retie.

3. Put a large sheet of extra strong foil in a 9 x 5-inch loaf pan. Place the pulse on top so it pushes the foil into the tin, then pour the stock around it before wrapping it up in the foil. Place it in the oven for 2½ hours.

4. Remove from the oven and put the foil-wrapped brick compress on top. Once cool, place in the refrigerator for at least 24 hours. When you are ready to serve, remove the foil and cut into thin, even slices.

TIPS

* This keeps and travels well, so it's ideal picnic, hiking, or camping food—which would be accompanied by a healthy shot of Gammel Dansk to warm you up.

CHRISTINA WITH HER MOM, HENRY, AND FLORENCE, 2006

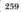

John Derham's Potato Cakes
(BOLINHOS DE BATATA)

MAKES 21 CAKES • PREPARATION TIME: 15–20 MINUTES • COOKING TIME: 10 MINUTES PER CAKE • V

John Derham aka "Pop" is Katie's dad. On Boxing Day, at dinner time, he puts on his apron, requests people make some space for him by the stove, and embarks on a dish that all the family would be bereft without. Serve with red currant sauce. (If you don't, Katie's sister Miggy will have something to say about it.)

2¾ lb **Yukon gold or russet potatoes**, peeled and chopped
1 **onion**, chopped finely
1 cup **shredded cheddar cheese**
1 **egg**
1¼ cups **bread crumbs**
a large handful of **fresh parsley**, chopped
all-purpose flour, for dusting
vegetable or **peanut oil**
salt and **freshly ground black pepper**

JOHN AND BROTHER TONY, TRUNKS, PAILS AND SPADES, CA.1960

1. First boil the potatoes—don't let them get so boiled that they fall apart, or they'll be too wet. Then drain and mash them dry.

2. Sauté the onion in a little butter until it's soft and translucent. Set aside.

3. While the mashed potatoes are still warm, mix in the cheese, egg, bread crumbs, cooked onion and parsley, and season well with salt and black pepper. Let cool.

4. Now form the cakes: In your hands, shape the cakes into large croquettes, about 2 inches long and ¾ inch in diameter, then dust in the flour. Heat 2 tablespoons of oil in a clean skillet, and cook the first batch of potato cakes on both sides until crispy and golden brown. You will find that they take up some of the oil as they cook, so you will probably need to add more as you work your way through the cooking. It's not an exact science. Just keep an eye on things, and keep adding oil between batches as you see fit. And make sure the oil's hot enough before you add the next few cakes. Serve, piping hot.

Frank Plunkett's Bubble & Squeak

SERVES: DEPENDS ON YOUR LEFTOVERS • PREPARATION TIME: 8 MINUTES • COOKING TIME: 25 MINUTES

Traditionally British "bubble and squeak" is made with leftover potatoes and cabbage. Kay says: "Dad's bubble and squeak is a family tradition. And it's only with much cajoling that I've managed to pry his closely guarded recipe away from him. He's been making it in one form or another since he was twelve years old. With both his mom and dad at work, it was often his turn to make the dinner, and this was a Monday night regular, using up the leftovers from their Sunday roast."

FRANK PLUNKETT,
EGYPT, 1952

leftover potatoes, and any other **leftover vegetables** from Christmas dinner, enough to make a ¾-inch layer in your biggest skillet
1 teaspoon **chicken bouillon powder**
1 teaspoon **anchovy sauce** (optional)
1 teaspoon **light soy sauce**
1 teaspoon **Worcestershire sauce**
1 teaspoon **oyster sauce**
½ stick **butter**
salt and **freshly ground black pepper**

1. Make sure all your vegetables and potatoes are at room temperature. Chop them all up, and put them into a bowl with the bouillon powder and the sauces. Mix everything together well. (You could use a masher, but you want some texture.)

2. Melt the butter in a nice wide skillet—the wider the better. When the butter's foamy and hot, put all the vegetables into the skillet and start moving them around, breaking them up, keeping things going over medium heat. You want the outside of the bubble and squeak to be crispy and the inside to heat through properly. The best way to do it is to keep it moving around to cook everything, then to leave it on the heat until crispy. Serve piping hot on its own or topped with a fried egg.

My dad, Frank Plunkett, has led an extraordinary life. Born just off the Old Kent Road, he's a Londoner through and through. An evacuee during the war, he served as a paratrooper in Suez, before joining Ford after the war. After becoming an overseas Ford service representative, he left the company to join the Ford dealership in Thailand, and over the years he worked his way up to chairman of the company until he retired. Every so often, when I was a girl, I'd be lucky enough to accompany him up-country, and he knew all the best food stalls from Ayutthaya to Yasothorn. So thanks, Dad, for a wonderful food education!

IF YOU'RE GOING TO CATCH ANYTHING, CATCH FISH.

10 THINGS YOU SHOULD KNOW HOW TO COOK BEFORE YOU LEAVE HOME

The thing about leaving home is that you suddenly realize just how expensive takeouts are. So we've pulled together a short collection of recipes to keep you going.

Mom's Roasted Chicken

AND HOW TO USE THE LEFTOVERS

SERVES: DEPENDS ON YOUR LEFTOVERS. THE CHICKEN ON ITS OWN WILL FEED 4
PREPARATION TIME: 10 MINUTES • COOKING TIME: 1 HOUR 30 MINUTES • ✓ ♥ WF GF DF

Roasted chicken is one of those dishes that everyone loves because it's a taste of home. Kay says: "My mom always used to make it whenever I came home to Thailand from school. And even now, it's the first meal I cook when I have been away."

a 3¼ lb **chicken**
1 small **onion**, peeled
a small bunch of **fresh herbs**
1 **lemon**, left whole, but stabbed a few times with a sharp knife
1 tablespoon **olive oil**
salt and **freshly ground black pepper**

1. Heat the oven to 400°F.

2. Pat the chicken dry and season the cavity with salt and black pepper. Then shove in the onion, herbs and lemon. Pour the oil over the top of the chicken, then season with salt and black pepper.

3. If you desire, you can now sprinkle the chicken with the dried herb or spice of your choice—sometimes we throw on a pinch of thyme, oregano, za'atar, Kay's Cajun Magic (see page 57)—something to give it a little extra zing. (Sometimes, Kay adds a pat of butter into the creases between the thighs and the body of the bird.)

4. Then slam it in the oven until it's done—about 1 hour 30 minutes in all—basting every 20 minutes or so.

5. Because a chicken must be properly cooked through, the best test is simply to stab it with a knife in the thickest part of the thigh and make sure the juices run clear. If they don't, just put it back in the oven for another 5 minutes or so.

TIPS

* You can't beat gravy with a good roasted chicken. We tend to skim off the excess fat in the roasting pan, then add about 1 cup of wine or chicken stock and bubble it up, scraping up all the yummy, sticky roasty parts. Our design guru Anita's mom used to stir in a Boursin cheese, too.

THE DAY AFTER
Homemade Chicken Stock

1. Strip the chicken meat off the bones. Then put the carcass into a big saucepan with 1 coarsely chopped **onion**, 1 coarsely chopped **carrot**, a **bay leaf**, a few **peppercorns**, and a pinch of **salt**.

2. Cover with water, bring to a boil, then simmer for an hour to an hour and a half.

3. Leave to cool, then strain through a strainer for a simple, clean chicken stock you can use for soup on pages 34–39 or any of the risotti on pages 102–5.

Quick Cheap Student's Risotto
(FOR 1)

1. Finely chop a small **onion**.

2. Bring your **homemade chicken stock** (see page 265) to a simmer on the back of the stove.

3. Melt 1 tablespoon of **olive oil** in a small saucepan and cook the onion until soft.

4. Add ½ cup of **risotto rice** and make your risotto following the basic method on page 103.

5. Finish the dish with **salt**, **black pepper**, the zest of ½ **lemon** zest, the chopped leaves from a sprig of **fresh rosemary**, and a good grating of **Parmesan**.

Chicken Curry
(FOR 2 IF NOT 4)

1. In a skillet, soften a finely chopped **onion** in 1 tablespoon of **vegetable oil** for about 3 minutes.

2. Add 2 chopped cloves of **garlic** and cook for 1 minute or so. Add 1 tablespoon of the **curry powder** of your choice, and cook it in the oil and garlic until fragrant.

3. Add ¾–1 lb of the **chicken**, toss it through the onions, and add 1½ cups **stock**.

4. Now add some **tomatoes** (canned if you like), maybe some **okra** or some **potatoes**. Simmer for 20 minutes, or until the sauce has reduced.

5. If you have it, add a little **coconut milk**. Stir it through the sauce. Then toss in a handful of chopped **fresh cilantro** and serve with **rice**.

Chicken Pot Pie
(FOR 2–4)

1. Chop an **onion**, a **carrot**, and a stick of **celery** and soften them in 1–2 tablespoons of **olive oil** for about 5 minutes or so.

2. Add 12oz **chicken**, some sliced **potatoes** (leftover ones are fine), some **dried herbs**— maybe thyme and oregano, ⅔ cup **frozen peas** and 1¾ cups **stock** (including any **leftover gravy**). Mix it all up together and season with **salt** and **pepper**.

3. Now you can either cook it right now or let it cool and cook it later. Either way, when you're ready to cook it, put it all into a large ovenproof dish. Then brush the rim of the dish with some **beaten egg**.

4. Roll out some **pastry dough** (shop bought is fine) and place it over the top. Pinch the pastry rim to seal. Brush the top with the rest of the egg. Cut a couple of holes in the top and bake it in a preheated oven at 400°F, for 35 minutes, or until golden brown on top. Serve piping hot.

Quick Convenience Store Curry

SERVES 2-4 • PREPARATION TIME: 10 MINUTES • COOKING TIME: 30 MINUTES • ✓ ♥ WF GF DF

There's almost always a bag of frozen spinach or peas lurking in the local late-night store. Maybe some potatoes or sweet potatoes. Some shallots and some garlic, too. A can of chickpeas. Or lentils. Or black beans. Or kidney beans. Or anything you find in your cupboards.

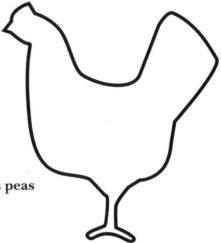

1 tablespoon **vegetable oil**
2 **small onions**, chopped
2 cloves of **garlic**, chopped
1 teaspoon **ground cumin**
1 teaspoon **ground coriander**
4 **cardamom pods**, lightly crushed
1 cup **vegetable stock**
1 teaspoon **chili powder**
1 large **potato/sweet potato**, chopped
2 x 15-oz **cans of beans**, drained and rinsed
1 (10-oz) package **frozen spinach**, thawed, or 3 cups **peas**
a handful of **fresh cilantro**, chopped
salt and **freshly ground black pepper**

1. Heat the oil in a skillet over medium heat, and cook the onions until they're soft and translucent. Add the garlic, cumin, coriander and cardamom, and cook until fragrant, a minute or two. Then add the stock.

2. Bring to a simmer, add the chili powder, potato and beans, and cook over low heat until the potato is soft.

3. Now add the spinach or peas and heat through. Season with salt and black pepper. Serve with rice, and garnish with the chopped cilantro.

John's Cheat's Chicken

SERVES 2-4 • PREPARATION TIME: 10 MINUTES • COOKING TIME: 30 MINUTES • ✓ ♥ WF GF DF

This isn't chicken for people who are unfaithful. It is chicken that is far lovelier than the effort that goes into it. Efficient. Good use of natural and human resources. It goes like this:

1. Put some **olive oil** in a skillet. Add a chopped **onion**. Or two. Add a few shakes of **curry powder**.

2. Fry 2 **chicken thighs** per person in the sizzling oil and onion. Add some more oil or curry powder if you think it is a good idea. Season with **salt** and **freshly ground black pepper**. Ta-daaaaa.

TIPS

* Try adding golden raisins. Or slivered almonds. Or minty yogurt. Any other top tips? Write to me. Or add them at www. leonrestaurants.co.uk

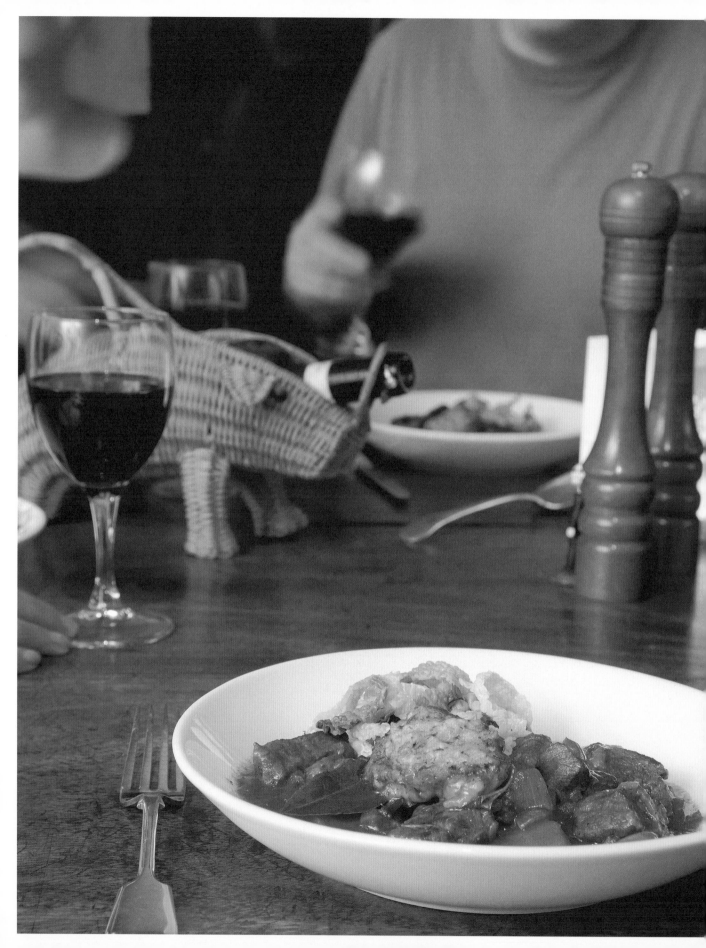

Bumper Beef Stew with Dumplings

SERVES 8 • PREPARATION TIME: 30 MINUTES • COOKING TIME: 3 HOURS 20 MINUTES

A rich, warming stew that goes a long way. Feel free to replace the all-purpose flour with buckwheat flour—the dumplings will be a little chewier, but in a good way.

1–2 tablespoons **all-purpose flour**
2¼ lb **boneless beef chuck**, cubed
¼ cup **olive oil**
1 large **onion**, chopped
3 **carrots**, chunkily sliced
1–2 cloves of **garlic**, chopped
a small handful of **fresh parsley**
a few sprigs of **fresh thyme**
2 **bay leave**
several good dashes of
   Worcestershire sauce

2–3 teaspoons **tomato paste**
2 **beef bouillon cubes**
salt and **freshly ground black pepper**

For the dumplings:
¼ cup **suet**
½ cup **all-purpose** or **buckwheat flour**
2 teaspoon **dried thyme** or **marjoram**
salt and **freshly ground black pepper**

1. Heat the oven to 400°F.

2. Put the flour into a large freezer bag and season it with salt and black pepper. Add the beef, hold the bag closed, and shake until the meat is well coated. Remove it from the bag, shaking off any excess flour, and set aside.

3. Put 1 tablespoon of the oil into a skillet over medium heat. Add the onion and soften until it's translucent, about 5 minutes or so. While it's cooking, put the carrots, garlic, herbs, Worcestershire sauce and tomato paste into a large casserole, and crumble in the bouillon cubes. When the onions are done, add them.

4. Increase the heat under the skillet and add 2 more tablespoons of oil. When it's hot, brown the floured pieces of meat in batches—don't overcrowd the pan— until they're nicely caramelized, then add them to the casserole.

5. Keep the skillet on the heat and pour in a small glass of water. Bubble it up, scraping up the cooking sediment on the bottom of the skillet, then pour it all into the casserole. Stir all the ingredients together, add enough water to just cover the meat. Put the lid on and put it into the oven for 30 minutes.

6. Turn the oven down to 350°F, and cook for another 2 hours.

7. When the 2 hours are up, it's time to make the dumplings. In a dry bowl, mix the flour and suet together with the herbs, a good pinch of salt and plenty of black pepper. Gradually add a little water and mix until you have a sticky dough. Too little water, and the flour won't combine with the suet; too much, and it will be too wet. You're looking for a claggy mess.

8. Take out the stew, turn the oven back up to 400°F, then divide the dumpling dough into 8 even chunks with a spoon and add them to the casserole. Baste them with the gravy, then put the casserole back into the oven, uncovered, for another 35 minutes. Serve with mashed potatoes and green vegetables.

Tagliatelle Aglio, Olio e Peperoncino

SERVES 2 • PREPARATION TIME: 5 MINUTES • COOKING TIME: 10–12 MINUTES

This is one of the world's simplest dishes to make, and one of the most satisfying, too.

8oz **tagliatelle**
2 tablespoons **olive oil**
1–2 cloves of **garlic**, peeled and sliced
1 teaspoon **dried red pepper flakes** or
   1 **fresh red chile**, sliced
1 tablespoon **fresh flat-leaf parsley**,
   finely chopped (optional)
salt and **freshly ground black pepper**
freshly grated **Parmesan**, to taste

1. Bring a large saucepan of salted water to a rolling boil and cook the pasta according to the package instructions.

2. Put the olive oil into a heavy saucepan over low–medium heat and add the garlic and red pepper flakes. Cook until the garlic turns a deep golden brown.

3. When the pasta's done, use a pair of tongs to scoop it into the garlic, red pepper flakes and oil. You want a little residual cooking water to go with it. Stir everything together, season with salt, black pepper and parsley, if using, and serve immediately with a good sprinkling of freshly grated Parmesan.

TIPS

* You can make this with most of the longer pastas, spaghetti, linguine, capellini … we wouldn't go for one that's much fatter than tagliatelle, and as for pasta shapes, well, there really isn't enough sauce here to get deliciously caught in their crenellations, so what's the point?

LEON IN PRAIA DA ROCHA, 1965

Simple Thai Pad Pak Ruam Mit

WITH JASMINE RICE

SERVES 2 • PREPARATION TIME: 10 MINUTES • COOKING TIME: 10 MINUTES • ✓ ♥ WF GF DF V

Pad pak ruam mit means stir-fried mixed vegetables. This is a really easy way to serve some of your five a day.

> 1 tablespoon **vegetable oil**
> 2–4 cloves of **garlic**, finely chopped, depending on size
>   (and how much you like garlic)
> 6 **baby corn**, cut in half
> 1 cup **snow peas** or **sugarsnap peas**
> 1 tablespoon **Thai fish sauce**
> 1 teaspoon **sugar**
> 1 head of **bok choy**, sliced

1. Heat the oil in a wok. Add the garlic and cook until fragrant, but don't let it brown. Add the baby corn, then, after a moment, the peas.

2. Add a dash of water for the steam, then the fish sauce and sugar. After a couple of minutes, add the bok choy, and another tiny dash of water if you desire. Keep stir-frying for another 3 minutes, until the vegetables are cooked. Serve piping hot, with jasmine rice (see below).

TIPS | * As a general rule, Thai mixed vegetable stir-fries don't feature chile. If you'd like to punch up the heat, add 1 sliced Thai chile at the same time as the garlic.

Jasmine Rice

SERVES 2 • PREPARATION TIME: 2 MINUTES • COOKING TIME: 12–15 MINUTES • WF GF V

> ¾ cup **jasmine rice**
> ¾ cup **cold water**

1. Rinse the rice by putting it into a strainer and splash it under cold running water, swishing it about with your hands until some of the starch has run off. Rinse until the water runs clear.

2. Put the rice and the water into a saucepan or casserole that has a tight-fitting lid. Place on the heat and bring to a boil. As soon as it's boiling, put the lid on, and turn the heat right down to a simmer. Cook for about 8–12 minutes.

3. When the time's up, taste it. If it's not quite cooked, add a dash more water and cook for a little longer. You should be able to smell when it's done—its wonderful perfume fills the kitchen.

4. Turn off the heat and let it rest for at least 5–10 minutes, so that each individual grain of rice can puff up to its perfect glory. It will happily sit and keep warm for up to 30 minutes.

Four Cheat's Desserts

Affogato Arabesque

SERVES 4 • PREPARATION TIME: 10 MINUTES • COOKING TIME: NONE • ♥ WF GF V

A Lebanese twist on an Italian classic.

1. Make your fresh coffee in your usual way, adding 2 cracked-open cardamom pods and their seeds to the grounds (we find one of those Italian, stovetop espresso pots the best for this).

2. Place a scoop of a good vanilla ice cream into each of 4 bowls. Serve with a shot of espresso on the side. Then pour the espresso over the ice cream, and enjoy!

Cheat's Chocolate Trifle

SERVES 4 • PREPARATION TIME: 5 MINUTES • COOKING TIME: NONE

2–4 **Flatplanet Brownies** (see page 80)
1 shot of **espresso**
1–2 shots of **rum** (optional)
1 batch of **Fred's Chocolate Mousse** (see opposite)
1¼ cups **heavy cream**, whipped
3 tablespoons **grated semisweet chocolate**

1. Lay the brownies in the bottom of a serving dish and pour the coffee (and the rum, if you're using it) over them. Smooth the chocolate mousse over the top of the brownies.

2. Top with the whipped cream and sprinkle with the grated chocolate. If you're feeling *really* naughty, you could also whip some rum into the cream!

TIPS

* Get retro and channel the 70s by sprinkling some bottled morello cherries between the cake and the mousse. And don't forget to balance one of the cherries artfully on top of the cream for a groovy Black Forest trifle. Serve wearing a medallion.

Fred's Chocolate Mousse

SERVES 4 • PREPARATION TIME: 25 MINUTES PLUS CHILLING • COOKING TIME: NONE • V

Fred says: "I first learnt to make a chocolate mousse from my sister's copy of the *My Learn to Cook Book* which featured a red cat and a blue dog guiding you through some simple recipes. Honestly, I think my chocolate mousse recipe has barely changed over the years, though it's probably included progressively less sugar."

3oz **semisweet chocolate**, with 70 percent cocoa solids
2 **eggs**
2 teaspoons **superfine sugar**
⅓ cup **heavy cream** (optional)

FRED, FAWLEY, 1975

1. Bring a saucepan of water to a boil. To melt the chocolate, break it up, put it into a large bowl, and sit it on top of the pan, making sure the bottom of the bowl does not touch a boiling water.

2. While the chocolate is melting, separate the eggs into two bowls. Whisk the whites into stiff peaks and fold in the sugar. Gently beat the egg yolks in the separate bowl.

3. When the chocolate has melted, take off the heat and mix the egg yolks into it and add the cream, if using. Fold the egg whites gently into the chocolate mixture, being careful not to knock too much of the air out of them—the lighter your touch, the lighter the mousse. Pour into individual ramekins and let set in the refrigerator for at least an hour.

TIPS

* If you don't like your chocolate mousse too sweet, you can halve the amount of sugar.

* This is a great dessert to make up to a day before you want to serve it.

Henry's Salted Caramel Bananas

SERVES 4 • PREPARATION TIME: 1 MINUTE • COOKING TIME: 15 MINUTES • WF GF V

4 **bananas**, peeled
2 tablespoons **butter**
½ cup **sugar**
a good pinch of **sea salt**
25ml **brandy** (optional)

1. Slice the bananas in half lengthwise. Heat the butter in a pan and fry the bananas until they're a little brown.

2. Sprinkle on the sugar and sea salt, and cook until the sugar has caramelized. Then, if you like, flame it with the brandy (not necessary, but fun).

3. Serve with vanilla ice cream.

YESTERDAY

This is a little bonus section. It is a collection of memories. Things we cooked on our first dates.

Technicolor memories from our childhood. The wisdom of grandmas. And recipes from our extended Leon families and friends.

Please share your memories with us at www.leonrestaurants.co.uk

MEMORY LANE

We could get all Proust about this, and go on about madeleines. But let's face it, he was a genius nineteenth-century French novelist, and we're just food writers. Suffice to say that the relationship between food and memory is well known. Something to do with the relationship between the olfactory bulb and the amygdala, where the brain processes emotion. So they say. I would argue it's a little less cerebral and a lot more emotional.

So here we have some recipes and memories from both Kay and John, as well as from some of the rest of our Leon family.

Marion's Bacon & Egg Pie

SERVES 4 • PREPARATION TIME: 40 MINUTES • COOKING TIME: 50 MINUTES • ✓

John says: "Between the ages of one and late teens, I spent most spring and summer weekends on and in the marshes of the Thames estuary, in a place called Tollesbury, near Maldon. It wasn't really a gourmet experience. In fact, I seem to remember that I ate a lot of crisps [potato chips], and when not drinking coke I drank a synthesized nonalcoholic version of rum and coke … for kids. And what's not to like about scampi or chicken in a basket? In *Leon Book 2: Naturally Fast Food* I included my Mom Marion's Scotch egg recipe, which she would make in London and which we would eat once we'd arrived. This recipe is for the bacon and egg pie we used to eat with it. You know, if I had to tell you which I enjoyed more, I am not sure I could. I hope you enjoy it, too."

4oz **unsmoked bacon**	*For the pastry dough:*
3 **eggs**	1½ cups **all-purpose flour**, plus extra
1 cup **light cream**	for dusting
3oz **Gruyère cheese**	a pinch of **salt**
freshly grated **nutmeg**	½ stick firm **butter**, cut into ½-inch pieces
salt and **freshly ground black pepper**	¼ cup **lard**, cut into ½-inch pieces

1. First make the pastry. Sift the flour and salt into a mixing bowl. Add the butter and lard, and rub lightly into the flour with the tips of the fingers until the mixture resembles bread crumbs. Add enough cold water to bind the mixture and make a firm dough, handling the pastry as little as possible.

2. Place the dough on a lightly floured board and gather it into a ball. Wrap the dough in a plastic bag and put into the refrigerator for about 30 minutes.

3. Now heat the oven to 400°F.

4. Sprinkle a small amount of flour on the board and roll the dough as lightly as possible, lifting the rolling pin between strokes. Line an 8-inch tart pan with a removable bottom (fluted if possible) with the thinly rolled dough, pressing it well into the bottom of the pan. Trim the edges and prick the bottom with a fork. Line the bottom with parchment paper and put pie weights on top.

5. Bake in the oven for 10 minutes, then remove the pie weights and let the pastry to cool. Precooking the pastry stops it from becoming soggy when the filling is added.

6. To make the filling, cut the bacon into ¾-inch strips and cook them in a nonstick skillet until the fat starts to run, then place them in the pie shell.

7. Beat the eggs lightly, stir in the cream, cheese, and seasonings, and pour over the bacon in the pan. Immediately transfer the pie to the oven and cook for 30–40 minutes. When cooked, the bacon and egg pie should be golden brown.

TIPS

* You can omit the bacon, if you desire.
* Add a good pinch of dry mustard (¼ teaspoon) to the mixture and omit the grated nutmeg.

Betty's Mah Jong Lunches

Who knows what Mah Jong is? Hands up? It's a Chinese game. And my mom and her gang played it back in the days. No, I don't know how to play it. I just remember the laughter, the clickety-clack of the Mah Jong tiles as they tumbled on the green baize card table, the shouts of "NORTH WIND; SOUTH WIND," the "serious" matchstick gambling, and the smell of compact powder and waxy rose-scented lipsticks.

Most of all I remember the food. The ladies would sometimes have sandwiches. Cakes always. Noodle soups from time to time. But the one dish that trumped them all was Som Tam. Here's my version of Mom's favorite.

KAY

Som Tam Thai

SERVES 1–2 • PREPARATION TIME: 20 MINUTES • COOKING TIME: NONE • WF GF DF

This is pretty much the dish Mom used to love—spicy, tart, and refreshing.

> 1 **Thai chile**
> 1 tablespoon **tiny dried shrimp**
> 1 **clove of garlic**
> 1 **large tomato**, sliced
> a small handful of **green beans**, chopped
> the juice of 1 **lime**
> 1 tablespoon **palm sugar (jaggery)**
> 1 tablespoon **Thai fish sauce**
> 2 large handfuls of **grated green papaya**
> a handful of **toasted peanuts**, to serve

1. Pound the Thai chile in a mortar and pestle. Add the dried shrimp and pound again. Then add the garlic and pound it just enough to break it open and release its oils—we're not making a paste here.

2. Put the tomato and the green beans in a bowl and stir in all the other ingredients, lifting and pushing back down with a spoon. Add the lime juice, palm sugar, and fish sauce, stir, then add the green papaya. Mix everything together well, stirring and pounding to bruise the papaya.

3. Taste and adjust for balance, then turn out onto a plate. Top with the peanuts and serve.

John's Chicken Ce Soir

SERVES 2 • PREPARATION TIME: 10 MINUTES • COOKING TIME: 30 MINUTES • ✓ WF GF

When Katie and I were first dating, I announced to her that I was going to cook. Now, I am from the 1980s. Well, from the 70s, too, but I grew up with two types of food. Traditional shepherd's pie, and liver and bacon on the one hand, and instant packaged goods on the other: dry goods that we could stash away when sailing across to Holland. So I really, really thought that buying a jar of Chicken Tonight and putting it onto some grilled chicken constituted cooking. I turned up at Katie's apartment in London one evening and when I whipped it out (that jar of mushroom and cream sauce), I sensed a little surprise. I am good with body language. Especially when people are laughing and pointing. So here it is, my Chicken Ce Soir, my attempt to make two things:

(1) An authentic version of that night's dinner.
(2) Amends.

> 1 tablespoon **olive oil**
> 2 **chicken breasts**, cut into chunks
> 2 tablespoons **butter**
> 1 **clove** of **garlic**, crushed
> 2 cups **sliced crimini mushrooms**
> ½ cup **white wine**
> ⅔ cup **heavy cream**
> 1 tablespoon **fresh parsley**, finely chopped
> **salt** and **freshly ground black pepper**

1. Heat the oil in a heavy sauté pan and cook the chicken pieces until they're golden and cooked through. Remove from the pan and set aside.

2. Now melt the butter in the pan and when it starts to foam, add the garlic. Cook, stirring for a couple of minutes, until you can really smell it, then add the mushrooms. Sauté for about 5 minutes, until you've cooked out their moisture, then remove them from the pan and set aside.

3. Now deglaze the pan with the wine, bubbling it hard and scraping up any cooking sediment from the bottom of the pan with a wooden spoon. Then add the cream, stirring it into the sauce, and let bubble and thicken.

KATIE AND JOHN, EARLY DAYS 1995

Leon's Poker Night Chili

SERVES 4 • PREPARATION TIME: 15 MINUTES • COOKING TIME: 10–15 MINUTES • ✓

Leon is John's dad. John's dad is Leon. We thought it was a nice name for our good fast food chain. And here we are. In the 1970s, Leon played poker. Every Monday evening. Well, for most of the night. Each week, a different wife would have the delight of catering for their husband's friends. (In a nice way.) Smoke would fill the house. And someone would walk away richer. But a little tired for work. Mostly the food would consist of sandwiches and pies, except on so-called "gala nights," when there was a more "exotic" offering, such as chili con carne. This is how it went …

2 tablespoons **vegetable oil**
1 **onion**, finely chopped
1 clove of **garlic**, finely chopped
1 lb **ground beef**
½ a **beef bouillon cube**
½ cup **water**
1 tablespoon **tomato paste**
1 (14-oz) **can of tomatoes**
1 (15-oz) **can of red kidney beans**, drained and rinsed
2 teaspoons **dried oregano**
1 teaspoon **ground cumin**
½ teaspoon **ground cinnamon**
½–1 teaspoon **chili powder**, to taste
salt and **freshly ground black pepper**

1. Heat the oil in a large saucepan over medium heat, and gently sauté the onion until it's soft and translucent.

2. Add the garlic and cook until fragrant, just for a couple of minutes, then add the ground beef. Brown the meat thoroughly.

3. Crumble in the bouillon cube and add the water. Stir everything together well, bubbling it all up, then add the tomatoes, tomato paste, beans, herbs, and spices.

4. Season with salt and black pepper, then simmer over low heat for 30–40 minutes, until it has reduced to a thick, fragrant, spicy chili.

5. For that final 70s touch, serve with rice or tortilla chips and a good grating of cheddar cheese.

LEON, EASTERN MEDITERRANEAN, 1957

Kay's Coq au Vin

SERVES 4–6 • PREPARATION TIME: 15 MINUTES • COOKING TIME: 2 HOURS • ✓.

This is the first meal that Fred cooked for me (or wooed me with, depending on how you look at it) on our second date. (The first one consisting mainly of martinis …) Suffice to say, I rushed back for a third … and we have been fighting over kitchen counter space ever since.

½ stick **unsalted butter**
a dash of **olive oil**
4oz **bacon lardons**
1 small **onion**, chopped
1 (3¼ lb) **chicken**, cut into 8 pieces
⅓ cup **brandy**
3 cups **red wine**
2 cups **chicken stock**
a bouquet garni of thyme, bay, and parsley
1 tablespoon **tomato paste**
2 **carrots**, chopped
2 **cloves** of **garlic**, finely chopped
8oz **baby onions**, peeled
8oz **mushrooms**, trimmed
3 tablespoons **flour**
salt and **freshly ground black pepper**

1. Heat the oven to 400°F.

2. In a heavy skillet, melt 2 tablespoons of the butter and a little olive oil (to stop it from burning). Add the bacon and onion and sauté until lightly browned. Scoop them out and transfer to a heavy casserole.

3. Add the chicken pieces to the skillet and brown thoroughly on all sides, in batches, removing them to a separate plate as you work. You may need to add a little more oil from time to time.

4. When all the chicken pieces have been browned, return them to the skillet. (Now for the fun part!) Pour in the brandy and, standing at arm's reach, set fire to the lip of the skillet. Gently shake the skillet back and forth until the flames subside. Then transfer the chicken to the casserole.

5. You should be left with a rich brown juice in the skillet. Add about a glass of the red wine. Bubble it up fiercely as you scrape up the cooking sediment from the skillet, and reduce it by at least half. Add the stock, stirring it together with the reduced wine over the heat, then pour all of this into the casserole.

6. Now add the herbs, salt, and black pepper, tomato paste, carrots, and garlic to the casserole, mix it all together, and pour in enough red wine to just cover the chicken. Cover the casserole and place in the oven for 30 minutes, then turn down the temperature to about 325°F, and cook for another hour or so.

7. While the chicken is cooking, sauté first the baby onions and then the mushrooms in about a tablespoon of olive oil. The mushrooms will release a lot of liquid in the skillet: make sure you cook all of it out. Set the onions and mushrooms aside separately when they're done.

8. When the chicken is ready, remove it from the sauce and keep warm on the side. Skim off any excess fat on the surface. Check the seasoning, and if needed, add a little more salt and black pepper.

9. Boil the sauce rapidly to reduce by at least a quarter. Then remove the bay leaf.

10. While the sauce is reducing, blend the remaining 2 tablespoons of butter with the flour to make a smooth paste (this is called a *beurre manié*). When you've reduced the sauce, vigorously whisk the paste into it to thicken it. Once the paste is all absorbed, you should end up with a sauce thick enough to coat a spoon lightly. Now return the chicken to the sauce with the onions and mushrooms and serve.

FRED AND KAY, GOZO, 2000

TIPS

* It's best to use a whole chicken when you make this because it adds a greater depth of flavor (keep the spine, and shove that in, too). But if you're in a hurry, a couple of packages of chicken thighs will work just as well.

* You can omit the onion and the mushroom step, but don't skip the *beurre manié*—it's a vital part of the sauce's silky mouthfeel, and it's worth taking a little time over.

Mary's Victorian Diable

SERVES 4 • PREPARATION TIME: 10 MINUTES • COOKING TIME: 40 MINUTES • ✓ ♥

Anita is our Leon design guru. She makes everything look good. She says: "My mom, Mary, was a great cook and was always trying out new recipes. One staple was a very posh sounding 'Victorian Diable,' which my brother, sister and I giggled at initially. Then it just became part of our vocabulary. Mom would often make this on a Monday using the leftovers from the Sunday roast, mostly lamb or beef. I particularly remember the capers, as we three would leave them on our plates at the end.

"Now I'm a mother, I have to bite my tongue when my kids leave the 'green bits or the black bits' that they don't want. They'll come round, eventually."

This is based on a *Reader's Digest* recipe from the 1970s.

¼ cup **gluten-free bread crumbs**
1 tablespoon **olive oil**
2 **onions**, finely chopped
1 **clove** of **garlic**, crushed
1 tablespoon **chickpea flour**
1 tablespoon **Dijon mustard**
1 tablespoon **white wine vinegar**
1 cup **beef stock**
2 teaspoons **packed brown sugar**
½ teaspoon **Worcestershire sauce**
1 teaspoon chopped **capers**
1 **bay leaf**
8–10 slices **cooked meat** or **poultry**
2 tablespoons **unsalted butter**, melted,
    plus a little extra to toast the bread crumbs
salt and **freshly ground black pepper**

MARY WITH STEPHEN, LISA AND ANITA, MALLORCA, 1974

1. Melt a little butter in a heavy saucepan. Put in the bread crumbs and stir, moving the crumbs around until golden and crunchy. Remove with a slotted spoon and set aside on a plate lined with paper towels.

2. Heat the oil in a large skillet over medium heat, and cook the onions and garlic until golden brown.

3. Add the flour and stir to blend. Add the mustard and vinegar and gradually stir in the stock. Bring this sauce to boiling point and stir until thick and smooth. Add the sugar, Worcestershire sauce, capers, and bay leaf, and season with salt and pepper. Simmer for 5–10 minutes, stirring frequently.

4. Meanwhile, heat the oven to 375°F.

5. Put the sliced meat into a buttered ovenproof dish. Pour the sauce (remove the bay leaf) over it, sprinkle with the bread crumbs, and pour the melted butter over the top. Bake in the center of the oven for about 20 minutes, or until golden brown. Serve hot, with buttered rice.

Stella Matthews' Stew

SERVES 8–10 • PREPARATION TIME: 230 MINUTES • COOKING TIME: 3 HOURS • ✓ WF GF

In Wales, this old recipe known as "cawl" is made whenever anybody is coming down with cold or flu symptoms. It banishes them! Or at least lessens them. It's the Welsh echinacea.

1¼ lb **beef shanks**
2 **onions**, peeled and sliced
6⅓ cups **water**
1 **small rutabaga**, diced
3 **parsnips**, diced
3 **large carrots**, diced
3 **leeks**, sliced into rings
4 **large Yukon gold potatoes**, quartered
a small handful of **chopped fresh parsley** (optional)
salt and **freshly ground black pepper**

1. Put the beef shank and onions into a large saucepan. Pour the water over them, bring it to a boil, then reduce the heat and simmer for about 2 hours, or until the meat is tender.

2. Take off the heat and let cool completely. Skim off all the fat from the surface, then shred the meat into small pieces and return it to the saucepan.

3. Add about 2 cups of the beef stock to the meat. Then add the rutabaga, parsnips, carrots, and leeks. You may need to add a little more water to make sure everything is completely covered. Put back on the heat and cook until the vegetables are nearly done—about 15 minutes, then add the potatoes and cook until they're soft.

4. Serve in bowls, sprinkled with the chopped parsley, with crusty bread and sharp cheddar cheese.

TIPS

* You can buy beef shank either on or off the bone. If it's on the bone, make sure you use the marrow!

STELLA AND GRANDPA, ANDREW, AND
JONATHAN, SOUTH WALES, 1979

Andrew Matthews-Owen is a classical pianist, a lover of fine food, and a great friend of Katie and John. His mom, Stella, grew up in the town of Llanberis, at the foot of Snowdon mountain in Wales. Whenever her kids where coming down with a cold she'd make a batch of this and it always kept illness at bay.

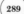

Pam Edwards's Date & Walnut Loaf

MAKES 8–10 SLICES • PREPARATION TIME: 15 MINUTES • COOKING TIME: 30 MINUTES • V

Glenn Edwards says: "Mom used to bake this loaf for the holidays [vacations] in the family caravan. While Mom reckons its best the next day, Dad always preferred it buttered, still warm from the oven (in fact, I'm not sure it ever lasted until the next day)."

1¾ cups **all-purpose flour**
2½ teaspoons **baking powder**
1 level teaspoon **salt**
1 level teaspoon **baking soda**
1 cup **milk**
⅔ cup **pitted dates**
⅓ cup **golden raisins**
½ cup **walnut halves**
2 tablespoons **light corn syrup**
⅓ cup **packed light brown sugar**

1. Heat the oven to 375°F. Grease and line an 8 x 4-inch loaf pan.

2. Sift the flour, baking powder, salt, and baking soda into a bowl. Put the remaining ingredients into a food processor and blend for about 20–30 seconds. Stir into the dried ingredients and, when they're well combined, pour the batter into the prepared loaf pan.

3. Bake in the oven for 30 minutes, then let cool on a wire rack.

4. It's at its best served the next day, sliced and buttered … if it lasts that long.

PAM AND GLENN, CUMBRIA, 1980

Glenn is a new member of the Leon team. He's very tall. You may find him at one of our shops dressed as a chef. Or "test-eating." Pam is his mom. Back in the 70s, she was a beauty queen. We think this cake's a beauty, too.

Crêpes Suzette

SERVES 6–8 • PREPARATION TIME: 15 MINUTES • COOKING TIME: 10-15 MINUTES • V

Surely this is the mother of all 70s dinner party classics. The 70s were when dinner parties were dinner parties. Half dinner, half party. And half Charlie's Angels-esque fashion show, if you can have three halves. Which you could back then. John remembers the tablecloth that used to be laid. The smell of cigarettes and perfume and alcohol. And the guests. Chaz and Jean. Paul and Rosemary. In fact, Rosemary used to make Crêpes Suzette at her dinner parties, too. It was a dish that got around.

1 cup **all-purpose flour**
2 **eggs**
1 cup **milk**
a pinch of **salt**
½ stick **butter**
the zest of 1 **orange**
1 tablespoon **superfine sugar**

For the sauce:
3 tablespoons **unsalted butter**
the juice of 2 **oranges**
the zest of 1 **orange**
1 tablespoon **superfine sugar**
3 tablespoons **Grand Marnier**, plus extra for flambéing

1. Sift the flour into a bowl and make a well in the middle. Add the eggs and a dash of the milk. Whisk in the rest of the milk and the salt until all the lumps are gone. Melt half the butter and add to the mixture along with the orange zest and the sugar. Let to rest while you sauce the sauce.

2. Meanwhile, to make the sauce, put the unsalted butter into a saucepan along with the orange juice, orange zest, superfine sugar, and Grand Marnier and heat gently until the butter has melted. Keep warm while you make the crepes.

3. Melt the remaining 2 tablespoons of butter in a skillet and add a small amount of the batter. Cook for a few minutes on each side. Pile up the crepes on a warmed serving plate covered with greaseproof paper. This amount of batter should make 16 thin crepes.

4. When they're all cooked, cover the folded crepes with the orange sauce. If you want to flambé the Grand Marnier, warm a small amount of the alcohol in a small saucepan, light it with a match, and pour over the crepes and the sauce.

To celebrate *Leon Family & Friends* and its whole *raison d'être*, we asked our customers to send in their food memories and favorite family recipes. The winner would have their recipe printed in this book. We were overwhelmed with entries, all of them fantastic. So much so that we've found it hard to choose just one winner. So we've chosen two. Meet Lucie and Ayaz—we're think they're fab.

Chicken à la Grecque

FROM LUCIE FIALOVA

SERVES 4 • PREPARATION TIME: 35 MINUTES • COOKING TIME: 2 HOURS • ✓ ♥ DF

Lucie says: "My mom's been making this recipe ever since I can remember. I'm not sure where the name comes from, as the combination of mustardy roast potatoes and root vegetables is probably as far as you can get from authentic Greek cuisine. But this dish has always had a special place on our Sunday table—and in our hearts."

4 **chicken leg portions**
2 tablespoons **herbes de Provence**
2 tablespoons **olive oil**
2¼ lb **Yukon gold potatoes**, peeled and chopped
   into ¾-inch pieces
3 tablespoons **Dijon mustard**
3–4 **lemons**
4 **carrots**, peeled and quartered
2 **parsnips**, peeled and quartered
1 small **celeriac**, peeled
   and cut into ¾-inch pieces
4 cups **sliced mushrooms**
2 large onions, quartered
2 **apples**, cored and quartered
4 cloves of **garlic**, sliced
salt and **freshly ground black pepper**

LUCIE AND MARCELA, PRAGUE, 1987

TIPS

* If you can't fit everything in a single layer, put the vegetables on top of the chicken for the initial hour. Then, when you take the foil off, give it a good stir and move the chicken to the top, skin side up.

1. Heat the oven to 400°F.

2. Season the chicken pieces well with salt, black pepper and herbes de Provence. Heat the olive oil in a skillet and brown the chicken over medium heat.

3. While the chicken is in the skillet, toss the potatoes in a bowl with the mustard and the juice of 2–3 lemons.

4. When the chicken's nicely browned, place it in a large shallow roasting pan with the potatoes, the rest of the vegetables, the apples, and garlic. (Lucie says: "My mom has one that doubles as an oven shelf, if you've got one of those you're golden.") You want just a single layer of ingredients in the pan.

5. Squeeze the juice of the remaining lemon over everything and season with salt and black pepper. Cover tightly with aluminum foil and bake for about an hour, until the potatoes are tender Remove the foil, and cook for another 30 minutes or so until the chicken skin is crispy and the vegetables are sticky, soft, and golden.

Nanabhai's Kulfi

FROM AYAZ HOSSAIN

MAKES 18–20 SMALL KULFI MOLDS • PREPARATION TIME: 10 MINUTES • COOKING TIME: 20 MINUTES • WF V

Ayaz says: "I am a thirty-two-year-old British Indian Muslim who grew up in the sunny Lancashire Pennines. From ages four to eighteen, my mother and father would take my sister and me to India, more precisely Kolkata, more precisely the black hole of. Having been dragged from our home to the dirt, noise, and overpopulated former outreach of the British Empire, which was actually its capital for over 100 years, my grandfather (or as we say Nanabhai) would attempt to cheer us up with his creation of 'ice cream.' It would take him the best part of the day, the excitement of a cold treat tantalized by frequent power cuts and water shortages that would mean freezing the end product became quite a challenge.

"Anyway, both my sister and I have now eaten kulfi at various restaurants but none bring back those memories of seeing my grandfather in his vest [undershirt] stirring away in the heat quite like the recipe below. One spoonful of this and I'm back in West Bengal. These days my mother (Nanni Ammi) has modified the recipe for the current generation of grandchildren, and is now a firm family favorite."

a good pinch of **saffron**
4 cups **whole milk**
2 tablespoons **cornstarch**
1 (14-oz) **can of sweetened condensed milk**
6 **whole green cardamom pods**, finely powdered or the seeds, ground
¼ cup **almonds** or **shelled pistachios**, soaked overnight, peeled, and sliced

TIPS

* Ayaz uses his grandfather's stainless steel kulfi molds. If you don't have any, you can use paper cups, half-filled, or small yogurt pots.

* To speed up the process, you can cool the mixture quickly by placing the pan into a large bowl of cold water.

1. Soak the saffron in a tablespoon of the whole milk and set aside.

2. In a separate small bowl, make a paste with the cornstarch and 2 tablespoons of the whole milk.

3. Mix the rest of the milk and the condensed milk together in a saucepan and bring to a boil, stirring continuously. Reduce the heat and simmer for 10 minutes, stirring all the time.

4. Add the cornstarch paste and continue stirring until the mixture thickens.

5. Remove from the heat, but keep stirring and let cool slightly.

6. Add the saffron in its milk and mix well. When completely cool, add the powdered cardamom and almonds *or* pistachios. Pour into kulfi molds and freeze.

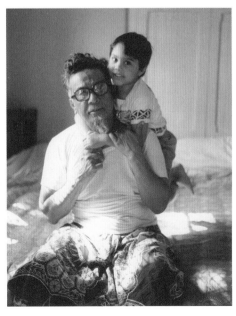

AYAZ AND NANABHAI, KOLKATA, 1983

RECIPE INDEX

INDEX

THANK YOU

FROM KAY

John Vincent—for giving me an amazing opportunity and for being a terrific partner in crime • Henry Dimbleby and the LEON team—for allowing me to play in their sandpit • Ottie Ise, for keeping JV on the straight and narrow • Anita—for designing a stunner of a book. King Size. • Georgi—amazing photography and giggles • Abi and Issy—the backbone of the whole Lymers operation • Willis, Arnold & Kimberly. You know why. • Alison Starling, Sybella Stephens, Jonathan Christie and all the fantastic team at Octopus • To my family—Dad, Kim and Nick, Alex and Alastair, The Kintbury Hogges: Gavin, Ann Marie, James and Sarah; Alice and Corinna, Joyce, Bramble and Philip for all being so supportive • My wonderful agent Felicity, and the redoubtable Becky • Jo Wander—TV beckons • Katie and the Vincent girls for allowing us to descend on their domestic idyll and, frankly, to trash the place • Wilcox and Hepburn, kitchen cats • And last but not least, Fred, without whom I couldn't have done any of this.

FROM JOHN

Big thanks to: Katie for being the most fiercely supportive wife a man can get • Natasha and Eleanor for caring very much about their Dad and what he does • Mom and Dad aka Marion and Leon for being positively brilliant • Henry D, a partner who becomes more wise each year, we have something special, so let's keep going day by day • Ottie for being committed beyond comprehension • Dave for great loyalty and friendship • Giancarlo and Katie Caldesi for hosting the kids cooking class with such flair • To all the friends and family I wrote about at the back of book 2 • To Migs and Will (and Wilf) for supporting the photo shoot with your presence. Special thanks to Hutch • To all of my Leon colleagues, past and present • To Brad Blum who is fast becoming a very special friend and collaborator. May your dream for "Good Food for the Planet" come true • To Vivian and Jacques for support and friendship and patience • Georgia for the photo magic • Anita for designing this book with such grit and determination and character under tough time pressures • And of course to Kay for being formidable and for your love of exclamation marks(!)

CONTRIBUTORS

Many thanks to the following contributors for permission to use the recipes they have contributed to the book: Giancarlo Caldesi: Impasto per la Pizza, Pasta Fresca • Christina Coleman: Rulle Pulse • Katie Derham: Sprout & Caramelized Onion Soup, Tarteflette • Qing Derham: Aunt Qing's Sushi Roll • Henry Dimbleby: Meatballs with Herb Salad, Sunday Dinner • Lucie Fialova: Chicken à La Grecque • Mamta Gupta: Mom's Chicken Curry; Eggplant Pickle-style Bhaji; Garam Masala • Anna Hansen: Pumpkin & Miso Cheesecake • Deb Henley: Chicken Enchiladas Verdes • Alice Hogge: Vegetarian Fall Pie • Fred Hogge: Classic Burger, Chocolate Mousse, Joyce Ann's Jamaican Curried Lamb Shanks, The Rude Boi, Ragù alla Toscana, The Wheel of Tomato-Based Pasta Sauce • Ayaz Hossain: Nanabhai's Kulfi • Vince Jung: Margarita • Jenny Linford: Sago Gula Melaka • Anita Mangan: Mary's Victorian Diable • Stella Matthews: Stew • Rachel McCormack: Tortilla Española • Ralph Monthienvichienchai: Mango Lassi • Justin Ovenden: Mackerel Ceviche • Benny Peverelli: Scotch Eggs • Apple Pickard: Easy Chocolate Birthday Cake • Frank Plunkett: Bubble & Squeak • Kim Pusinelli: Spanish Style Chicken • Phillip Regan of KellyBronze Turkeys: turkey cooking times • Gill Siebert: Muenster, Spinach & Chorizo Salad • Robert Elliott Smith: Shrimp Creole • Susanna Usai: Almond Macaroons • Bryn Williams: Bread Sauce.

SUPPLIERS

Philip Regan at Kelly Turkeys for our amazing Leon Christmas bird; Dodie at The Cool Chilli Company for pure corn tortillas and Mexican magic, Chris Hughes at Parson's Nose Putney for being my supertop butcher who supplied all the meat I needed for this book with inimitable good humor, and Georgie at LDR London PR for the Appleton Estate Rum. Matilda Harrison and Bee Bedford for the generous loan of their lovely props. Thank you all.

THE LEON TEAM

Salvatore Bellavia • Meriem Benouguef • Nawal Boukhemma • Agne Bucmyte • Mara Casolari • Arsenji Cechonin • Justina Ciuksyte • Marc-Alexis Constance • Edes Dutra Torelli • Fabiano Gonilde • Talita Sahai Heshiimu • Francisco Javier Iglesias Mori • Peter Jablonski • Alejandro Garcia Jinorio • Natalia Koc • Egle Ozolaite • Sarah Rees • Lauren Roverts • Salvatore Scarpa • Anastasia Voronina • Olivier Aka-Kadjo • Matthew Alp • Steve Bage • Luch Buckingham • Holly Clare • Lysette Cook • Samuel James Field • Elisabeta Gjovani • Nora Ivette Goboly • Tom Green • Eszter Hajmal • Vadim Ivanov • May Kovacova • Jirina Kralova • Nicholas William Kraus • Robert Lorik • Kristel Maley • Tia Paige Marks • Joshua Martins • Ashley Kathleen Peters • Istvan Szep • Guenzit Reives Arthur Tanoh • Birgit Arumetsa • Bozena Bobowska • Oriana Catino • Simona Cijunskyte • John Paul Corrigan • Nicolle Dawkins • Alexandra Elzbieta Kralewska • Valentina Manea • Anna Miller • Amita Shrestha • Gytis Sirinskas • Jurgita Sirvinskiene • Andrius Venclovas • Maria Trinidad Anca Julian • Bernando Aragao • Pedro Barchin • Michaela Boor • Yok Ming Chung • Rute Cristina Coelho Da Rocha • Kristina Dabkeviciene • Claire Didier • Kimberley Frost • Meritxell Gabarra • Margarita Kvasaite • Yinghua Luo • Florent Magnoux • Carlos Martinez Munecas • Sini Marika Mulari • Elizabeta Pac • Roberta Rimkute • Alvaro Santamaria • Lydia Rachel Turner • Gwendoline Blandine Vinard • Simona Vysniaukaite • Christopher Ali • Matthew Ali • Vadims Belovs • Pawel Bojanowski • Remi Chmieliauskas • Mirela-Ana Hapsa • Vydmante Kalvynaite • Viktor Kanasz • Nicola Kibble • Maciej Marek • Rodrigo Menezes De Carvalho • Evijs Ozols • Anna Robero Carro • Marton Vandlik • Maria Alcolea Fernandez • Nina Amaniampong • Yeray Bautista Armas • Claudinei Da Silva • Anax Gregory Da Silva Jorge Matias • Karolina Driessen • Lucas Drotar • Reda El Guebli • Patricia Ferreira Martins • Ema Claudia Gomez Pinto • Ali Grossi • Thomas Anthony Holden • Anna Kireeva • Katre Aurika Kurosu • Bernardo La PortaDa Silva • Acacio Machado Oliveira • Edvinas Marma • Tamara Morero Ruiz • Julia Nauer • Tran Nguyen Hoang • Nadia O'Mara • Justas Pokvytis • Anu Rego • Renan Rodrigues Lozano • Fernandinho Roberto Santo Veronese • Navina Senivassen • Michal Mikolaj Tobiczyk • Daniel Trevor Benjamin • Ineta Bliudziute • Ursula Bowerman • JulianGomes • Katrina Hassan • Monika Jaworska • Mariana Kastrati • Menlin Kook • Taz Kucuk • Simon Marin Montoya • Hong Thi Ngo • Oxana Popa • Egle Rimaite • Anna Sobczak • Ayanetu Degefa Tollesa • Martyn Trigg • Ruth Zenaida Yuste Alonso • Kayan Ayob • Maija Bika • Alessandro Bonny • Jenna Brehme • Nilton Caboco • Alessia Cardace • Soozi Carter • Fabio De Micheli • Terhi Evakallio • Valentina Fiorio • Dean Leacey • Thomas Malley • Mary Catherine Mannion • Lauryna Massionyte • Emanuele Mazzocca • Rafael Mollfuelleda • James Norris • Nuria Olmedo Nieto • Justy Ovenden • Bernardas Rindokas • Jennifer Karen Shearman • Thiago Turibio Da Silva • Megan Bailey • Nickie Bartsch • Agnieszka Chmieliauskas • Vasilica Cirican • Tom Davies • Henry Dimbleby • Simon Drysdale • Glenn Edwards • Toph Ford • James-Lee French • Steve Superstar Oakley • Ben Oliver • Georgie Sanderson • Tom Ward • Renan Amorin • Pedro Candida • Maria Capuano • Olga Chwilowicz • Davide Dabala • Marta Goszczynska • Annie Elizabeth Grant • Marion Christiane • Jennie Helly • Malgorzata Herda • Marta Klosinska • Saga Levin • Rasa Raskeviciute • Deivid Santos Grigorio • Denszso Zrinszki • KadijaBegum • Zoheir Benalia • Steph Brown • Katrina Bulman • Oliver Thomas Callway • Lukas Cholewinski • Agata Cyminska Thomas • Micheline Essomba • Abdelhadi Fekier • Helen Susan Foan • Liliya Georgieva • Cecilia Julia Amanda Holmgren • Andrew Hyman • Ben Iredale • Zoe Langley-Brown • Tom Lee • Bruno Lupi • Hester Mary Alice • Macdonald Thomas • Robert Arthurt William Machin • Philippe Rui Mesquita • CarolineMikkelsen • Sandra Navaro • Olufunmilola Grace Opeyemi • Clara Magdalena Ostman • Isabela Santos • Francisco Luis Gomes Silva Ramos Barbosa • Kamila Webb • Matthias Abdel-Haiat • Anna Anuscenko • Fred Balbi Amatto • Amy Browne • Charles Casey • Joao Carlos Da Cruz Moreira • Alaric Benjamin Demmer • Natalia Joanna Farnaus • Fayomi Fashanu • Anderson Gomcalves • Kayleigh Goodger • Nerea Hoyos • Osiur Khan • Svetlana Kokotkina • Lacey Lawson • Nicolo Lenzi • Orlan Masilu • Mourad Moukhalis • Olumide Otti Otusajo • Alicja Maria Pawlitko • Mark Prove • Benoit Ratinaud • Dominic Sherington • Nora Szosznyak • Eimear White •

To the memory of my beautiful mom Betty, and to moms everywhere

KAY

To my mom, Marion, who is, I truly believe, the most positive person I will ever meet.
To my dad, Leon, whose principles, honesty, and values are steadfast, and an inspiration.
Plus you are very funny. Thank you for all the adventures and laughing.

JOHN

BETTY, JON TIEM, 1962

JOHN AND LEON, 1981

First published in Great Britain in 2012
by Conran Octopus Limited
a part of Octopus Publishing Group
Endeavour House, 189 Shaftesbury Avenue,
London WC2H 8JY

An Hachette UK Company www.hachette.co.uk

Distributed in the US by Hachette Book Group USA
237 Park Avenue, New York NY 10017 USA

Distributed in Canada by Canadian Manda Group
165 Dufferin Street, Toronto,
Ontario, Canada M6K 3H6

Text copyright © Leon Restaurants Ltd 2012
except the recipes listed on page 302 where
the copyright belongs to the contributors

Design and layout copyright
© Conran Octopus Ltd 2012

Illustrations copyright © Anita Mangan 2012

Special photography copyright
© Georgia Glynn Smith 2012

The right of Leon Restaurants to be identified as the Author
of this work has been asserted by them in accordance
with the Copyright, Designs and Patents Act 1988.

British Library Cataloguing-in-Publication Data.
A catalogue record for this book is available from
the British Library.

Publisher: Alison Starling
Senior Editor: Sybella Stephens
Project Coordinator: Fred Hogge
Design and Art Direction (for Leon): Anita Mangan
Art Director (for Conran Octopus): Jonathan Christie
Illustrations: Anita Mangan
Photography: Georgia Glynn Smith
Production Manager: Katherine Hockley

ISBN 978 1 84091 619 5

Printed in China

A note from the authors…
We have endeavored to be as accurate as possible in all
the preparation and cooking times listing in the recipes
in this book. However they are an estimate based on our
own timings during recipe testing, and should be taken
as a guide only, not as the literal truth. We have also tried
to source all our food facts carefully, but we are not
scientists. So our food facts and nutrition advice are not
absolute. If you feel you require consultation with a
nutritionist, consult your physician for a recommendation.

DOES THE BULL LOOK GOOD IN THIS?

ABI AND ANITA DOING THEIR BEST DRAWING

THE THREE SISTERS

EEYORE MISSING ELEANOR

ISSY ON THE TABLE

CY WITH A PASTA FACE AT CALDESI'S

ABI GOING IN FOR THE MOULES SHOT

WHERE'S THE DISH?

ISSY GETTING INTO CHARACTER

KAY NOT WASTING THE PROSECCO

UNUSED PROP TRYING TO GET A LOOK IN

OUT ON DAY RELEASE